To Thyself Be True

Bill Murrell

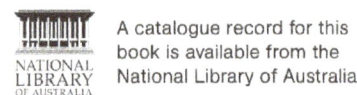 A catalogue record for this book is available from the National Library of Australia

This book is copyrighted. Apart from any fair dealing for the purpose of private study, research, criticism or review, as permitted under the Copyright Act, no part may be reproduced by any process without permission from the publisher and editor. All effort was made to render this book from error and omission. However, the author, publisher, editor, their employees or agents shall not accept responsibility for injury, loss or damage to any person or body or organisation acting or refraining from action as a result of material in this book, whether or not such injury, loss or damage is in any way due to any negligent act or omission, breach of duty, or default on the part of the author, publisher, editor or their employees or agents. Every effort has been made to trace copyright holders and to obtain their permission for the use of copyright material. The editor and publisher apologise for any errors or omissions and would be grateful for notification of any corrections that should be incorporated in future reprints or editions of this book.

For feedback or copies of this book, please contact the editor, Thomas Murrell below.
8M Media and Communications
PO Box 8086
Subiaco East WA 6008
Australia
Phone: +61 08 9388 6888
Email: 8m@8mmedia.com
Websites: www.8mmedia.com and www.fairviewofsubiaco.com.au

Frontspiece: Eric Wright, *Portrait of My Father Alfred Wright*, 1921, charcoal and pastel on board, 36 x 27 cm. From the Collection of Andrew Douglas Ambrose Murrell and now in The Fairview Art Collection.

Copyright © 2023 William John Calvert Murrell
ISBN-13: 978-1-922727-63-3

Linellen Press
265 Boomerang Road
Oldbury, Western Australia, 6121
www.linellenpress.com.au

Contents

Contents iii

Foreword 1

Chapter 1 - Life and Death on the Kitchen Table 4

Chapter 2 - Kindergarten and Primary School Days – Depression into War 12

Chapter 3 - Days at St Peter's College – 1943 – 1948 24

Chapter 4 - My First Paid Jobs – 1947 – 1950 31

Chapter 5 - Working for General Motors - 1950 - 1958 33

Chapter 6 - Working Post GM – MRD – AMI – NH – CAL – 1958-76 60

Chapter 7 - A New Career – Industry Training 82

Chapter 8 - Fill-ins – Finding a Job at 60 90

Chapter 9 - A New Career WAWA 92

Chapter 10 - Retirement – The Story Continues! 120

Chapter 11 - Family and Friends 130

Chapter 12 - Introducing Me 172

Chapter 13 - Convicts, Norfolk Island Family Trees 174

Chapter 14 - Life Through the Lens 198

Appendix 1 - Bill Murrell, The Art Collector by Thomas A.C. Murrell 236

Appendix 2 - My Norfolk Island Connection – Searching for Meaning and Stories 258

Appendix 3 - Mother's Memoirs 274

Appendix 4 - Letters of Bill Murrell from USA to Adelaide 299

Foreword

My uncle, Bill Murrell, was a loving and kind man who was a pioneer of the Australian car industry.

He was also a very keen observer of life and loved taking photographs of the world he was passionate about: his family, his travels, and his cars.

This book came about at the encouragement of his daughter, Lucy, who requested he capture his life story for future generations.

He was very proud of his handwritten book, full of his wisdom, career insights, family stories and, of course, photographs. In fact, he kept a written record of the people who had read it and a summary of their comments.

This version took all his original writings, letters and photographs. It was carefully edited and then published after his death with the full support of his family.

It provides a deep insight into the social changes happening in the world from the 1930s until his death in 2020 at the age of ninety.

A blood transfusion from his father on the kitchen table of their home in Thebarton, South Australia saved the life of Bill Murrell. He was born a "blue baby" in an era before blood matching and blood banks, and the quick-thinking but inherently risky actions of the local doctor were later cited as a case study to medical students on how to treat haemolytic disease in newborns. It was this near-death experience as a baby that gave Bill Murrell a positive can-do attitude to life.

He was an avid art collector, industrial engineer and pioneer of Australia's early car manufacturing industry, matching a love of visual design and creativity with hands-on engineering problem-solving.

Educated at St Peter's College, Adelaide University and the General Motors Institute of Technology at Flint, Michigan in the United States, which later became North Western University, he was a house prefect, school champion shot putter and represented South Australia in the Junior Under-19 Rugby Union team of 1948-49.

The second of five children, his father John William Murrell was an engineer who was responsible for setting up the sewage system in Adelaide and played football for Geelong, New Town – the Tasmanian State team – and Norwood. His mother, Beatrice Alice Calvert, was the daughter of noted Huon Valley orchardist and politician, The Hon William Henry Fairfax Calvert.

Bill turned down a scholarship at Roseworthy Agricultural College to take up a mechanical engineering cadetship at Adelaide University, which paid £5 a month. In 1950, he became a technical clerk at the Plant Engineering Department of General Motors Holden Woodville and, in 1951, applied for an Engineering Scholarship through General Motors Overseas Operations.

After winning the two-year scholarship, he was tasked with designing a pencilled 'schematic' plant layout for the proposed new Elizabeth facility. In Michigan, he studied metallurgy, processing, metals, foundry management, tool tryout and side-gate body assembly, and he worked on the iconic Buick and Pontiac models at a time when General Motors was producing 240 cars a day. This experience ignited a lifetime's passion for studying the interaction of human beings with industrial processes.

Murrell travelled extensively in the US, visiting San Francisco, Chicago, Miami and New York. This gave him a real insight into how the motorcar was transforming lives and lifestyles during the 1950s.

On returning to Adelaide, and after three years as a supervisor in the Production Engineering Department at GMH, he took on the role of Director of a South Australian Management Consultancy. Bill then worked at Australian Motor Industries in Melbourne as Chief Production Engineer when they were assembling Mercedes-Benz, Rambler, Fiat tractors, Triumph Herald and Vanguard cars and he planned the assembly of the first 6-cylinder Vanguard car.

In 1960, he moved to Standards Manager at New Holland in Dandenong and lectured part-time in Industrial Engineering at the Royal Melbourne Institute of Technology.

Bill moved back to Adelaide with Chrysler, where the 'S' Model Valiant was the car of the moment. There, he supervised Methods and Processes and, in 1963, was promoted to Industrial Engineer then Special Project Manager and was later posted to Sydney to run the Far Eastern and African Operations, making five trips overseas to places as diverse as Karachi, Canada, Detroit, the Philippines and New Zealand.

Back in Adelaide in 1970, as Chrysler's Australian Service Manager, he launched the 'Chrysler Cares and Service Excellence' program which saw the introduction of standard blue uniforms for mechanics, customer service awards for staff, the first computer recall system and an innovative "Women on Wheels" program created especially for women who drive.

Some of the production challenges faced during his sixteen years at Chrysler where the "Hey Charger" advertising campaign was making a big impact, included visiting 300 out of the 400 dealerships around Australia seeking ideas to lower warranty costs while improving customer service attitudes and finding engineering solutions to performance issues. For example, the VG Valiant had a curl-pin that held the gearstick in and, once it wore, the gearstick could come out in your hand, which drivers found a bit disconcerting!

Bill was also involved in the recall of Chryslers because wheels were literally falling off. A wheel nut runner on the assembly line did not work properly for a short time, allowing the wheel nuts to loosen while on the road.

After this, he worked for the Australian Productivity Council and became State Manager of the South Australian Construction Training Committee, a body established to develop and train personnel to higher competence at all levels from management through technical to trade levels in the building and construction industry.

He came to Perth in 1990 to become an Industrial Engineer and Project Manager with the Asset Management Branch of the Water Authority of Western Australia and was a former State and Federal President of the Institute of Industrial Engineers.

A keen art collector, he supported South Australian artists Colin Russell Gardiner from Stirling in the Adelaide Hills, Mary Millicent Wigg from the famous E.S. Wigg stationary family and his younger brother Andrew Douglas Ambrose Murrell, a notable art and antique dealer and oil painter.

Community service roles included WA President of Better Hearing Australia, co-ordinator of the men's group at St Christopher's City Beach and a life member of the UWA Sports Recreation and Fitness Centre.

He was a faithful man who lived to the motto "to thyself be true".

Enjoy this book as it is his legacy, dedicated to his sons James and William, daughter Lucy, adult step-children Alison and Geoffrey, and his seven grandchildren.

May his life, his words and his images continue to inspire future generations.

Thomas Andrew Calvert Murrell,
Nephew, December 2022.

United by a love of visual arts.
Left to right: T.G.C. (Tim) Murrell, T.A.C. (Tom) Murrell, W.J.C. (Bill) Murrell
pictured at a St Peter's College Old Scholars Dinner in Perth in the early 1990s.

Chapter 1

Life and Death on the Kitchen Table

It was on a sunny November morning when the shrill, agonising cries of my distressed mother pierced through our quiet household.

"Save him ... save him ... please," she helplessly sobbed, her voice laced with ardent desperation despite her exhaustion.

Before this fateful day, the 8th of November 1930, my mother decided that she wanted her second born, me, to be born at our cosy home along Port Road, Thebarton, South Australia.

Anticipation turned to horror as my supposed-to-be birth story turned into a near tragedy.

My dad looked on helplessly as Dr 'Wacka' West chaotically scrambled through his various medical instruments. He anxiously glanced at my vulnerable infant form, my skin turning an alarming shade of purple.

He looked at my dad, his gaze frantic. "We need to do a transfusion ... now!"

I was an Rh-ve 04 blue baby, which meant the antibodies in my mum's blood attacked my own blood cells due to an incompatibility between our Rhesus (Rh) blood types.

As I lay on the kitchen table, close to death, Dr West transferred Dad's 04 blood to me, and after some difficulty, the greatest miracle of my life occurred: I was granted a second chance to live.

I have lived! And I'm so glad, as I've had a very fortunate life, as you will discover.

Well, the first event I remember – I went with Dad to the Blind & Deaf Association in Hackney, Adelaide, where he bought a large two-handled cane basket that could carry the newborn twins, Tim and Ruth. I remember Dad loading this basket into the rear seat of his red 1926 Fiat Impala. I was 2½ years of age.

About eighteen months later, the twins had grown out of the basket so it was stored down in the cellar, where I would bring it to the top stair, sit in it and toboggan down the eighteen or so steps. Great fun! Dad erected a swing that he made – he was a very handy carpenter – and erected it on the side verandah.

**Here I am about two years in the swing in 1932.
Helen (four) is on her tricycle – later mine.**

Note the blind on the left hand side. My job each hot morning was to lower this and the two larger ones on the front verandah.

A studio portrait of me, three years, and Helen, five years in 1933.

John William Murrell, three years old

History must be repeating itself. There is a studio portrait of my own father, John William (Jack) Murrell when he was three years old in 1903. The portrait was taken in Geelong but my father's dad was born in a tent on the Ballarat Goldfields. Can you see the likeness between me and my dad at three years old?

A snap with Mum's sister Auntie Mollie holding Tim, 2, aside Ruth, 2, Helen behind and me, 4, in 1934.

Dad with Tim & Ruth about 12 months on LHS of seesaw, which Dad had made.

A family snap in 1935 on the side tennis court lawn. L to R: Ruth, Me (five years), Mum, Helen & Tim. Much fun was had on this lawn as a swing was strung up high on a large branch. We played on the swing for hours.

Sometimes I played with Helen's dolls house, which Dad made. I'm about 3½ years in the photograph below. At four years old, I went to Miss Leal's pre-kindergarten. I walked with Paddy, our Irish Terrier, who guarded me well. Mary Schafer is on my right. She, way later, married John Haigh, of Haigh's chocolates.

Right Paddy was a marvellous dog. As I walked around the Sewers Yard (approx. five acres). He would be beside me. If anyone put their hand on my shoulder, he would growl at them.

Me about twelve months on Dad's knee beside Mum with 1930's hat.

On the rocks on a day at Seacliff in 1935. Me (about five), Dorrie the maid, Mum, Tim, Ruth and Helen.
We went to the beach often, mainly to Brighton.

Left: Here we are in 1936 at Port Elliot back beach on the double swing.
Me with hat at back (about six years).

Right: The four children snapped at the corner of the tennis court (asphalt), me with my first pair of glasses about six years.

Left: On the beach esplanade. I'm at the back, approx. 5 ½ years.

**On the beach paddling at Queenscliff Victoria with Dad's sister Auntie Chris.
I'm with tie – in beach mode!
L to R: Tim, Helen, Ruth, Auntie Chris, Me**

At the SA-VIC border in 1936. L to R: Me, Ruth and Tim

I'm on the running board of the 1932 Morris Oxford 6 that Dad bought so we could tow the caravan (6 berth) he made. I helped him build it over a period of two years. We often travelled at Christmas to see Dad's elderly parents at Geelong. We also had several holidays at *The Falls* Guest House at Apollo Bay, Victoria. It was owned by Dad's sister – Auntie Belle and her husband, Ted Hughes.

**In 1943. I'm on the right-hand side with others shelling peas at Auntie Nell's farm near Geelong.
R-L: Next to Ruth, Tim, Helen, Auntie Nell, Mum and my other aunt, Auntie Chris.
I'm about thirteen years old.**

We had great fun with the younger guests. I learnt to body surf.

I have very pleasant memories of my early days, from three to five years old.

We were given jobs around the house at Port Road, but they were not too onerous.

I went to Sunday School Kindergarten at Holy Trinity run by Miss Beryl Julge. We had a birthday candle ladder – the older you were, the more candles to light up the ladder. It was a big success.

I forgot about Christmas at Miss Leal's. Before Christmas, Miss Leal took us (about 15) pre-kinders outside to show us a plane flying.

"That's Father Christmas's plane," she said, and we went back inside. In the classroom were fifteen individual presents wrapped and laid out carefully.

Fabulous! That's the magic of Father Christmas.

Chapter 2

Kindergarten and Primary School Days – Depression into War

There are many experiences a child is privy to, but rarely can a juvenile say they have lived through a war. Despite being besmirched by some ominous traces of war, my early years have mostly been coloured with the euphoric hues of bliss, excitement and exuberance.

This period covers my 5 – 12 years (1935 – 1943).

I joined the cubs (1st Torrensville) and Miss Morgie, aka "Arkele", was the leader.

I was a very keen cub. I eventually led my own "red sixer" group, and through my enthusiasm, I was able to earn all thirteen activity badges. I had to do a lot of fun-discovery hikes to get these shiny badges.

One of the fondest memories I had from my club-member years was the inter-club races. My dad had a wooden chariot made for these races, but our kingly chariot was too strong and heavy. Hence, we were easily beaten by those riding lighter-constructed chariots.

Although SA was just coming out of the thirties depression, it was the start of my "Salad Days". I was into everything.

Kindergarten (five years old) was run by Miss Hastaxell at Thebarton Primary School, now School of Languages, Department of Education.

In year three, Miss Cochlander cracked my left knuckles if I picked up the pen with my left hand. As a result, I now write right-handed, although I'm ambidextrous. Interestingly, I play tennis and bowling with my left hand (single-handed), but I bat and play golf with my right hand.

Grade 5 teacher was Mr Laurie Arther, also a very keen bandmaster. I was a corporal in the B flat fife section. I could never grasp sheet music and had to rely on "doe-re-mee".

Under sugar fig tree by tennis court – Port Road about 1937.

L to R: Helen, Tim, Dad, Ruth, Mum and myself in my 1st Torrensville cub uniform.

Dad bought this '39 Pontiac for £339 just before the war started. Me: I'm eight years.

After the depression, as war approached, Dad joined the volunteer reserves as a Lieutenant. I'm eight years old beside him in these two photos (above and left).

Dad in his military uniform with Ruth (left) and Helen (right)

In my band uniform.

**The Thebarton Primary School Drum, Fife and Bugle Band.
I'm in the back row 7th from the left-hand side.**

Dad sold the Morris Oxford and bought a 1939 Pontiac Silver Avvous fawn colour S.A.2067 just before war broke out in September 1939. He paid £339. It was an excellent car, large enough for four kids and two adults. A good hauler of the caravan. I learnt to drive it when I was sixteen.

During the war, we did many Christmas trips to Geelong while towing a trailer packed with small drums filled with petrol, a very dangerous feat. Dad saved up his petrol ration and stored the drums in the cellar all year.

A memory that didn't seem so haunting back then, but is presently unsettling, was when I was on my way for a holiday in Broken Hill to stay with the Careys. Theo was chief engineer of the zinc copper mine and was showing me around when, at the Terowie Railway Station, there was a buzz all over that "war has been declared."

Ah, the things one remembers so clearly. I was eight years old at that time.

At "Thebby" Primary School, I remember being given a free mug of warm milk each day in kindergarten and grades. I walked approximately one mile to and from school. Eventually, after much pestering, I got a beaut red bike, (like the photo) except the handlebars turned 180° up.

I had to "dinky" Tim on the crossbar, at least until he won a Cathedral Choir Scholarship to attend Pulteney Grammar School. I rode to and from cubs, riding back in the dark, so I had to light up an acetylene carbide lamp – the same as in the photo.

It was quite effective – but not as good as the flashing battery lights of today.

In the E&WS yard, I spent many hours watching the smithy, Jack Tilbrook, and his punch-drunk ex-boxer striker. They worked over an anvil (not painted) like in this photo. The striker one day produced two pairs of boxing gloves and proceeded to give me elementary boxing lessons, for which I've always been pleased.

Talking about boxing stirs up a fond memory of "Thebby". I was sitting on a bench having my lunch when Colin Winning, my year's school bully, came to me saying, "You can't sit there. This is my area of the schoolyard."

I looked at him before steadily replying, "Well, we'll see about that."

I challenged him to meet me at my place for a boxing match. About half our class turned up to watch this box off.

Winning didn't win, but neither did I. One had a bloodied nose (me) and Colin a black eye. We shook hands absolutely tired out, and struck a deal to have half the school yard each. Ah, the things boxing can resolve.

Early in the war, "Thebby" encouraged drives for scrap metal, batteries, old tyres and the like, so I went around "the yard" (E&WS Dept) and collected stuff willingly gathered up by the employees. Hence, I was eventually awarded two silver aeroplane badges and bars for my feats – best in school.

I became very interested in aircraft identification and became an Air Raid / Warden's Despatch rider on my bike. We did several mock air raids, so I saved my pocket money and bought simple aero-modeller kits.

First gliders, then more complex engine craft similar to the photo on left), but nowhere as big – about a two-foot wingspan was the largest that I built.

At the outbreak of war, Dad (39 years) was pulled out of the army by the South Australian Government and made 'Controller of Essential Services', such as water, electricity, gas, and sewerage. He established a central control room in the basement of the E&WS Head Office in Victoria Square, which was always a thrill to visit. He held mock air raids. My dad and I also visited "damaging" bomb sites with mock sewerage and water mains blown up. Mock repairs were made by special crews. All essential pump stations were manned by Dad's army with ex-Boer war -300" rifles. So far for our "made-up" war. Not so made-up as we had to evacuate in 1942 to Aunt Mollie's house at Belair Road in the nearby Adelaide Hills.

I had a horse called "Prince" at the time, so I had the job of riding the fifteen miles to Belair. All started well until I was alongside the Mile End railway shunting yard when a stream engine driver saw me on Prince and, for fun, blew the whistle.

Off went Prince at full gallop. He didn't stop for two miles. When he was eventually puffed out, I had to dismount and walk him a mile before remounting for the rest of the journey at walking or trotting pace.

Three on Prince

This photo is of Aunt Mollie's fibro house. It had quite a large backyard full of long grasses that Prince enjoyed. After a while, he had consumed all the grass inside the wire fence.

To compensate for the sudden lack of food, he reached his neck through the tight wires to munch the wild oats growing on the verge. He also stepped with one foot between the bottom two wires, effectively trapping himself badly. When we came home from school, his hock was bleeding. We had to cut the wire with bolt cutters to free him.

There were many dead long trunks of gum trees about, so Dad and I cut them up to suitable lengths for chopping. We used a big crosscut saw like this one with a handle on each end to pull and punch.

Dad pushed me a lot on this, but I was fit.

At an early age, about six, I joined Our Boy's Institute (O.B.I) for gym every Saturday morning. These controlled exercises, with parallel bars, trapeze and equestrian vaulting, helped develop my muscles. It was good fun.

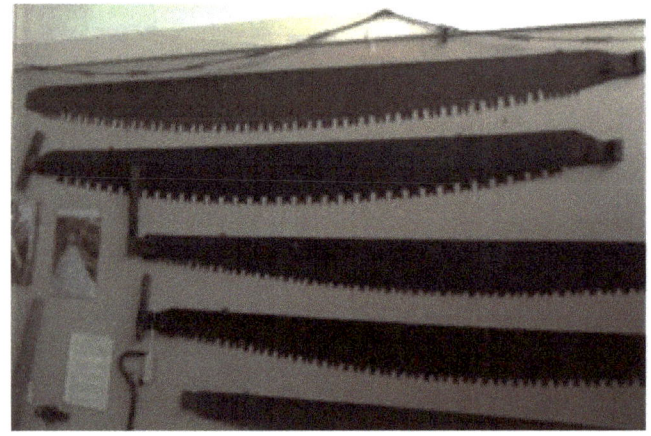

I remembered how we usually went roller skating for an hour before going to the gym. There was a board running track above and around the large gym area. From one side up into the rafters and down the other side of the track was a very scary rope ladder track. I attempted to transverse it several times but in vain. I have to admit that I'm still afraid of heights even now.

Sythe they used to cut the Lucerne

The type of separator to separate milk and cream

Grinding wheel to sharpen scythe and sickle

The sort of butter churn I used to make butter

Before going to gym on Saturday mornings, I had four main jobs that needed to be done: one, fill and light the copper tub for washing, two, polish the cross fender and wood box, three, help milk the cow and four, feed my chooks and ducks. My other delegated jobs on the weekdays after school were to cut the Lucerne, chaff the Lucerne, mix out Lucerne chaff with pollard and bran and feed chooks, separate milk and cream, and churn the cream into butter.

We were extremely lucky to have a cow, named Buttercups, through the butter-rationed war years. We also got plenty of free eggs from my chooks. I soon turned this into a business, with my very own entrepreneur's logbook – a notebook with one page labelled as "buys" and the opposite page labelled "receipts". I sold eggs to Mum and many of her Red Cross friends and delivered them myself by riding my bike. Once, the string bag full of eggs got caught in the front spokes. Oh dear, what an absolute mess and what a loss of profit!

Anyhow, I still had to pay Dad back for all the bran, pollard and wheat the chooks ate. I eventually sold the chooks, turkeys and ducks that I bred or bought to Dad. Together, when required, we would chop off their heads, pluck the feathers and drain the innards – a good anatomy lesson.

A classic, scary trick I used on my sisters was to let go of a chook without its head on – blood flies everywhere! I had a very dark sense of humour.

I had to help mum with the washing by pumping the old type washing machine handle as seen at the rear (right).

I also had to turn the wringer handle for this e.g. Shown at back, right.

Mum used a ribbed scrubbing board, shown on the left-hand side, front.

Again, the type of butter churn I used.

On many Christmas holidays, Dad would tow the caravan to a block at Brighton (adjacent to Lady Mawson's home), with only some sandhills and the road separating the beach. A tent was used as the outhouse and a kerosene lantern, like the one shown on the right, provided light at night.

The night watchman at the yard cut firewood, but I cut a deal to light the wood stove that Mum used which looked like that one but was black, not green enamel (pictured left).

The sink in the kitchen was like this, with cupboards underneath.

Ruth and I mainly washed and dried, Tim and Helen escaped to do their important homework.

Top – the type of mincer and kitchen utensils used in Mum's kitchen.

I omitted to explain why we were evacuated to Belair. Well, right adjacent to the yard across the road was a huge red gasometer. Dad was afraid the Japs would bomb it and take our house and many yard buildings with it. The gasometer had been dismantled long ago with the change from coal to natural gas.

Another change that occurred for war preparations: our cow and horse paddock were fenced off, and in their place, zig-zag air raid trenches with bunkers were dug. Dad and I helped dig air raid trenches in the "entoucans" tennis courts at St Peter's Girls College.

Tim and I enjoyed our OBI Christmas camps in tents near the Hindmarsh River at Victor Harbour. One year, Tim was terribly sunburnt with huge blisters on his shoulders. I never blistered but turned brown.

When I was twelve, I changed to the gym at YMCA because my school buddies went there. It was in this particular gym that I learnt the elements of wrestling. Dad used to take Tim and I to see "Big Chief Little Wolf" wrestle "Johnny Paradise", and I loved it.

By the way, you could catch a tram to "Paradise" in Adelaide.

We always had a great time at the yard Christmas parties. A policeman from the Police Training Barracks opposite, on Port Road, would be Father Christmas. He'd hand out presents of various kinds to everyone. Dad usually gave a thank you speech to his yard employees (about 500) as depicted right.

When 12 or 13, I made a Crystal Set Radio exactly like the one pictured. Later I made a valve wireless set. It worked!

For about a year, Grandpa Calvert (Mum's dad) stayed with us as Mum nursed him with cancer of the cheek. When it grew worse, he went to the Memorial Hospital and lived on painkillers. He died in 1942 and is buried at South Arm, Tasmania.

Over the war years, I became interested in collecting birds' nests and eggs, coins, beer and watch box labels, and badges. I suppose anything that would be considered a war relic. Dad provided a foreman's hut with lots of map slots which was very suitable for storing my collections.

By 1940, I charged one penny a visit, for the Red Cross (not for me). Many of Mum and Dad's friends gave me stuff. When Mum and Dad moved in 1953 when I was in the USA, Mum unilaterally gave it all to a boy at Trinity, and let me tell you, I was quite annoyed at the time. My collection of bird's nests and eggs, coins, beer labels, badges – all gone.

Dad took us for early morning swims to the Adelaide City Council pool in King William Street (no longer there). He offered me a fishing rod if I could swim five lengths. I did and got my rod.

One Sunday, I diverted on my way home from Sunday School to the railway yard beside the River Torrens. Vacant land was filled with tents of the unemployed. A circus tent was up and I went in. I willingly helped to put up the lions' circular performing cage. I didn't realise how long it took to get home. Meanwhile, Mum was worried and rang the police to look for me.

After coming home from school, having a growing boy's appetite, I always felt hungry. So, I would get slices of fresh bread and cover them with dripping (always in a pot beside the stove), pepper and salt. It was delicious! Also, I would climb the loquat tree and gorge myself.

My mum used a weight scale similar to the blue one shown below. She also used a beancer and a mincer – I turned the handle – and also flat irons as shown below, which she let heat on the flat black wooden fuelled stove.

When we went to stay with Grandpa Ambrose, a Murrell, at 256 Pakington Street, West Geelong, there was a mangle like this one and we would take turns to flatten the washed sheets and linen.

Also, as grandchildren, we would make a bee-line for the stereo viewer and slides, just like the one shown below.

One day I was playing with the knife sharpeners when Aunt Chris called out, "Don't do that! You will cut your thumb."

I didn't stop and sure enough, I've got today scarring on the top side of my thumb. At the time it bled and bled – I remember holding it up in the rear seat assist straps all the way back from Geelong to Adelaide.

One Christmas morning at Auntie Nell's (Dad's sister) and Uncle Alf Coundry's farm, they gave themselves a new kapok double mattress for Christmas which the children used in the lounge room to sleep on. Being up bright and early on Christmas morning, we arranged jumping competitions from the top of the lounge to the new mattress. By the time we had finished, all the hold-down buttons and associated stitching had parted. We received a severe dressing down!

At Geelong for Christmas dinner, sixpence and three pence were cooked in the pudding. There was always a demand for extra serves. Dad would occasionally point to a non-existent "fly" on the ceiling, and while we were all looking up, he would sneak a Florine under the pudding.

We had great fun catching the tram to the Corio Bay baths in the sea. We would spend the whole day there and would return by tram, all unsupervised.

I was an active member of Holy Trinity (H.T.) Youth Fellowships, a member of the Christian Missionary Society (CMS) League of Youth and also President and Secretary of the H.T. Youth tennis club. We played at our place on Saturday afternoons. Mum and Dad also played tennis on Sunday afternoon at Port Road when it was their turn.

Mum and Dad also hosted bridge parties. I used to shell the almonds. We had two almond trees, and I helped mum make devilled salted almonds for their bridge companions.

I was surprised to get the first prize in Grade 7, which was the SA Progress Certificate. Dad, as president of the Parents and Teachers Association (P & T.A.), presented it to me on stage at the Thebarton Town Hall.

Only two people in our class went in to private schools.

It was on the year of 1943 that I developed my first crush: Jennifer Barratt.

Most of our class went on to Thebarton Technical School, and it was also my wish to attend the said school. But my dad had other ideas, so I ended up going to St Peter's College instead.

Many tradesmen in the depression had to sell their tools to get money for food. Dad bought many carpenter tools like these, as shown on the next page.

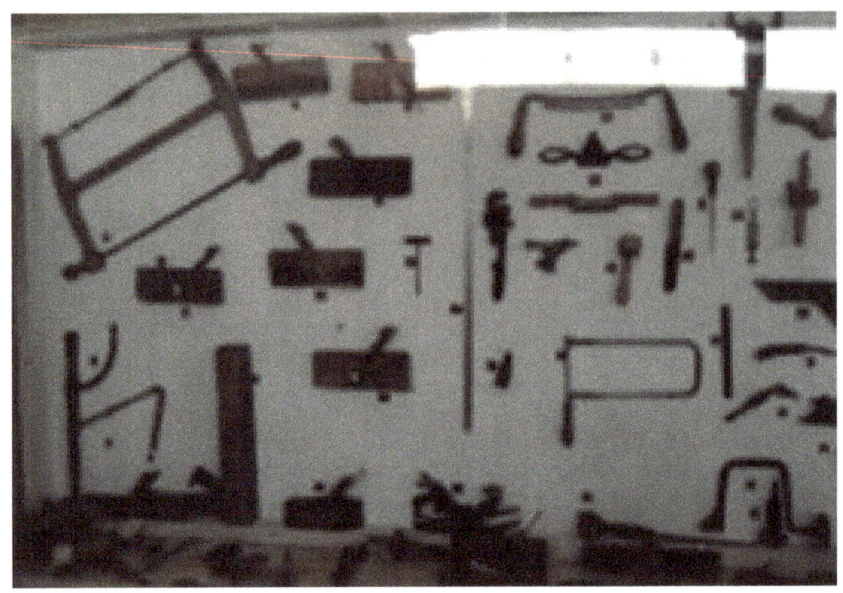

He had a well-paid SA Government job as Engineer for Sewerage in the Engineering and Water Supply Department.

In the street south of our Brighton beach block lived Mr and Mrs Shepley and their daughters, Margot and Christabel (my age). We often played hide and seek in the adjacent sand hills while our parents had afternoon tea. 'My Story" connects with Mr Ray Shepley, a civil engineer several times later.

In my wanders around the yard, I watched many tradesmen perform many engineering jobs. For instance, white metal bearing, running, fitting and turning, grinding, hacksawing, key cutting, wheel changing and tyre repairs, circular sawing and engineer over-hauls as I clambered over excavators, trench diggers and an old Abion chain drive 1925 truck. It was great fun, watching and learning. The men were pleased to show me things. The carpentry shop had a band saw, chain saw, planer, and mortising machines. All good grounding to be a handyman/engineer.

On some holidays, I went in the trucks with the sewer inspectors and visited injector stations, pumping stations and sewerage treatment plants. All exciting experiences for a young 12-year-old.

**Above and over the page: St Peters College
Schoolhouse for boarders; Main Oval; Memorial Hall; Headmaster's House, now Development Office.**

Chapter 3

Days at St Peter's College – 1943 – 1948

I glared at my father and crossed my arms over my chest petulantly. He gave me an impish smile in return, his stance victorious.

"Come on now. It'll be great," he said, patting me on the shoulder.

I sighed dejectedly as I trudged to the fitting room, reluctantly slipping the winter and summer "Saints gear" my father handed to me.

My longing to attend Thebarton Technical School, the school that most of my mates will be attending, went unheard. Instead, I'm currently sporting the colours of St. Peter's College.

I wrinkled my nose as I stared at my reflection in the mirror. Of course, the gear perfectly fit me, goading me to acknowledge the inevitability of my impending "doom".

As an act of rebellion, I made sure that I had my head down as my parents dropped me off for my first day.

I was placed in the 'Tich' Schubert computer room at Saints (see photo over page) for boys from State Primary Schools with Dr Koch Emergy as our master. What a stroke of luck this was as Dr Emergy was marvellous. Meanwhile, I was assigned to McDermott House with "Dicky" Holtham as Housemaster. He took a bit of getting used to.

Proving the statement that "parents always know best", I came home thrilled to be attending "Saints" after the first day and thanked Dad for insisting I attend. My dad merely nodded, but I think I saw him huff out his chest in pride for my gratitude. Since my Dad didn't go to a private school, he was determined that all his children did if he could afford it.

Tim, Bill, Ruth and Helen – all in school uniforms. Approx. 1944

Left: "Titch" Schubert Computer Room at "Saints".

Right: All throughout the war dad had a gas mask
hanging on the back door.
I used to put it on and scare my sisters.

Since I couldn't join the Cadets until I was 14 years old, I had to attend "Balxx" McIntosh's first aid classes for a year instead.

Here we are on the front lawn with "Paddy" and John Carey (far right)
who was Exeat as a boarder at "Saints". He later married Margot Shepley.
L to R: Paddy, me, Tim, Dad, Helen, Ruth, John.

As I relished in my "Saints" experience, the year 1944 brought an unexpected, welcome surprise – Mum found herself pregnant again twelve years after she had my twin siblings.

Andrew duly arrived on the 22nd of July 1945. Mum decided on Andrew Douglas Calvert Murrell (ADCM) but when Dad told his father, my grandfather Ambrose Murrell, of the proposed name, a telegram soon arrived with the message "Another Murrell and still no Ambrose."

The name Calvert was quickly dropped, and Ambrose was added. Hence Andrew's initials then spelt ADAM. Later, as a talented oil painter, he signed his artworks with these initials, including the word Dom, short for Dominus – the Latin word for master or God, and the cross of St Andrew.

Left: This photo was taken at Andrew's christening with his godparents standing at rear. Aunt Belle (Dad's sister), me, Mrs Villiers (Mum's friend) and Mr and Mrs Kellett (Mr Kellett was the yard superintendent). Mum is holding Andrew in the front.

Right: A few years later at Corio Bay beach with Grandma Murrell, nee Helen Cuthberson, and Mum, Ruth, Tim and Andrew.

Above: Later still, approx. 1948 with Mum and her younger sister Aunt Mollie.
L to R: Helen, Me, Mum, Aunt Mollie, Tim and Helen.

Right: Approx. 1947 Tim left-hand side, and me in Cadet uniform.

Amazingly, we could take our 300 Boer war (ex) rifles home. This was stopped in 1948 when I became Quartermaster Sergeant Major.

I was responsible for the correct storage of all 303 rifles and bayonets, 3" mortars, bren guns and Vickers machine guns. I did such a good job that I was awarded the Neville Swift Medal as the "most efficient cadet" in 1948.

In 1947, for passing Year 11, I was gifted a holiday to Tasmania to celebrate my success.

During this trip, I phoned Mr Shepley, who was the Chief Civil Engineer of the Tasmanian Hydroelectric Commission.

"Fine timing. I'm going inland to view Clarke Dam being built, then travel by jeep to Tarraleah to cover the site of larger water mains being built for the new Tungatinah Power Station opposite Tarraleah, so bring a pack and join me," he said. I agreed without hesitation.

It was at this moment that I realised I was graced with an advantage that not everyone is as fortunate to have – clear foresight. What I wanted to be was becoming clearer, as if the fog obstructing my vision for the future was starting to slowly unveil.

As instructed, I quickly packed my bags and joined Mr Shepley for one of the most stimulating experiences of my life. It proved to be an absorbing three days, after which he offered me a job as a Civil Engineering Cadet.

I thought about it long and hard. But, in the end, I refused. I wanted to spend another year at Saints.

I had to pass English which I had failed twice. It was required to start Engineering at the University of Adelaide. In 1948, I attempted Leaving Honours but failed four subjects. I did pass Leaving English eventually, so I was finally able to enrol in a university engineering degree at last.

Failing during my latter Saints years isn't my proudest moment. Being a cadet, Quartermaster in Automotive, a member of Science, Debating and Drama, Athletics and Rowing clubs, plus having girlfriends, left little to no time for studying. Not to mention, I was also a house prefect. Failing was easier than passing due to my incredibly chaotic, busy schedule.

A L/Hons class trip to Broken Hill and down 1800 feet north mine.
It was a good group experience with master "Snitch" Stevens.

Me in mining garb, about 17 years old.

My teachers for intermediate were specialists in Maths, English and Science, with R. Cameron as acting headmaster. I passed eight subjects, namely Ma 1 & II, Pc Ch, H, Com Ph & Credit Drawing.

I performed quite well in Credit Drawing as I gave up Latin and took up this subject only eighteen months prior. Philology was listed as the last exam in December, so I enrolled and studied Holem's textbook during the Test Cricket at the Adelaide Oval in the members' stand as I was a junior member of SACA.

I copied her prac book to hand in. The teachers at "Saints" thought it was a misprint when my name came up as Ph was not taught at "Saints".

I passed Leaving to matriculate next year (1947) in Ma 1, 11 & Special, P, C, German. However, as I have mentioned earlier, I failed English. I took special coaching to remedy this but alas, also failed the supplementary exam in January 1948. As you could probably tell through my writing, I was no English scholar. I finally passed English in November of that year.

I had several birthday parties at Port Road over my "Saints" years. At one of these parties, Dad hired a penny-farthing bike, like this one over the page.

I soon caught the knack of getting on and off without falling. Getting off the bike was surprisingly harder. My girlfriend at the time, Helen Angwin, the daughter of my dad's boss, once tried it and got her dress caught in the big front wheel. It was an utter disaster.

I was always broke at Saints. I always brought a packed lunch and almost never bought anything from the tuck shop.

A couple of other broke boys formed a gang with me. We would put our pennies together and go into town after our first aid class on Monday afternoon. One would buy a \-9 ticket to the 1-hour News at the Savoy Theatre, go in, sit down then go to the back toilet. He would then open the escape door where the eight of us would be waiting – we would space out our entry. Such cunningness and bravery!

I rode my bike five miles to and from Saints until the athletics coach "Joc" Volugi said I was back kicking when running. So, I took the tram thereafter.

In 1946, I was the Under 16 Champion, winning the long jump at 18' 6", second in the high jump at 5' 10", 100 yards of hurdles and 100 yards flat. From then on, my athletics performance failed except for the shot put. I think I gained too much muscle for my height (I was 5' 9").

The annual Blue and White formal balls, consistent with what you see in films, were always popular. And as in films, I was that one guy who always took a different date to each one. I asked a different girl each year as my partner: Jennifer Barrott, Nan Wellington, Nora Chamberlain, Helen Angwin and Rachel Bowen. I attended Nora Stewart's dance class, called the "in place", for first- or second-year college gals and boys.

I was eighteen when I finally graduated from "Saints", one of the eldest in my class.

At the end of 1948, Dad entered me for a scholarship at Roseworthy Agricultural College. The application took the entire weekend. I went to see the grounds one Friday afternoon. It was impossible not to marvel at the institution's grandiosity. The structure resembled a castle that towered high with pride, bringing whispers of success to its future students. The next morning, I was academically tested to ascertain whether or not I was qualified through an exam, and on Sunday, I visited the college to see more of its grounds and then overcome the more daunting agenda for the day: to find out my results.

On the ride back home that Sunday, I could feel my father's anger pierce through the once placid atmosphere in the car. His rigid posture, his pursed lips and his cold gaze made me squirm uncomfortably in my seat.

"I want to be an engineer," I said, my voice firm despite my fear.

My dad was silent for a moment. "A full scholarship … for three years," he said in disbelief. "Not everyone would have been as lucky."

I stayed silent. Although I got the scholarship, I refused it as I was determined to become an engineer.

"I can't pay for your university. You'll have to pay for yourself," my dad said with an air of finality.

All night, I thought about the situation. Helplessness turned into determination and the next morning, I phoned the Professor of Mechanical Engineering for an appointment.

We had a really good chat. Ah, the power of good conversation. That day, I left his office employed as a Cadet on the princely sum of £5 per month, and free courses in B.E. for which I had to work a minimum of twenty hours per week in the Mech Engineer lab and workshop.

I was filled with elation as the realisation set in: I can study engineering! However, accompanying this huge achievement was the harsh slap of becoming an adult: more responsibilities. My mum told me that she wanted a portion of my £5 per month for weekly housekeeping. Oh, how I missed the sweet ignorance of childhood.

Aside from these events that served as significant turning points in my life. Another memorable moment was when I attended a Youth for Christ rally in a city theatre in 1947. There, with Reverend Hyman Appleman (an American evangelist), I accepted Christ into my life. Up to this date, I have never regretted this significant step. I believe God has given me guidance throughout all the ups and many downs in my life and I owe him everything I have ever accomplished.

As a family, we played many games e.g. fiddlesticks, knucklebones, tops, skipping, Kudo, Chinese checkers and, of course, Monopoly.

Chapter 4

My First Paid Jobs – 1947 – 1950

I looked at my dad, looking for any signs of jest.

"A job?"

"Yeah, I got you a job," he repeated, grinning with self-satisfaction. "There ain't no way I'm letting you do nothing during the holidays."

It was the Christmas of 1947. Feelings of exhilaration threatened to overwhelm me as I thought of being able to earn money. My very own stash of cash. I grinned back at my dad, hoping that my gratitude was conveyed.

"You'll be a farmhand," he said.

"Alright," I nodded, thinking of the work and cash that lay ahead of me. Shouldn't be too hard.

"It's in Islington … at the Sewerage Farm."

I looked at him. "That's about eight miles away," I stated.

He looked at me, confused. "Yeah. You have a bike, don't you?"

And so, for my very first paid job, I would ride my bike from home to the farm and vice versa. Each trip took about forty minutes.

Accompanying this long, arduous journey was a set of equally strenuous tasks at the farm. For eight hours, I would either stack hay in the paddocks then pitchfork them into a large truck and conversely, pitchfork hay from a truck and into the haystack. After two days of pitchforking, my uncalloused schoolboy hands were covered in red, angry blisters.

"Piss on them," one of the men working on the same farm said. "Makes 'em hard," he added before pitchforking away.

And so I did. By the end of the week, I had hard hands.

I can't remember how much I got paid, but it was enough pocket money to compensate for the hard labour I had to do.

My pitchforking days came to an end as I transitioned into my university life. To earn extra money during my "uni" years, I joined the Adelaide University Regiment. I got the money I needed by participating in the weekly parades, camps and rifle shoots.

However, the main job I had in university was the one offered to me by Jack Kern. He worked in the university's mechanical engineering workshop and owned a foundry.

"You'll work Saturday mornings, from 6 to 9 for £5," he said.

And so, every Saturday, I forced myself to wake up at 4.30 am. I ate breakfast and got picked up at 5.15 am to be driven to the foundry, which was about eight miles from home.

There, I loaded pig, scrap iron and charcoal in set layers into the top side opening of the cupola furnace. The furnace was always lit by the time I got there. It was sweaty, hard work as I would load the barrow of iron or charcoal on the ground, climb the ladder, wind the loaded barrow up the hoist, then swing it round out, empty the contents into the side hole of the cupola and then repeat these steps for the next load and the subsequent loads after that.

I would be exhausted when I got home at about 9 am. But I would still persevere. I would take a shower, do the house chores, ride my bike to the University Rugby field and play 1:50 – 3:00 in seconds, then be the reserve for A's 3:15 – 4:45 and more often than not be called on the field. The shower after the second match would be pure bliss.

On good days, I'd ride my bike home, ask Dad if I could borrow the car then pick up John Callaghan at St. Marks College. We'd go have a good meal at a pub and buy a bottle of port on the way out, then on to Burnside Town Hall to attend a dance. I'd try my luck with picking up a couple of girls. It would usually work out. I'd drive, park, then fall asleep with my arms around a girl. Such were my glory days.

1948 I was selected in the SA Under-19's State Rugby Union Team.

Chapter 5

Working for General Motors
1950 - 1958

Scholarship in the United States

I trudged through the busy corridors, seamlessly blending in with the sleep-deprived crowd.

"What do you mean it's due tonight?" I vaguely heard as I passed the notice board, the bold letters of the word **SCHOLARSHIP** forcing me to a sudden halt.

I shifted the weight of my backpack as I approached the announcement:

SCHOLARSHIP IN THE UNITED STATES

The Galway-Mayo Institute of Technology (GMIT) is pleased to announce that it's granting three engineering students a scholarship for a period of two years in the United States. To be eligible, the engineering student must:
- have passed their second year of engineering

AND
- must have worked for two years at General Motors (GM) Holden.

For more details, please visit the student administration office, which is open from Monday to Friday from 9.00 am to 5.00 pm.

I nodded my head, determination coursing through my veins.

I checked my watch before quickly heading to the library, intent on finding some GM Holden job ads in the paper.

I combed my fingers through my hair as I searched the classified ads, worried as I contemplated my academic progress. So far, I was passing Physics, Chemistry, First Aid and Management Engineering. It was Maths I was most worried about as I was currently on a failing mark.

I glanced at my watch again. I had cadet duties to perform at around 4.00 pm.

I sighed as I abandoned my search. "Just find time for this later," I muttered, shouldering my backpack as I headed out.

Being a cadet, coupled with being a member of the Rugby Club and the Evangelical, I had little to almost no time for studying.

"William!" a familiar voice called out to me. I turned around, automatically grinning.

"Mr Bula," I said, nodding as a form of greeting. Akhiyan Bula MD, my lecturer for my Kelvinator unit, was definitely a personal favourite among the teaching staff. It was his unit that inspired me to pursue my ambitions of becoming an Industrial Engineer.

"Busy working hard on those assignments?" he asked, a warm smile gracing his kind features as he slapped me on the back.

I laughed humourlessly. "Not enough apparently. I need to try harder for Maths."

"Ah." He nodded understandingly. "You'll manage," he said, looking at me with confidence and assurance. "Well, don't try too hard now. You might easily top your class."

I laughed heartily as he headed off, waving as he went.

The days went quickly as I was swamped with both curricular and extra-curricular duties and soon enough, I found a job advert as a Technical Clerk in the Plant Engineering Department of GMH Woodville.

I straightened my back as I regarded the man before me. He was silent as he read the document he held, his face impassive. I tapped my oxfords against the wooden floors in an attempt to calm my nerves.

Get it together, I thought before he looked up. I held my breath.

He considered me for a few seconds more before he cracked a smile. He extended his hand.

"Congratulations, Mr Murrell. Welcome to GMH."

I couldn't help the grin that broke out as I shook his hand eagerly. "I won't disappoint you, sir."

Since I was still studying, GMH only required me to work for half the day.

For the next months, I found that the majority of my time revolved around my university and work life. It was hectic, but I found myself enjoying the challenge. It was a year later when I received my academic results back, and the saying 'you reap what you sow' couldn't be more accurate. I grinned widely as I stared at the outcome of my hard work.

"Like what you see?" a friend of mine asked, smirking.

I snorted before I grinned. "I passed."

My friend gave me a clap on the back.

1st-year Engineers were painted, then had to pull other year Engineers on brewery carts through Adelaide streets without trousers.

Pat Forbes, me and Geof Sutherland were all painted inmates.

Since I'd met almost all the required prerequisites, I wasted no time applying for the coveted 1951 GM Overseas Operations Scholarship.

I examined my appearance in the mirror; straightened the collar of my white oxford shirt. I exhaled slowly to help retain my calm composure. I checked my watch. *8.30 am.* I needed to go if I wanted to make it there in time. Today, I had an interview scheduled with Mr Earl Dawn, a high-ranking employee working in GMIT.

During the trip, I focused on trying to calm my nerves. I fervidly sought to be admitted to the scholarship program, but I knew I wouldn't be able to do so if I was on edge.

An hour later, I found myself staring back at Mr Dawn's intimidating stare. He sighed before he leaned further back into this chair, his stance unimpressed.

"Have you read what's required of you to be considered for this scholarship, Mr Murrell?" he asked in a monotonous tone.

"Yes, sir."

He tilted his head to the side before he leaned forward. He clasped his hands on the desk, his intimidating stare never leaving my determined ones.

"Mr Murrell …" he started in a chiding voice. "You haven't worked here for two years, nor have you completed your second-year engineering subjects. Why have you applied?"

I took a deep breath in before I offered him a bold smile. "So you'll remember me next year when I finally have the qualifications."

He raised an eyebrow, surprised, before giving me a slight smile. He regarded me with renewed interest.

"Colour me impressed," he muttered. "I'll be seeing you next year then, Mr Murrell," he said before offering me a firm handshake.

"I'll see you next year, sir," I promised.

The day after my interview, Mr Dawn had ordered my position be changed to that of a trainee Cadet Engineer. I consider this as my very first promotion in my career life. Every month, I was rotated to a different department, from press maintenance to the tool room, welding, gun manufacture, weld gear maintenance and special projects.

Throughout the year, I continued to work hard. Due to my predictable schedule, I was able to follow a monotonous routine – I worked for half the day, then studied and fulfilled my extracurricular obligations for the rest of the day. That is until a pleasant change disturbed the monotony of my days. I was assigned to complete a special project in work alongside a colleague named Theo O'Reilly.

"Well, it's goin' to be an uphill climb, Murrell, I'll tell you that," Theo said after we'd been given the instructions. We were tasked with streamlining the exhaust box manufacture line, which entailed conceiving, engineering, constructing and trying out different slide conveyors between the machines. It was an arduous and mentally-taxing task, but my interest in the subject was a strong enough motivator that pushed me to exert an outstanding performance.

At the end of the project, Theo and I got called to Mr Dawn's office. We nervously stood before him as he smiled from his desk, reading through some documents.

"Do you know what you've both done?" he asked us, raising an eyebrow.

Theo and I both stayed quiet.

"You were able to increase the output by 200 per cent."

My heart stilled. Theo and I looked at each other with wide eyes before grinning at each other. I turned to the smiling man before me.

"You may want to start packing, Mr Murrell," he told me casually.

I wrinkled my brows in confusion.

Mr Dawn merely grinned at me. "Congratulations. You'll be heading to the US soon."

I spent a week in Fisherman Bend Plant where I met the other three winners of the scholarship.

"Well, I'll be damned," I heard my mate mutter as we boarded our flight to San Francisco on a Pan Am Skymaster. I gawked at the pretentious opulence our first-class tickets had to offer – comfortable beds and a menu containing the most delectable dishes and refreshments more suited to a restaurant rather than a flight.

The next few days were a whirlwind of adventures. For the first few nights, we all went sightseeing and attempted to familiarise ourselves with U.S. currency. San Francisco was a jungle of towering buildings, extravagant cars and bustling professionals. Its streets whispered promises of dreams being fulfilled, and the scent of money, success, and excitement permeated the air.

Ignorant of the city's ways, we rode a cab and paid the driver a ten-dollar note for a trip that only cost two dollars. He grinned and thanked us for our generosity before driving away, leaving the four of us gawking after his boldness.

The day after, we boarded the Californian Zephyr in Sacramento before changing trains in Chicago. In there, we were met by Veanmette Smith. He kindly drove us around the sights for an hour or so before we had to board the train to New York, the final destination of our trip.

FOUR MORE GMH MEN TO DO 2-YEAR COURSES AT GM INSTITUTE IN U.S.A.

FOUR more employees of General Motors-Holden's Ltd. will go to the U.S.A. in September for two years' specialised education at the General Motors Institute of Technology, Flint, and practical training in various plants of General Motors Corporation.

The men, selected for 1952 under the GMH Oversea Scholarship Plan, are:—

FRANK ROBERTSON POUND, 22, of Victoria Road, Northcote. An Experimental Engineering Technical Assistant in GMH Engineering Department, Fishermen's Bend, he was with the Government Aircraft factories for three years during the war.

PETER JOHN GREEN, 25, of Brickwood Street, Elsternwick. An Equipment Engineer in GMH, Fishermen's Bend, he served his apprenticeship in six years with the Commonwealth Ammunition Factory.

WILLIAM JOHN CALBERT MURRELL, 21, of Port Road, Thebarton, Adelaide. A Technical Cadet in GMH Manufacturing Department, Woodville plant, he was formerly a cadet in the University of Adelaide Mechanical Engineering Department.

DONALD CHARLES ENDERBY, 22, of Grandview Grove, Seaforth, Sydney. A Plant and Equipment draftsman in GMH Pagewood plant, he served his apprenticeship with E.R.L. Products Pty. Ltd., Sydney.

Four other GMH employees—ROBERT G. BRIGGS, formerly in Manufacturing Dept., Fishermen's Bend; ALAN J. McMILLAN, formerly in Engineering Dept., Fishermen's Bend; ROBT. W. HOLDEN, formerly with Engineering Dept., Fishermen's Bend; and LEONARD PERKINS, formerly at Woodville plant as Technical Trainee—completed their training at the GM Institute last month. Another four employees are in their second year at the Institute. They are HERBERT MARTIN, Experimental Engineering, Fishermen's Bend; GERALD DOBELL, Manufacturing Dept., Fishermen's Bend; DONALD K. WYLIE, Technical Trainee, Woodville; and BRIAN L. STANTON, Layout Draftsman, Woodville.

Above: FRANK R. POUND, of Fishermen's Bend plant, who joined GM in June, 1951.

Above: PETER J. GREEN, also of Fishermen's Bend plant. He joined Company in March, 1951.

Left:
WILLIAM J. C. MURRELL, who joined GMH at Woodville plant in February, 1950. He was for three years a member of the Adelaide University Citizen Forces.

Right:
DONALD C. ENDERBY, of Pagewood plant, who joined the Company in February, 1951.

Overseas Scholarship Students, Class of 1954

Seated, left to right: Walter Pihan, Opel; R. G. Block, Continental; J. A. Ariztegui, Mexico; J. M. Schaub, Opel; F. R. Pound, Holden's; Keith Seymour, Vauxhall; W. J. Murrell, Holden's; R. H. Andrade, Brasil—Standing, left to right: Gerhard Rehkugler, Opel; B. L. Corbel, (France); D. C. Enderby, Holden's; Joachim Schildwachter, Opel; W. V. Dutra, Brasil; P. J. Green, Holden's; Roy Springham, Vauxhall; T. P. Roland, New Zealand; W. J. Blervacq, Continental — Not shown: R. W. Bradley and J. B. Smit, South African

I never understood why New York was dubbed the city that never sleeps and the city of dreams until I'd seen it for the first time. The city was breathtaking. The towering buildings we admired in San Francisco suddenly looked ordinary compared to the monumental structures that surrounded us here. The murmurs of rushing, energetic professionals with the continuous hum of honking cars created a cacophony that was emblematic of ambitions being realised.

Postcard of the sights

We had a week of orientation scheduled in the city and on the first day, we were able to finally meet up with the other employees for GM Holden.

After the orientation week, I decided to contact and arrange a meeting with an old classmate from Saints I knew had moved to New York, Hans Gruenberg. He served as our personal tour guide in New York City. He took us to the landmarks every traveller would dream of seeing in America, such as the Statue of Liberty and the view from the top floor of the Empire State Building. It was a wild couple of days with Hans, but the nights were even wilder.

I hooted as a fellow of mine downed another drink, music blaring in my ears.

"Holy shit," I heard someone mutter in awe as hoots and whistles filled the nightclub. I felt my jaw drop in shock as I gazed at the woman dancing seductively on the stage.

"That's Winnie Garret," Hans stated in wonder before whistling and cheering.

I nodded, dumbstruck. For the next few hours, we found ourselves busy with more alcohol, attractive female entertainers and dancing.

Our group stumbled through the exit, guffawing at our lack of balance.

"Hey!" we heard as we trudged through the quiet night. We turned around, the action making some of us stumble. I sniggered at my drunk friends, amused.

"Fellows! The tip you gave me ain't enough for the subway ride home," he complained to us, holding up the couple of dollars we left for him.

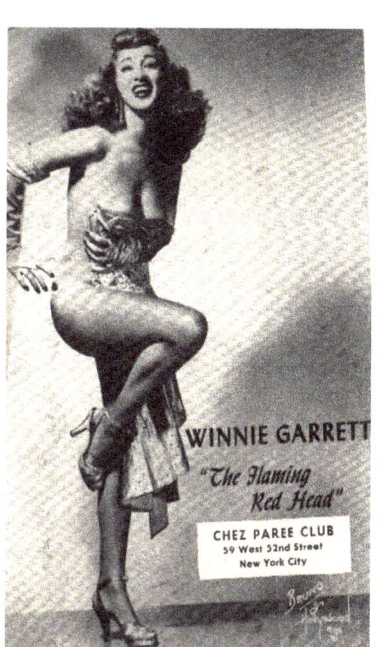

We all looked at each other, silent.

"… Well, better save 'em up. After a couple, you'd soon be able to ride the redhead!" Frank said dismissively.

We all guffawed before clumsily walking away, our merriment echoing through the sprightly alleyways of New York.

A few days after, we found ourselves on a bus headed to Detroit where we were scheduled to meet with several GM ex-executives, including BMH MD Earle Dawn.

"Where are you allocated at, Bill?" Frank asked me after we left the meeting, scratching the back of his head while looking at his scholarship brief.

"The Buick Motor Division … then the Fisher Body Pontiac next year," I told him as I read through the document. We were expected to spend one month at tech, then another month in a cooperating GM Plant.

Postcard: Buick Motor was a huge complex producing 2400 cars per day.

Postcard: Pontiac Motor Division and Test Track. Fisher Body Plant, Pontiac – the white conveyor conveys bodies from F.B.P to the Motor Division.

For the two years, I was in America, I worked hard and studied hard. Every six months, we had to complete progress tests. I built up a steady routine of immersing myself in textbooks, lectures and doing some work experience.

Postcard: GMI

"Oi! Enough of that," Frank chastised me, grabbing my book.

I glanced at the clock. "Frank … mate, it's literally four hours away."

He rolled his eyes. "And you're wasting those four hours on a book? Bill, you're in the US … Live a little. You don't get another shot at this."

I sighed before I nodded, conceding to his point.

He grinned before pulling me up. "Who knows? Maybe we'll find you a girlfriend at dinner tonight."

Every year, GMOO organised a dinner for all the scholarship recipients. The GMOO supervisors, Mr Charlie Strauss and Mr McBirnie, were present at each dinner to meet the new boys and bid farewell to the older ones.

"So … how are you enjoying Buick so far?" Mr Strauss asked me as Frank eyed the attractive woman who walked by our table.

"Yeah … not too bad. It's pretty busy … but I'm enjoying the work."

Mr Strauss nodded. At Buick, my assigned monthly work areas were safety advisory, foundry, stamping plant, fabrication plants, the forge pit and the process planning department.

"I expect you should be transferred to Fisher Body Pontiac soon. It's really exciting. You'll be assigned to manufacture, maintenance – both assembly gate and weld press, planning, design and the try-out panels."

I nodded before I took a bite of my dinner. Change is always exciting. Daunting, but nonetheless, exciting. I was pretty eager to have a change in my routine.

The rest of the dinner flowed smoothly. It was filled with amicable chatter, pleasant food and some fine-tasting wine.

"See an American girl you like?"

Frank snorted. "I have yet to find one … I'll be damned if I don't have a girlfriend before graduation."

I snorted. "Well, you've got time," I said, patting him on the back.

I was fortunate enough to have received a work assignment during the first month of my scholarship. On overtime, I was paid about $90 per week.

That was a godly amount in 1952.

In fact, I had to lend the guys some money to tie them over until they earnt the following month.

I bought an old 1949 Chev Coupe Green with the help of a loan from the bank for around $600. I had the car fixed in the GMI repair shop as a student assignment and it worked pretty well after.

I groaned as the sound of my alarm clock filled my quiet room. It was 5 am and I had to be at the Buick Foundry at around 6. After twelve hours of gruelling work, I would trudge through the snow to go back home. I'd normally stop at a deli to grab some evening tea, and by 8 pm, I'd be snug in bed exhausted from the day's events.

"I'm sick of this man," Rod Braddly, one of my scholarship mates, muttered.

I grunted in agreement, looking at the clock on the wall. Four more hours to go.

He looked at me, tilting his head to the side. "You wanna go for a ride?"

I raised an eyebrow in surprise, intrigued. "Where to?"

"Hmmm … how about Miami?"

I felt my jaw drop to the floor. "Rod … mate. That's a long way from here. You don't even have a car," I blurted.

He chuckled, amused at my surprised face. "Well, I'm going with Rod, Bob, Rene and Ron. We're using Ron's car … ten days. We could escape this for ten days."

I furrowed my eyebrows as I processed his words. "Well. We take shifts driving then."

He grinned at me before he clapped my back excitedly.

And so, a couple of days later, we found ourselves on the road to Miami. Ron's green 1948 Hornet had a fold-down rear seat, so as promised, each of us took turns to drive.

On the way to Miami, we stopped at the Great Smoky Mountains. The view of the mountains was majestic. Soon enough, I found myself intoxicated by the alluring smell of pine and the gentle caress of the cool breeze.

Above: The Hornet type

Us outside our Miami Motel.

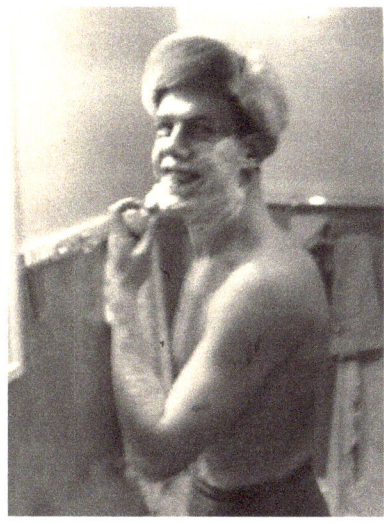

Shaving with my winter hat on, 1952.

Clearing snow @ 1633 Elwood, Flint (our accommodation).

We had time to play golf – 2 Scotties and me – Bill Dobell & Brian Stranton (both 2nd year).

"What the …" I heard Bob mutter in alarm.

We all turned to his field of vision and gawked.

"Is that … real?" Rene asked hesitantly.

"Of course it's real! It's chained up for fuck's sake," Bob exclaimed, taking a step back.

I snorted at his lack of courage. "What a wuss," I muttered, taking a step forward.

"Bill!" they all exclaimed.

I shook them off as I stared at the bear chained up to a nearby tree. The bear growled at me, standing up to its full height. I looked at it with interest before all of a sudden, it pounced at me.

All the boys yelled in alarm. I took a staggering step back.

"What the hell, Bill!" Ron yelled.

I stared at my tattered overcoat.

"Lucky it wasn't your knee," Rene muttered before we all started to slowly walk away.

As we continued on our trip, we decided to stop at Niagara Falls. Unfortunately, it was honeymoon season and all the motels were booked.

"Well, this is awkward …" Bob muttered as I groaned, horrified.

We finally found a B&B. The catch? It was a honeymoon double bed. At least we'd get breakfast in bed.

"We're never speaking of this …" I muttered.

"Agreed," he said uncomfortably before we both guffawed.

After coming back from our trip to Miami, I met up with a pen pal of my girlfriend. Her name was Gale Harris. I was invited over to their home in Winnetka, north of Chicago. I brought my mate, Frank, with me.

Frank and I on the "Old Lady" 1953

There, we spent the weekend sailing. Bringing Frank proved to be a great idea as he was a champion Jubilee sailor. The Harris's had two yachts, the "Old Lady" – a small one based in Wilmette Harbour about five miles from Ben Harris's home, and the newly bought "Banshee".

Frank about to step into the dingy to go to the "Old Lady". Gale in the stern.

Gale and friend on "The Old Lady"

Lake Charlevoix, Michigan.

Soon enough, our weekend sailing trip became a regular activity we'd try to do whenever we were free. The biggest sail we did lasted for two weeks, where we traversed the shoreline of the Great Lakes to Okeechobee Lodge.

We arrived at the lodge on a Sunday, a time when alcohol was banned from being sold in Canada.

"Get dressed; we've got to go somewhere," Frank said as he threw me my jumper.

I raised an eyebrow curiously. "Where to?

"Apparently, the MD of Carrier Air Condition bought the whole cellar of this lodge … He's giving out free drinks."

This was how Frank and I found ourselves amid a rowdy dinner dance.

After downing a couple of shots, I somehow ended up dancing with the MD's wife while Frank was nowhere to be found in the room.

She leaned into me as the music slowed.

"Come out to my cabin …" she whispered sensually after a few seconds.

45

My eyes widened in surprise.

"No," I blurted out abruptly. Her eyes widened at my blunt rejection.

I hesitated before taking a step back from her, putting some distance between us.

"Pardon my rudeness … but why would you ask me?" I asked, uncomfortable.

She smiled sadly. "I wanted to feel young and wanted again."

I pursed my lips before looking at her currently inebriated husband, laughing boisterously as he eyed the women in the room hungrily.

I nodded my head in understanding before muttering, "I'm sorry."

She just smiled before walking away.

I stood there, astonished. It was the first time I'd ever been propositioned, and it was by a married woman.

My days alternated between leisure and work.

During the busier workdays, we'd normally eat outside during our break hours as there were no eating facilities at 1633 Elwood. We'd normally go to a place we affectionately called "Australia House", as almost all the Australian students stayed there.

However, when a visiting GMH executive dropped by to check on our progress, we normally ate at "Gromer" where our lunch would be paid for by him.

During my weekends, I would meet up with my mates, and we'd try to make the most out of our stay in America.

I tried my hand at skiing and ice skating during the cold winter months. Ben was the one who taught me how to ice-skate on a small frozen lake in Winnetka one chilly day. I never truly mastered that skill.

I also went to the Adler Planetarium in Wrigley Field, Chicago with Peter Green and Sam Horrobin.

All in all, I've visited Chicago a total of eleven times. I hitch-hiked down there three hundred miles the first time to visit some dear friends of mine, the Smiths.

Gale also taught me how to ride her tandem bike. We kept in touch for birthdays and Christmas cards until she sadly passed away from stomach cancer in mid-2011.

Post Scholarship

I held my breath as the man on the podium, the GM Director, smiled at the crowd.

"This isn't the end. This is only the beginning … In fact, we just gave you several appointments with opportunity."

Everyone in the crowd cheered and hooted. I found myself standing next to Frank, grinning broadly as I voiced my excitement loudly.

Today was the day I graduated from GMI.

I had a wonderful time. I've learnt so much during my stay in America, but I'd be lying if I'll say I didn't miss home.

"Home sweet home in two days," Frank said, smiling.

"Yeah … home sweet home."

In 1952 in Flint, Mich USA

Dad filed my first 18 months of letters from Flint. Interesting reading. See Appendix 4. Turn to page 349 for my letter regarding the Flint tornado.

While the new arrivals are still on expense accounts for the first week in Flint, it is a tradition that they take the 2nd year GMOO students to dinner. The 2nd year I was the convenor, and we had a very good wind-up at Potter's Lake. The 1st year's dinner was at Zehender's (postcard below).

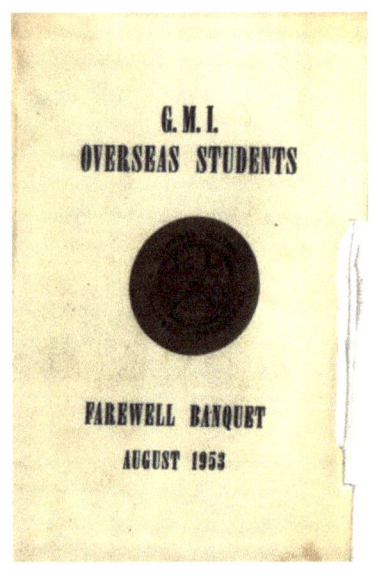

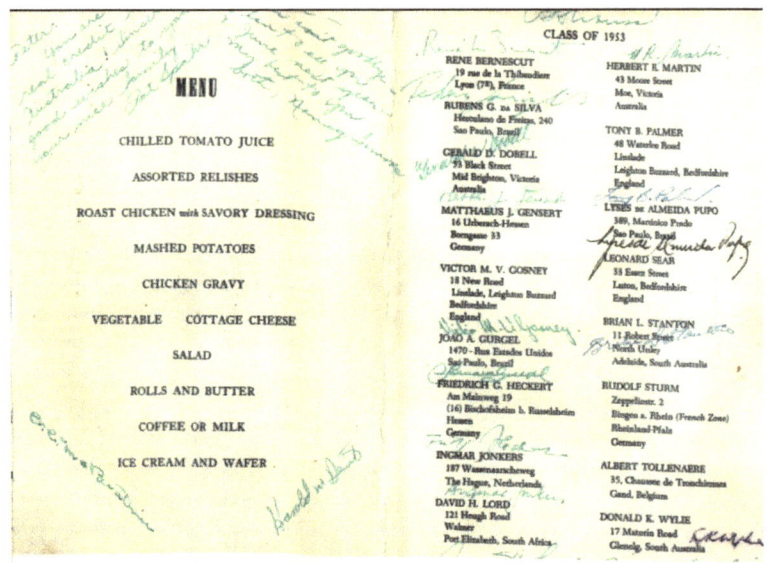

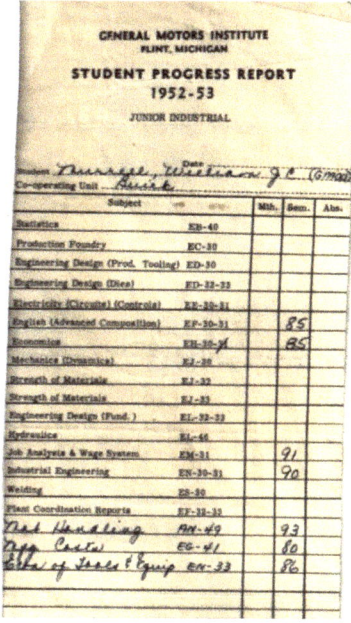

My final GMIT Results

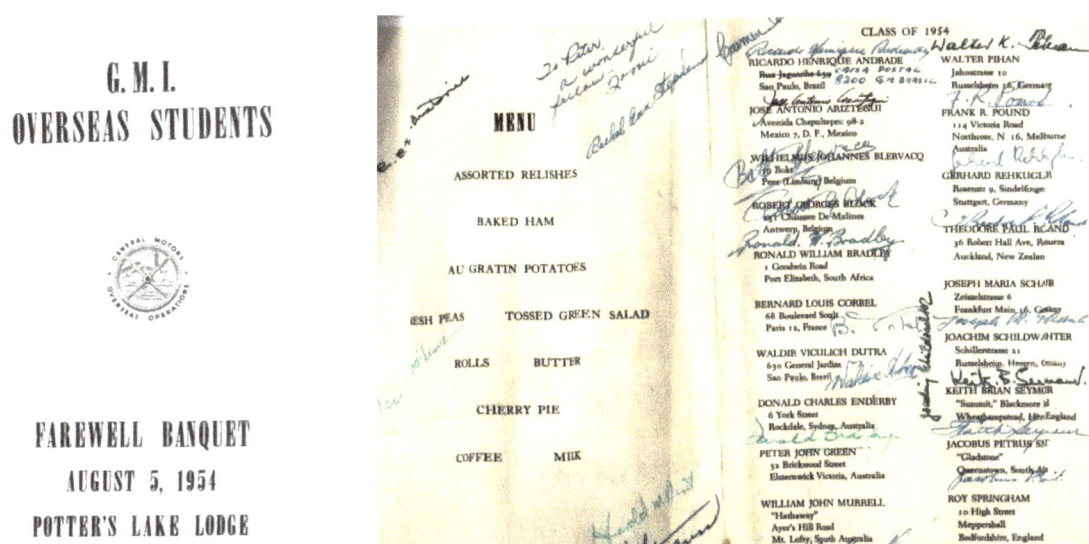

We worked hard, studied hard, and played hard for two years. A marvellous time. Progress tests were made each semester (six months).

Jean-anne Ewing

Jane Hamilton went overseas just after I returned to SA and we lost interest in each other. It was hard leaving Jean-anne Ewing. She was a great girl but I knew she was not the one.

**Jean Thompson next to me (my date) at the Engineer's Dinner.
Jean, now Jean Giles, was U of A's photographer, so I saw her often as a Cadet in Mech Engineering.**

**This is me walking in downtown Cleveland, Ohio.
There to see Brian Stanton.**

Travel back to Australia was the reverse over two weeks.

We had a huge welcome party when we got back home.

1954 – On returning from Engineering Training at GMI Flint, Michigan, USA – Claude, Me, Neil.

After a few days of catching up with my friends and family, I got a job in the Standards Department of GMH setting labour budgets with Jack Bourne. I also assisted Claude McNeil with "make or buy" decisions on the new FE models. After a couple of weeks, I was told that I'd impressed the management of GMH with my work ethic. Thus, I was given a small section to supervise the total handling of all suggestions.

Initially, I couldn't afford a Holden, so I bought a two-stroke 178cc Excellsion motorbike. I had an accident while riding it once and ended up in hospital emergency with a grazed knee.

A few months after my return from the USA, I moved into a foreman's shed alongside "Hathaway", Mum and Dad's new home. I had a cosy little space, with light brown Caneite soft board lining. Being separated from my parents gave me a sense of independence, albeit only being a short distance from them.

Eventually, I did save up for a deposit on a green FJ/215 Holden, below.

While driving one of my mates, Wally Scott, back to Victoria, I noticed an oncoming Ford a little too late. As I rounded the curve in the centre of the Great Ocean Road, in the Ottaway Range, I crashed into the Ford. My FJ's front suspension (right-hand side) was buckled.

My FJ was towed to Geelong where we proceeded to stay with my Auntie Nell. I left the car at the Holden dealer to get it repaired while Wal and I had a merry time hitchhiking back home.

We made it back on Ash Wednesday.

"You ought to sell your car you know," my mum said one day while she was cleaning the dishes.

I looked at her in confusion.

Seeing my baffled expression, she merely smiled. "Green's a very unlucky colour."

And so, the next day, I sold my green FJ and bought a grey one.

The week proceeded with me following my usual routine. I worked; I caught up with my parents during dinner and cleaned my small dwelling space. Little did I know that my life was about to change the coming Saturday morning.

Married Life

"Huh."

I looked at the man in front of me, leaning back nervously as he regarded me with cool, steely eyes.

"Marriage is a huge responsibility …" He trailed off and scratched his chin, unsure.

I cleared my throat. "I understand. But …" I hesitated before looking at his eyes levelly, "I love your daughter."

Mr Morton George Wollaston nodded. There was a tense silence before he smiled and said, "Her kindergarten training … she'll need to finish it first."

I felt the burden from the possibility of rejection lift off my shoulders. I relaxed my tense stance and shared a smile with the man in front of me.

I met his daughter, the sparkly-eyed and bright-witted Phillippa Murray Wollaston, nicknamed "Phil", on a sunny Saturday during the year of 1955. A friend of mine, Rosemary Haigh, rang me and invited me to a tennis party on Haigh's lawn court at Mt. Lofty.

I immediately became besotted with Phillippa. A newfound friendship steadily turned into a serious relationship and, after a year, I found myself asking Mr Wollaston for Phil's hand.

A few weeks later, I was kneeling in front of "Phil", my impassioned gaze mirrored by her misty ones. At that moment, everything else ceased to exist. It was just me, her, and the vast blank canvas of our future together, waiting to be painted on.

"Will you marry me?" I said, my voice doused with every emotion I felt – love, excitement, passion, adoration, fear.

She nodded, her smile radiant. "Yes."

And just like that, our futures became inextricably entwined.

Philippa at 18 years

Engagement night at a party

Photo in *The Advertiser* on our engagement announcement at an Overseas League function.

The days quickly progressed into nights, and before we knew it, the 5th of May 1957 made its arrival. We had a long engagement, a year to be precise, but it didn't matter for, at this moment, I was going to be a wedded man.

My nervousness was temporarily muted by awe as I gazed at the scene before me. The children Phillippa taught at Stirling kindergarten lined the way to the church. I marvelled at how many people were present to share this glorious moment with me.

I was ushered to the end of the aisle, and my nervousness increased tenfold. I pocketed my sweaty palms, a pathetic attempt to ease my stress and anxiousness.

Soon enough, the euphonous tune of our wedding hymn enveloped the vast hall of the church. I held my breath as my bride Phillippa, radiant and ethereal, appeared at the entrance of the church. I was awestruck as she walked down the aisle, our eyes never leaving each other.

The bride – radiant on "the day"

The rest of the ceremony passed blissfully. It was hard to tear my gaze away from my wife. It still felt surreal at that moment, identifying her as such.

We had our wedding reception at the historic Olivet Guest House, opposite my parents' home 'Hathaway'. Every moment of that reception was filled with laughter and excitement, except for one. I nervously rose from my seat and grabbed the microphone with shaking hands.

Olivet House, Stirling, circa 1950s.
Source: State Library of South Australia B35719 used with permission.

I had written a poem for my wife in "Snooksi's" autograph book a year before.

I looked at the crowd, feeling slightly intimidated. I felt my heart increase its pace due to undue stress before my gaze landed on Phil. I felt some of the tension from my body drain away as she smiled at me encouragingly. I smiled back.

I cleared my throat before I started,

"Phillippa

Blue-grey eyes most wistful,
Tiny waist, and small hands,
High cheeks freshly flushed
With a spirit so blithe,
And, youthful.
On Haigh's tennis court, per-chance
I met you,
Interested in no man.
Brown short hair ever changing;
Moods, and attitudes too,
I became fascinated
By a charm so unusual
Yet, endearing
In an automobile you tenderly answered;
"yes: and I love you"
Bright, gay lady of mystery,
Many dreams and kind heart,
Sensuously noticing nature
Sweet Phillippa Murray

"Snooksi" to me.
Before God our love we will promise
"Till death us do part."

William John Calvert Murrell
11/5/1956

The early stages of our married life proceeded with utmost passion, joy and excitement. For the first night of our honeymoon, we went to Tintinara, a beautiful small agricultural town. Our adventure continued on to Mt. Gambier, where we explored the city's beautiful volcanic landscape and vast crater lakes. It was such a refreshing trip that was rekindled by a profound admiration for nature. Our ensuing trip to Warrnambool did not make my top favourites as the bed had bugs, which made for a very 'interesting' and 'memorable' sleeping experience.

Our trip continued on to the Great Ocean Road, to Apollo Bay and finally, onto Lorne. I fondly remembered how Phil slipped on the algae-covered rocks as we explored the magnificent Erskine Falls. We then drove to Geelong to see my uncle, Chris, and my aunt, Nell, who were very pleased to see the both of us. After the brief family reunion, we toured the Grand Oriental Hotel in Melbourne, famous for its sophistication and grandiosity. It was where Melbourne's first pavement café was accommodated. Thus, the hotel end of the street was endearingly termed the 'Paris End' of Collins. After checking in to have a brief taste of luxury, we drove to the fern forests of the Dandenongs to hunt for Lyrebirds. Although the hunting experience was enjoyable, we, unfortunately, did not encounter any Lyrebirds. We were lucky enough to find nest briars though.

The scene after our hunting trip was one of my fondest memories up to date – we returned to our hotel completely drenched, laughing as rainwater gently cascaded down our clothed bodies. Needless to say, we were able to make good use of the huge, deluxe bath of our hotel room after. We spent a few more days indulging in the grandeur of the hotel before we finally returned home.

For our house, we had bought an old piggery which had been converted to a weekender. Hence, it was a humble one-storey structure containing one bedroom, a kitchen, a small dining area and a bath with a chip heater. We did not rely on town water or sewerage. Rather, we depended on rainwater and a septic system. I also paid a stonemason approximately £75 to enclose two sides and one end of the carport. To go on our honeymoon and buy the Heather Road piggery, I sold my FJ Holden and bought a secondhand '54 Renault 750cc – a sweet little car.

Our "750" outside the motel on the first night of our honeymoon. We were both virgins - unlike young people these days.

**The "750" in the carport before being enclosed as a lounge room.
It was an unusually cold frosty morning.**

Since Phil had errands to run while I was at work, I bought her a pre-war circa 38 Austin 4.

"Bill, you didn't?!" she gasped in wonder, excitedly rushing to the car. She gently trailed her fingers along the car's fawn-tinted exterior in awe. She looked back and grinned at me, her eyes shining with mischief.

"What?" I asked cautiously and curiously. She just laughed in response.

I stood there, dumbstruck, wondering where her sudden playfulness came from until one day, the answer presented itself willingly.

I came back home and halted in front of the Austin, stupefied. Phil smiled at me broadly. "Isn't she a beauty?"

"How did you even manage?" I asked, still staring at the car in shock.

"I remembered we had a tin of paint in the shed."

I looked at her grinning face, the now red-tinted car and smiled broadly. "Not too bad … it is a pretty shade of red. Though I'll admit, I'll miss the fawn."

Meanwhile, I bought an old 26½ Essex with a few friends, Brian Stanton and John Farmer and boy, it was a beauty. We endearingly called it "The Beast". We would drive the beast on the run down or up the hills daily, laughing as we did so. The car served us well for several years before we eventually sold the Beast to another engineer, Darcy Clear, at Holden.

Soon enough, Phil found herself pregnant even though we weren't planning to have children at the time. I was beyond elated by the news. It was during her sixth month of pregnancy that she started to feel ill.

"I'm scared, Bill," she found herself saying as I frantically drove us both to the clinic. Tears were streaming down her face as she gently cradled the bump on her stomach.

For the next few hours, we were frantically embracing each other as the gynaecologist hung his head low, muttering a low apology as he pronounced the baby dead.

"A missed abortion." Phil sobbed as I enveloped her smaller, vulnerable form. The embryo, our baby boy, was removed through curettage.

After her miscarriage, my wife was never the same. She became desolate, depressed and silent. Her smiles became scarce while her sullen expression became frequent. Seeing her in such a pained state ultimately pushed me to make a decision.

"What in the –" Phil muttered, coming out of the house as she heard my car pull up in our garage.

I grinned at my wife excitedly. The cocker spaniel bounded up to her, its tail wagging with adoration and anticipation.

"Bill, are you mad?!" she exclaimed, looking at the dog.

"Come on, Phil. It'll be great," I coaxed. She glared at me before regarding the dog curiously.

"Alright," she relented, having been won over by the dog's sweetness. "But we'll be naming him Shelley."

Shelley became our family dog for many years to come. Although most memories with him are fond, there were times when he wreaked havoc. One of these was when he ran in front of a motorbike. It was a disastrous crash, causing the bike's eventual destruction. It was a blessing that both the rider and Shelley were not hurt during the accident. However, I did have to pay for the bike's repairs.

Life carried on with the same vigour and bliss until one day, I came home to find Phil sitting in the dining area with a pensive look on her face. She looked at me and then smiled, the warmth not reaching her eyes.

"Hey. You alright?" I asked, shrugging off my work shoes and coat as I walked toward her.

She licked her lips, hesitating.

I sat at the chair parallel to her, leaning forward to grasp one of her hands on the table. She squeezed my hand in reassurance before looking at me determinedly.

"I think that ... you should quit GMH."

I leaned back in surprise. "Sorry?" I asked.

"I think you ought to quit GMH ..." she trailed off. I gave her a look of reproach before she put a finger up. "Honey, GMH ... it's inflexible. These big businesses ... all they care about is profit. They're not willing to compromise on anything if it's for the benefit of their workers ... for your benefit," she explained.

I mulled over what she said before I shook my head slowly. "I like my job, Phil. I ain't quitting," I said.

**Shelley.
Note the rainwater tank**

She just sighed and shook her head.

To get to work in time, I had to take the 5 am train from My Lofty to Woodville. The next available train service is scheduled to leave at 6.30, which would arrive in Woodville at 8.05 am. Since my job starts at 8 am, taking the 6.30 service would result in me being 5 minutes late to work. As I considered this dilemma, the memory of Phil's comment about GMH being inflexible nagged at the back of my mind. The next thing I knew, I was walking towards my boss' office.

"Bill?" my manager asked, looking up from the stack of papers he was currently studying. "What can I help you with?" he asked kindly.

I explained my current predicament and offered a reasonable compromise – considering that I would be five minutes late to work in the morning, I was willing to put in an extra fifteen minutes regularly in the afternoon to make up for the lost time.

My boss nodded at me sympathetically before leaning back in his chair. "Bill, you've been performing very well in this job." He paused. I smiled in gratitude.

"However, rules are rules. No single employee will be above the rules. The company expects you to start at 8, and so you have to be here at 8. I'm sorry mate," he said apologetically.

My heart sank. My wife was right – no flexibility at GMH. "Yeah … alright. I understand," I replied.

And so, the seeds of discontent were sown. As soon as I got home that day, I started to look for other opportunities in the job ads. A particular one stood out among the rest. There was an opening for a management consultant which offered a higher wage. I applied and was contacted for an interview.

"Well?" Phil asked excitedly as soon as I got home.

"I got offered the job," I said, grinning. She squealed in delight.

"Are you taking it?" she asked after giving me a congratulatory embrace.

"Still thinking about it."

I pondered about it for days and after much thought, I dialled their number and accepted the job. It was one of the worst decisions I've ever made throughout my entire lifetime. "To yourself be true" I wasn't, I really liked my work at GMH and had a great future. My school and GM "Salad Days" were over.

Chapter 6

Working Post GM – MRD – AMI – NH – CAL – 1958-76

The die was cast, and Phil and I drove one weekend to Melbourne to meet Mal Denson, MD of MR Denson and Associates and discuss my immediate training plans. On the way back, Phil said, "You know that you signed up to a crook?" As things turned out, her hunch was right.

Anyway, I was now SA Director of MRD with a good salary, 2000 shares in MRD and a new FC 21T green business sedan, again unlucky, as it was repossessed after twelve months as MRD had not paid a repayment. On the way driving the little Renault just outside of Ararat, I was dozing and the car suddenly shook like it was on severe corrugations. Aroused, I looked up to see the front wheel running ahead as Phil stopped the car. All five wheel nuts had come off. I walked back and luckily found four, then jacked the front LHS, straightened the inner hub five-fingers with a large shifter from the toolbox, then used one nut as a die to reform the bruised threads, put on the wheel, attached four nuts tightly and limped into Ararat. There, I found the Renault agent, who said flexing of the inner wheel was a common fault. He found the correct nut, so we continued safely back to Adelaide.

GMH played hardball once I resigned and offered immediate dismissal: hand back my GMI textbooks (they only got a few) and one week's pay. As I was on monthly pay, I legally was entitled to a month's pay even if they did not want me to work the month out. I threatened legal action. I won and got one month's pay plus minimum other benefits. So I started at MRD's a month early, December 1957. Denson gave me several follow-up assignments, plus I had to look for an office and furniture. In January 1958, Phil and I went to Melbourne again for my training. We had an apartment at Toorak. It was hot and Phil had about five showers a day!

I was kept very busy learning and practising the techniques of time study, the Bedaux rating system, and MRD procedures.

All new to me, a much tighter system, than I learnt at GMH and GMI. I felt on familiar ground when I helped set up our incentive program at Dependable Accessories, which produced mufflers and tailpipes, among other auto parts.

Back in Adelaide I set up the office, hired a secretary and began following up on old job leads and seeking new assignments. Hard and frustrating work!

I trained with Peter Mendes – setting time standards at Harrison Shoes.

I was amazed by the speed of the Harrison Shoes sewers on incentives with approximately 200 per cent increase – frighteningly fast.

When the owner, Mr Harrison, took me aside and asked my opinion on the proposed expansion plans and layout, I gave my opinion freely.

Back at the hotel, Peter Mendes warned me not to give "free advice". I queried this ethically as Harrison was paying MRD a goodly fee for our services. I resolved that I would give "all" in my operating as an MRD consultant in SA.

The first new company I succeeded to enlist my consultancy services was Ford Dry Cleaners, in Norwood. We nearly had a strike as the clothing union would not agree to the processing times I had set. After a lot of negotiations, things were resolved. The advertising Ford man was my idea and an example of my "extra service". Another new assignment was at Schartinger's Cooperage. I, with Ray Renonds from MRD Melbourne, set up incentive standards for all ops. Again, as Geoff Schartinger had just inherited the business after his father had died suddenly, we talked about many subjects including insurance, marketing and product lines.

Other assignments were Tyrell's Laundry – Mr Nancarrow was a wily owner/manager, but we helped him.

Another one I found was Rosefield Smallgoods. We didn't have a factory assessment, but a marketing ore. "Rosefields For Better and Worst" was the slogan I dreamed up. It worked wonders.

I arranged a big seminar for SA companies. Denson was the main speaker. We got several new leads for business from these registrations. Haigh's chocolates, and Fricker Bros builders: I was well into the latter, regarding the layout of their salvage yard when MRD rang and demanded I close up shop in SA and come across to Melbourne to assist him with paying assignments there. On arrival, I found that Mal D had been raiding the set-aside superannuation fund to pay wages. About six of his consultants had packed up and left. I helped as much as I could – worked at a dress company, and at AB Johnsons – dustcoat and overall manufacturers. This contract came in very useful later in 1970 at Chrysler Aust. While I held the above seminar, Marc was born ten weeks prematurely. Phil had to go to the Queen Victoria Hospital when her waters broke, and she had to lie still in bed for ten days, listening to the yelling and screaming of young wives in the labour room next to her room. Not good! Because Marc was under 4lb weight at birth, he had to be in a humidicrib for six weeks until he was okay and over 4lbs.

Phil had to express milk with a pump, and I dropped it into the hospital each morning. Of course, a lot of to and froing from Heather Road, Longwood to see Marc. (Later he changed his name by deed poll to Marc). And from here on in this book he shall be called Marc.

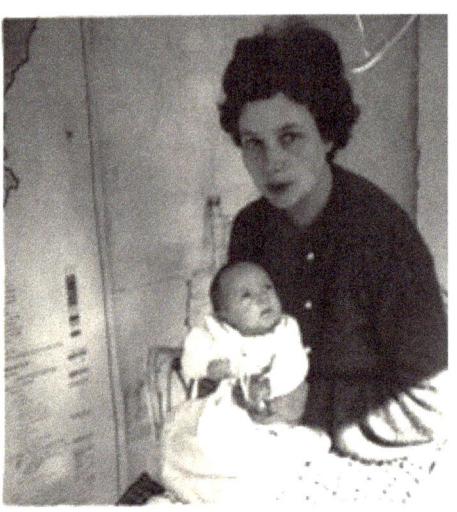

Phil with Marc Wollaston Murrell at about two months.

So, after about three months, we packed everything we could in the Holden, sold the Piggery furnished for a good profit, paid off the mortgage and drove off to Heidelberg where an apartment outbuilding awaited us. MRD arranged this through a friend.

After about six months, men came early one morning and repossessed the FC that MRD had not made the monthly payments on. Eventually, finance was freed, and I got the car back.

After about six months in the apartment, we bought "White Woods" at Canterbury Road, Heathmont. This was a modern white weatherboard two-bedroom house with a modern kitchen and bathroom and a big lounge/dining room with a large fireplace in the inner wall – our central heating. We were happy here, but work with MRD was very dubious. Eventually, a position at

Australian Motor Industries, Standard Motor Division, as Production Engineer Manager was advertised. I applied, was interviewed and started in January 1960. Now back in the car game, I was pleased although I did not crack it with my dour English boss, Mr Geo Harris. He insisted the Vanguard was a better car than the Holden and VW beetle. Sales told a story: Vanguard 25/d, FC Holden 25/day, VW 100/day.

Leaving MRD, I had to hand in the FC, so I bought Mrs Wollaston's Standard 8, 4-door, which Mrs Wollaston had rolled over, but it still went okay. I drove it back to Melbourne and had the dents repaired by apprentices at Standard Motor Co. They encouraged using their product and did repairs.

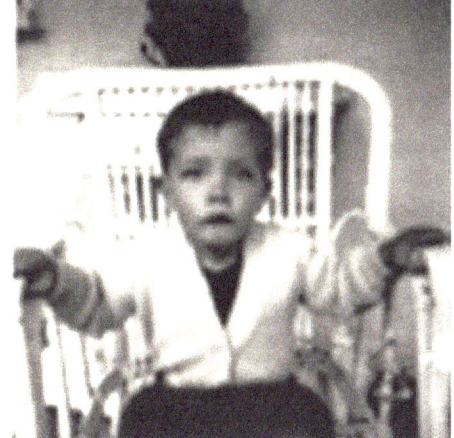

Left: Marc, about one-year-old at Heathmont

Right: Marc as a toddler on the right, Mallen on my left at "White Woods", Heathmont, Vic

The black car is the Standard, the green FJ is Wally Scott's – very similar to the one I crashed with him as a passenger. Margaret Sutherland, Winifred Balfour-Olgilvy (nee Calvert) and Phillippa – at a picnic in the Barossa, 1960

Things went swimmingly at AMI for a while producing Mercedes Benz (they withdrew from assembly due to quality problems), Vanguards including engine 4 & 6 cyl assy, Tricups L Herald 3 models, Fiat tractors and vans.

Quite enough to keep me and fourteen staff very busy. Then the credit squeeze happened in mid-1960 and sales fell drastically. There were significant quality and engineering problems with the Herald models, so by November, I was asked to put off one production engineer per week. At this time, Phil was pregnant with James. On the day he was born – 22nd December – I phoned Mr Harris and told him I would be late in as I wanted to visit the Queen Victoria hospital in Lonsdale Street. He said, "Fine. Come by my office when you get in." I did and he gave me my notice and I went to the Company Secretary for my payout. Again, I arranged for more pay to tide me over Christmas and I got it.

I did something of long-term significance at AMI. Ross Wishart, my brother-in-law, was an agent for Sheridan textiles in Australia. He had received a brochure and pricing on the Subaru car range and asked me what I thought of the specs. They were very good and the prices were even better. He did not want to proceed so gave me all the info. I took them to the AMI MD, Mr Greenlaugh, and suggested he and a team go to Japan and arrange for car assembly in Australia. He later did just as I suggested, and the team returned in 1961 with signed agreements to set up a Toyota car assembly in Australia. What a success this has been! Initially, though, my idea.

So, the hard slog of looking for work again. I answered an ad for temporary work with Utah Construction (they built the big Boulder Dam in Colorado). An interesting job précising all the employees' CV's so they could give thumbnail sketches on quotes they presented for construction sites. I was part-time and took time out for job interviews. Utah actually offered me the position of Construction Project Manager on a new carpet radiation cleaning plant. I thought I didn't have Project Management experience so said "No" reluctantly, as I had three mouths to feed, my family, and no job.

By mid-January, I had six different job interviews and decided on New Holland at Dandenong as Standards Manager.

While out of work, Mum's brother, my Uncle Doug, right-hand side of the picture, came to stay. It was difficult to keep a stiff upper lip with no job, no income and not levelling with him. His daughter Winifred and her daughter are also in this photo.

So New Holland here I come!

New Holland hay rake and baler.

This turned out to be a very interesting and challenging job. I made the job as there was no Standards Manager before me. PA management consultants quoted the MD at Lugo fee-behind me instead.

We got on fine. I went with him and the product engineer to see equipment trials and get to understand how cutters, balers and rakes worked.

My boss, the production manager, allowed me a free hand providing I kept him informed with a monthly report. I re-organised the baler and cutter assembly lines; reduced the assay time of the baler from 65 hours to 16 hours using time and method study techniques. At one stage, I had 65 cost reduction proposals on the go over the two years I was there.

I also suggested two significant product improvements as cost savings which were implemented. At the end of '61, the MD offered me the job of Australian Service Manager. I declined, thinking I would be out of my depths – little did I then know I'll be in that depth in 1970 at Chrysler. I was headhunted by CAL, flew to Keswick and Tonsley Park to see the facilities and meet executives and was offered a position of "Methods and Processing Supervisor" in all five plants. I accepted. "Wacko, back in the automotive manufacturing business!"

We sold our house by auction but did not get what we hoped. Phil was in tears. We packed up and drove our 403 Peugeot back to Adelaide. Phil was really pleased to go, as her mother "Timmy" was not well. She died six months after we went back.

Mrs and Mr Wollaston were pleased to see us and the two grandchildren again. I had, after leaving MRD, applied to return to GMH but they replied, "Thanks, but no thanks". That door was closed, unfortunately. After leaving CAL in 1976, I again applied but again "no go!"

While at NH, I lectured on Method Study at RMIT in Melbourne city. Interesting, but made a long day – Heathmont – Dandenong – City – Heathmont. I liked teaching, and the experience helped later.

Left: Wendell James Murrell was a delightful little chap.

Right: Mr W handing a plate to Mrs Wollaston, Aunt Mab is on the right.

Left: The "Wooly-bug" gang in Adelaide. Phil with the Halls, Wisharts and Pawseys. (In-laws)

Right: Phil with her Dad, Morton George Wollaston

Left: This is the 403 Peugeot model I had. I had a blue one with a white stripe along the side mouldings. It was an ex-Redex trial car and I had to have the engine re-ringed, then it was okay.

Phil's four sisters and brother were thrilled to have her within visiting distance in Adelaide. We first rented an apartment on the beachfront at West Beach, near the airport. Then after looking around for a place, in Clovelly Street, North Glenelg. It was nothing special but served its purpose as a home for several years. It was walking distance to pre-kindy and shops, plus I could leave Phil the 403 as I got a ride with the neighbours to CAL.

Valiants SV1 and SV2

These were the Valiants SV1 and SV2 that were assembled in my 1st year at CAL. They were a great sales success. So much so that when we announced to dealers, one Sydney dealer said that he would take the whole lot of 2004 SV1s (the one with the dummy spare tyre-shaped boot lid). Based on the Valiant acceptance over Holden and Falcon (we could not build SV2s quick enough for the sales department), rushed plans were put in place to design an Australian Valiant plant plus build a new Press Shop, Tool Room and Assembly Plants at Tonsley Park. Meanwhile, we had to make do with the old plants at Keswick and Mile End.

The paint shop was a big problem, being limited in capacity and producing poor paint quality. I was asked to solve the white spots and black spots paint problem. I looked and thought about it, and hunched it was a +V or –VE paint polarity problem. I discussed this with Dave Pawsey (my brother-in-law) and he came into the ME plant armed with +,- measuring equipment. Sure enough, by earthing the bodies and the paint guns, the spotting problem was solved. Dave and I were pleased. I was a hero at CAL.

Another unsolved long-term problem was thrown at me. The end of the ATA truck bumper scoured badly on forming in the press die. I had been to the doctor and had a rectal examination the week prior and recalled that he used some slippery gel on his glove. I went to the chemist and bought several tubes of this gel, went to the press shop and smeared the two ports of the firing up die with the gel. The press superintendent thought I was mad, but bingo, it worked! So they quickly got the lab to analyse the gel, made up bulk quantities and have used "Murrell's magic drawing compound" ever since.

I had to supervise six method engineers located in five different plants viz Keswick, Mile End, Truck and Steel Pressings at Trinsbury, then Tool Room and Engineer assay at Tonsley Park. I could keep the six providing their total savings amounted to four times their total salaries per year. It was a challenge I accepted, and in the first year, 1962, I achieved 10x. Not bad!

After about a year, I was promoted to Industrial Engineer – in charge of H.O. and Plant IE's, about 25 at the time. This was a big jump in responsibility, as I had to set direct labour, indirect labour, other manufacturing expenses (OME) and material handling equipment budgets. Once Tonsley Park was built and in service, this was over $65 million p.a.

The VC 1966 model

As the AP5 was developed, I was brought in to advise on any cost reductions I could find.

The design and layout called for a lot of industrial engineering input. How many cars were in each car park?

How big should each of the four car parks be? What size and configuration of the large press shop? How large the work-in-progress sheet metal stone should be? How to stack plattetage and transport and store the many sheet metal parts without damage? How long were the metal finish booths, paint booths and prime dip tank? How long the trim assay and fixed assay? How large and what configuration should the final car storage be? What size the receiving docks and where? What size canteen for D.P employees and what for executives? How to manage lockers for daily paid employees? What size change rooms? Where and the size of D.P. change rooms? Size of labs and Engineering, Tool Design, Planning and other H.O. functions? The office layout of all staff departments? Should there be lifts, stairs, or escalators in the two-storey H.O. building? Etc, etc – quite complex but interesting work to supervise as Chief Industrial Engineer.

Over this period, I had a lot to do with the MD David Brown (an excellent leader), the Treasurer, Laurie Scholtz, Manufacturing Engineering Manager Colin Adey (my direct boss), Production Manager and Product Engineer Roy Gedunery, Plant Engineer Ian Scott, Tooling Manager, Product Engineer Manager Roy Rainsford and of course the Manager of Tonsley Park Task Team, Roger Stapleton. We all had our differences from time to time but overall worked on a very good team under a lot of pressure.

CHL assembled Simca sedans and wagons, Dodge Phoenix Deans, Dodge trucks, air conditioners and Valiants of course. I was enjoying CAL but becoming a "workaholic" without realising it. I worked Easter 1964 changing body assembly from the Mile End plant to the new Tonsley Park plant.

We had the offer to mind Auntie Mab's house at 22 Edwin Terrace, Gilberton for an extended period whilst she travelled the UK, so we quickly sold the North Glenelg home and moved. I was President of the P&T at the St Leonard Pre-School Kindergarten at the time, so I resigned.

22 Edwin Terrace was full of clutter, so we stored our stuff. We saw a 1932 Daimler for sale in pristine condition for £300 – a bargain I thought. I arranged a bank overdraft but did not proceed as it was winter and we had no cover for it, with a cloth top, in Aunt Mab's driveway. The next move was to buy an old, stately, roomy blue-stone "Kensington" in Burlington Street; two houses from Ruth and Bob's place in Walkerville (see photo left).

It had a big, big shed with two '48 Hillmans in it (below right). Lots of work fixing corroded holes in the roof, painting inside and out etc. In the old chook shed, while cleaning it out, I trod on a rusty nail that went right through my thong. Gee, it was sore. I went to the company doctor the next day and he gave a tetanus injection and ordered me off my foot for a week.

Just after this, my darling Lucy was born – 27/06/1966. Unfortunately, Phil got hepatitis shortly after, so Lucy was nursed at Phil's sister Julie's place for a few weeks while Phil recovered. I was very busy guiding a specially selected team of specialists on a lock-up secret project to design a new assembly plant at Mt Druitt in Sydney (see photo below).

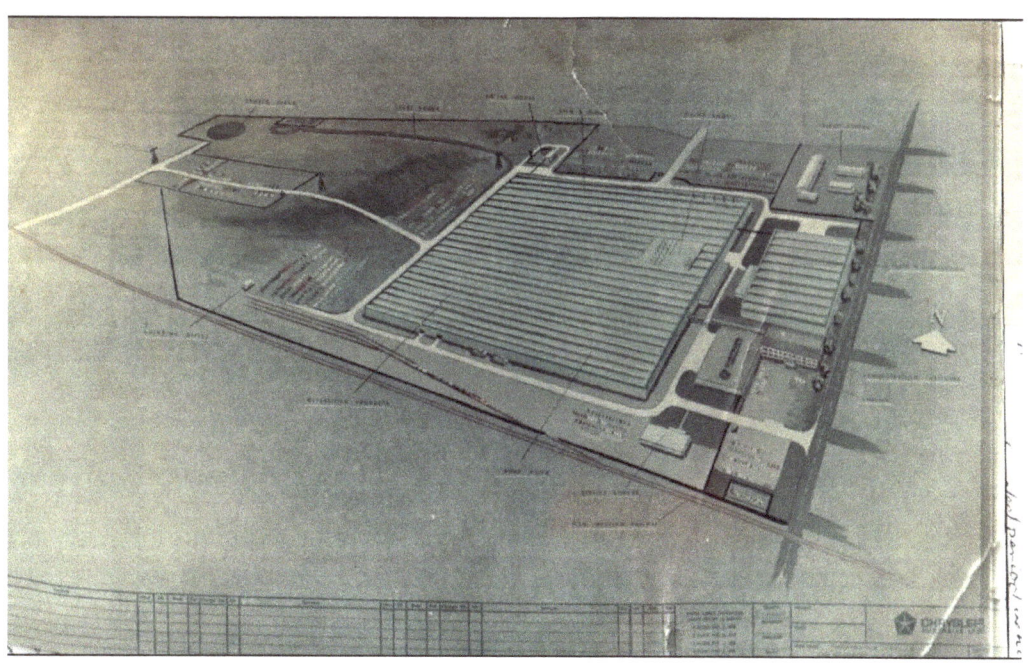

I remember I squibbed actually seeing Lucy born and saw her and Phil just after the birth then went back to work until 10 pm. The Thompson girls, next door, were willing babysitters.

Nothing ever eventuated on the Sydney plan, as sales of Valiant were starting to drop.

In my quest for cost reduction, another project at CAL was to restyle the roof join of the VE to a simpler 3-line approach for styling the VE. Engineering agreed, and CAL saved $44,000 p.a. on the reduced metal finish. While still at Kennington, I bought "Fair Winds" with a bridging loan (high interest, never do it) from the National Bank. "Fair Winds" was a weatherboard, built on the steep slope at Mt Osmond. It was the old Golf Club House. It had a magnificent panoramic view of Adelaide across the width of the house where we made our dining/living room. Fantastic city lights at night. I lined the underneath shower/change rooms with "strawit" and made two cosy bedrooms with showers attached for the boys, who now went to Junior School at Scotch College, Mitcham. Eventually, I sold the Walkerville house to the Jones's (Simon Barbor is a friend of the Jones boy) and I smiled when I paid off the bridging loan.

We were well satisfied when Will was born in 1968.

Lucy (11 months)

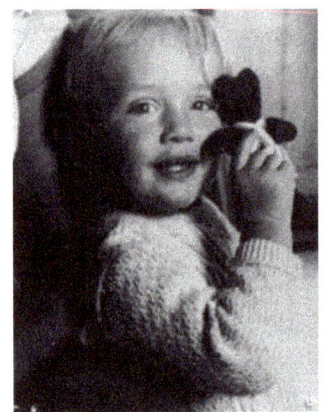

Will

Right: Lucy (3 years) and Will (18 months).

The next BIG surprise. I was headhunted by Chrysler International for East and African Operations (FEAO) in Sydney to be 'Manager Industrial Engineer and Quality Control'. A big rise to $10K p.a. lease car, overseas travel, and an excellent office on 44th floor of Australia Square Tower, so I said "Yes". Immediately CAL sent me to a Quality Control course run by Dr J Juran, a Work Quality guru. He set up Japan's quality revolution. He also trained me in quality auditing at CAL. So we set a fair price at a fair profit for "Fair Winds" and had six buyers bidding on the first opening day. So much for the NAB manager saying "weatherboards in isolated positions are hard to sell". Sell we did. Looking back, though Phil supported the move to Sydney, I think she was reticent to move away from her family again.

So we packed up, used a removalist provided by FEAO and off we went. Shipped Phil and Hillman imp free. I got a new VIP Chrysler in Sydney on lease. I actually moved across about two months early to look for a house (very dear in Sydney) and to get to know the ropes at FEAO. My boss, Mr Dick Newell, was a great man, very extensively travelled and he made me very welcome. He introduced me to FEAO's bank manager, who said there would be no worries regarding a loan for me on my salary and to go ahead and buy a house. So I did, only after several fell through due to high demand, and after long phone calls to Phil, and mailing photos. I even went up in a friend's plane and flew over promising North Shore suburbs. Finally, 15 Tipperary Court, Killarney Heights was ours. Photo below.

A very modern project-built home designed by the 2nd in charge architect of the Opera House. It had copper guttering and a view of the Middle Harbour tributary from the bathroom window. There were several jobs the builder promised to do, such as the driveway, that I had to get a lawyer David Stratton to ensure happened as I headed overseas in January 1969.

I again squibbed being at Will's birth. Unfortunately, William Ashley Randell Murrell (WARM) was never actually christened. He is by nature a very warm and lively alert person with a happy disposition. He was only a 7-month toddler when we moved to Sydney.

My trip to the US started by reviewing Valiant assembly quality at Haroon Motors in Karachi. It was surprisingly good for such low volume. I took a finished car off the assembly line and drove it through the streets into nearby hills. When I stopped to turn around the bandits appeared on horses about 300 yards away. I quickly vamoosed! At the farewell Chinese meal they gave me, I must have picked up a bug.

I was distressed on the plane to the UK and more so across the Atlantic, so by the time I reached my hotel in Detroit I was a cot-case with dysentery. I spent one day in hospital (very poor care) and the rest of the week withering in bed.

On my visit, my eyes were opened to real high production and I passed on these ideas at FEAO and CAL.

Having just returned to Sydney, I was immediately sent with an American to NZ to evaluate Todd Motor Operations. After review, FEAO decided not to buy it as it had severe capacity and expansion restrictions at Wellington. They did have a good size, well-located block of land in Auckland.

**Snow on the Dodge Dart
I was allocated for US trip.**

**Above: Roma and me, in the centre,
on the way to Pagsanjan Falls**

**Right: P. Roma, self and MD
at a thank you farewell.**

I had just settled back into our new Killarney Heights house and seeing the family again when I was called to review the Chrysler Philippines truck plant. They were building very poor quality units and had a yard full of unfinished trucks. Pepe Roma was the IE and was very cooperative. In the two weeks there we improved the build. The MD was pleased and said so. I returned just before Easter 1969 packed up the family in the Chrysler and drove to Adelaide. We had a good family time with "rellies" and then it was back to Sydney. No more overseas that year, thank goodness. But 26 budgeted for in "TO". We had a good FEAO staff viewing of the Man on the Moon mid-year. Chrysler worldwide was having a sales slump so they decided to drop two overseas offices, ours FEAO and Mexico, which handled South America.

All the world was to be administrated from the London office, which was not allowed to increase staff. Luckily before I left CAL I had a good chat to the MD David Brown – he didn't recommend that I accept the FEAO job as "they live too high on the hog, Bill!", but he didn't oppose me going and said, "If you ever want a job, ring me." So I did, and true to his work he said, "Pack up and there will be a job at FCAL." He appointed me Manager Service Division CAL. Although I didn't know much about service operations, I soon learned. Marketing had a survey of Holden, Ford and Chrysler customers and found the service of customers cars rated 1, 2, 3 in order, Valiant last. I immediately prepared a Customer Case Program to lift CAL service rating to No 1 in five years. By reorganisation, new service policies and customer programs plus a lot of travel, talks, dealer cooperation and sweat and team effort, we achieved No 1 in 1973. The new service image is shown here.

New "Chrysler Care" programs (see below) were radically different from the oppositions approached at that time. I had long discussions with the CAL's lawyers, and simplified the wording of the warranty, redesigned the glove box manuals (modernised), introduced formal dealer service apprenticeship training, and "WOW" (Women on Wheels), and addressed dealer principals to up their service game. Lucy had "WOW" stickers all over her childhood room. She remains very proud of me for this program that gave women the confidence to drive.

Most visually, I introduced Chrysler blue service dust coats and overalls. These were dirt-resistant and a hit with men and wives. I got the idea from my time at Johnson's with MRD. This blue concept was extensively copied by Holden and Ford and Toyota service people. Chrysler had just under 400 dealers, and my aim was to spruce themselves up so, camera in hand, I visited widely which meant to my detriment I was often away from home. In 1971, I had 85 interstate trips. I wished they'd had Frequent Flyer points then! Phil at home became restless. Marc and Jim were back at Scotch.

I never achieved seeing all the dealers but saw about 200 in three years.

The map on my office wall had many real pins where I had visited.

At a Service Managers Conference dinner "Service Excellence".

This dinner was for all CAL executives. Due to more liberal service replacement parts policies, the Warranty costs grew from $2 to $9.50 per car. There were quality and product problems with the new VB model.

I had the full support of the new MD, Paul Moore, whom I had fortunately met during my FEAO trip to USA three years earlier.

MENU 16/10/72

Appetizer
NATURAL OYSTERS
AVACADO SEAFOOD

Entree
WHITING CAPRICE
KIDNEY ROYALE

Main Course
BARON OF BEEF SLOMBE
Yorkshire Pudding; Horse Radish Sauce
Jacket Potatoes; French Salad

Cheese and Greens
COFFEE
AFTER DINNER MINTS

Me presenting a Service Manager with a Service Excellence Award. Note: service blue-coated man ½ hidden at back.

Lucy on Mum's Simca on return to SA.

I first bought Phil a '45 Dodge (pictured left) but she left the hand brake on and the engine grease caught fire. Luckily, I was following, so when she stopped, I ran into a front garden, grabbed a hose and put it out. We immediately traded this big car for a more suitable-sized Simca.

During my period as Service Manager, I used to take home cars offline and imported vehicles to do quality audits on.

We bought a house with a city view in the heights of Beaumont. It had four bedrooms and an unfinished en-suite, which I had a plumber complete. It served us well, but Phil was restless, and to get a bit closer to Scotch and kindy, we sold well and bought an old but renovated bluestone at 53 Eaton St, Malvern. This had four bedrooms, with dining and lounge plus a small trap door cellar under the kitchen.

One night while eating in the kitchen, I looked up and saw flames coming from Will's bedroom. I ran in – the curtains were aflame – a curtain had caught fire on a radiator – and rang the fire brigade. They were only ten or twenty minutes coming and quickly extinguished the blaze. Damage to carpet, curtains, lamp stand and of course walls smoke damaged. Luckily the whole house didn't go up in flames. Insurance, after an argument, came to the party and all was repaired.

About this time, we met up with an old Sunday School chum of Phil's viz Col Gardiner, artist, partner in practical jokes, electrician and landscape gardener. This eventually had severe implications for our marriage. Again, Phil was wanting a change, so we sold and bought "Heathleigh" in Emmett Road, Crafers. This was a sprawling two-bedroom and two out-bedroom house with city views and a large, steep, five-acre block.

At one stage, we visited Robe and stayed with the Scales at their beach house.

We saw a very old property advertised and went to it. We were impressed at "Burlington" and the cheap price and decided to ask the bank for a loan. When we returned to Adelaide, I got cold feet on the idea and we never proceeded.

About this time, we were invited to Col Gardiner's opening of his paintings at Hahndorf. Colonel Beresford Nyman opened the exhibition. We met Berry and his wife Jennifer during the show. We were invited to dance in the Officers' Mess at Woodside the following Saturday. Things developed between the four of us and we drifted into a foursome, having BBQs and dinners at each other's homes. One Fathers' Day, Phil asked me 'if I had had it off with Jenny.'

"No," I said.

She replied, "You may as well, as I have with Barry and I don't intend to stop."

"Unto yourself be true" I was not, and Jenny and I became an item, with very unfortunate consequences for two families. When I travelled interstate, the Colonel's jeep and driver would park outside while Berry "attended" Phillippa inside, so our good neighbour, Ann Hart, later informed me. I was dopey enough to buy a return ticket to Melbourne for Phil to visit Berry. My false thinking was "She would get him out of her system." She did not and only felt more strongly for him. We battled on as a family, and occasionally went camping (see photos below).

Ann Hart

I could see that I must stop my travels to save my marriage. I still loved Phil. So I asked for a transfer to a non-travelling job, having explained my reasons. I was made "Manager – Manufacturing Engineer and Quality Control" at the Lonsdale Plant within a week. Another new challenge for me. Lonsdale has a large foundry, small tool room, and engine manufacture, assay and testing operations.

I'd had a lot to do with the plant's location and internal layouts at IE years before. I retained my company car and leased a Valiant for Phil. We all enjoyed going to CAL Christmas parties each year as a family. Then one morning in January 1975, I received a dreaded "Dear John" phone call from Phil at the airport, with Lucy and Will, saying, "You had better go home as I am leaving you for Berry."

Above: Will, 12, and Lucy, 14 years. They were 6 and 8 at the time of my separation.
Right: Our camp tent and station wagon in earlier days. With Marc and James camping

It was a long dreadful drive home from Lonsdale to "Heathleigh" that morning. Marc and Jim had ridden their bikes to school so they weren't home, only an empty house with almost half the oddments taken, much of which was stored at Julie's place, as she was "in the know".

Two weeks prior we had boarded the neighbour's dog. Some strange act of torture, his fleas began to bite my ankles and lower legs. I couldn't find anything to kill them until someone suggested Baygon and it did the trick. Thank goodness.

I was absolutely gutted. When Phil and I married I would have bet millions that our marriage would not fail, so strong I felt our love was for each other. However, it was not to be. It was very difficult explaining to Marc and Jim the situation. They were extremely angry, disappointed and missed their Mum greatly. Due to financial stress, I had to remove Jim from Scotch to Urrbrae Agricultural High School. Marc continued at Scotch on reduced fees, but his work effort fell off notably. Jim got mixed up in a drug and alcohol culture at the high school.

The CAL came to my rescue and I was transferred back to Tonsley Park again as "Manager of Industrial Engineering." This I relished and headed a corporate cost reduction program. I had my company Valiant and, as soon as they could drive, I leased a Charger each for the boys. Jim at that stage had taken up wool classing at TAFE. Marc struggled at Flinders Uni in Arts.

To try and be Mum and Dad, I went to cooking classes after work at TAFE. At lunchtime, I would get the double serve ingredients for two recipes, so that I had enough food for four meals following at night; that, plus Fish & Chips and Hamburgers got us through. But me trying to be mum was a complete failure. I had often wondered what the different result would have been had I resigned from CAL and taken a single-parent pension. Less stress? Who knows?

Ann Hart (our neighbour) helped me immensely. I would hang the washing on the line in the morning and on return home from work I would find my shirts ironed and all washing folded neatly in piles.

James had to have formal work experience so I spoke to Dave Brown, and he readily agreed to have him work during Jim's holidays at his farm in the southeast at Padthaway. This was very successful and I would drive us down at the weekend, stay overnight with Marcia and David Brown, then return the next day, and repeat the route a few weekends later to pick him up. I got to like Dave's icy cold Coca-Cola's! Jim went down a boy, and came back a man! He learnt a lot, including how to ride a horse.

I finally after pressure, joined the Institute of Industrial Engineers (IIE) and soon found myself SA President. I kept this association up until retirement. Later I was elected Federal President then, in 1990, WA Branch President, and Federal Councillor. I was awarded a Fellowship in 1986 and an Honorary Fellow after retirement.

I joined CAL, a large industry Productivity Group which met monthly at different plants and swapped ideas for better productivity. The contact I made in this group would serve me well a few years later.

A big drive was on to reduce the build hours of the Valiant '75. We built a car in 40 hours, down from 85 hours for SV2 in '62. The new small US "H" car was being built (we were told) in 19 hours so I was sent to the USA to find out how we could match them. I discussed my absence with Marc and Jim and they both thought they could cook, wash and get to and from school ok.

After Phil left, I was so devastated, that I would hardly talk to any girls, let alone date them.

After six months, I received a call from a friend who wanted a partner for a friend of his wife to go to the Scotch Parents Ball.

"No way," I said but on the third call I reluctantly said 'Okay."

The time came and I picked up Nonie Whiteburn and we clicked. We had a good time, then went out occasionally. She was also recently separated and had a son and daughter, both younger than Marc, at Scotch. Then, we became an item together. She called at CAL and took me to the airport.

Noni even drove with me to Melbourne when I went to see Lucy and Will and to plead with Phil to come back home. This was what our children wanted – all one family again. However, it was not to be!

Nonie and I drove home through the Grampians.

One day she was patting her dog when she suddenly said, "Bill, I love my dog more than you!". That was the end of our relationship, although years later I introduced her to a friend. They never clicked; later still she married an Englishman.

After a few months, the SA Service Manager introduced me to his wife's friend, Mary Summers. She was single, and we got on well together. We went camping, dancing and bush walked. It was a good relationship for nearly two years. My mum wanted me to marry her. Mum had taken my breakup as a great shock, even though Mum was quite off-putting to Phil when we were first engaged. Once we were married, Mum warmed to Phil. Dad was always okay.

Mum was a member of a spinning group and made many items of clothing at Victor Harbour, where Mum and Dad had a townhouse. Mum willed me her good Huon pine spinning wheel which I have lent to Ruth. It is now sold.

Left and Centre: Nonie Whitburn

Mary Summers

I found that the US assembly's actual time for the H car was 25 hours, 17 hours was their budget time. While I was away my boss, Colin Adey, was sent to Japan to study the Galant time. He came back and said, "Forget 25 hours – the Japs do a small car in 11 hours." Anyway, we settled to drive the Valiant assembly time down to 30 hours. When I left IE sometime later, we had achieved a 29-hour car. Hooray! I was again driving experimental and imported cars home. Pictured below left is an example: a Simca "Bahkera" 4-cylinder, high-powered, mid-engine sports car that looks and drives well. It has three seats only in front. You can see (below right) how the Charger shape was similar.

The "Hey Charger" slogan and car were a great success. It was an all-CAL design.
Budgets were tightened and retightened.

The then General Manufacturing Manager Graham Spurling called into my IE office to see the OME budget which I had cut very hard. He looked at it and said, "Cut it by 15 per cent."

I objected and said, "If I do, all you will see is a 15 per cent red bottom line."

He left and within a week I was transferred (demoted) as 'Product Control and Material Handling Manager' back at Lonsdale. Unfortunately, I remained in Spurling's black book. Although I was managing 88 employees, in lieu of 44 IE's, I lost the two lease cars (the boys) and company car but I did not like the job. Marc had dropped out of Uni, and Jim was away a lot wool classing. I took him away with me to our IE conference at Wrest Point, Hobart then visited my cousin Dianne and Donald Marshall's farm near Launceston. He clicked with their son and they went out on the town several nights.

Back in Lonsdale, there were many problems getting the right size pisface ring in the Saturn 4-cylinder engine, and several times Tonsley Park nearly ran out of engines. The blame went to me. Just when I thought I had mastered the job, CAL decided to retrench 750 employees, including 100 staff. I was called into the Plant Manager's office and offered a redundancy packet to leave immediately, no farewells, which hurt, and a security officer by my desk. I could return Saturday morning and clear out my desk. So another long, sad and horrible drive to Crafers to tell the boys "I'm out of a job." They rallied and tried to help. Marc cooked thankfully. I stayed in bed for several days (he says three weeks) licking my wounds. I calculated my payout and found an $18,000 underpayment, which on phoning and checking, CAL made good.

I read ads; tried several interviews to no avail, then I recalled the Productivity Group Scheme of Dept. of Productivity. I rang my contact and he said, "Leave it with me" and in a few days rang back with a proposal. I would work as an hourly paid consultant, with mileage allowance, to contract companies and form new Productivity Groups in different areas of Adelaide. The full-time government employees were failing to achieve any new group. I took to the task, listed Co's in the yellow pages, drove around, visited receptionists and found names and direct phone numbers of MDs and data about the company, usually in their annual report.

I soon, within two months, had my first Productivity Group (PG) up and running and handed it as a going concern to an operational government servant to run. So on to my next group, another two months, and another group organised, until the Manager of the Dept of Productivity concerned said, "Stop, Bill, you are getting so many groups we cannot move them and support them." Stop means no pay, no good!

At the time I was retrenched from Chrysler, I had met a girl who'd been making eyes at me in a cook shop, so I got her phone number. A week later. Mary Seales rang and asked me and my partner, if I had one, to a BBQ. So I asked Valerie Jane Brooke Esau to Sealers BBQ. A fateful evening it eventually turned out to be. The next weekend, she was having a house party at her 1/3-owned beach house at Aldinga Beach. She had Simon as a partner and organised one for me. As the weekend progressed, she (Val) and I clicked. By the way, I collected my things from Lonsdale on the way down that Saturday, so I could not have been in bed for three weeks, Marc!

Mr Wollaston was retiring from his wholesale opal business, while I was still at CAL. He offered it to me, walk-in-walk-out. I had general attempts to grade the rough opal into three saleable grades.

MGW checked my gradings to find that I would not have lost money, but I wouldn't have made any. It was too big a gamble for me with a family to support so, "Thanks but no thanks" again.

The SA Director Dept of Productivity had seen the work I had done with forming Productivity Groups and he wanted to recommend me as Tasmania Director DoP, providing I got a Police clearance, which I quickly arranged. I had to become a member of the Australian Institute of Engineers, again which I did by interviews, as I did not have a B.E. I thought about this new change, but decided selling "Heathleigh", disorienting Marc and James to Tasmania was too big a price. So again, I said to the Director "Thanks, but no thanks!"

Chapter 7

A New Career – Industry Training

It was in 1978 that my work starting up Productivity Groups ceased. Mr Allan Shevens, who headed an industrial and commercial training program of the South Australian Department of Productivity, had been watching me and offered me a full-time job as Assistant Training Manager. Supervisor Productivity Achievement Program (SPAP) was the main product, and I was to sell it to companies.

My boss, Allan Stevens, trained me to run SPAP too, which I found satisfying. Eventually, I sold SPAP to companies, and ran the training programs as well.

By the end of 1978, I was dating Valerie Esau frequently, and stayed over occasionally. She would not stay at Crafers for fear of bushfires. We did have one night, the fire flames from the paddock opposite woke me. I went outside in my PJs to find a Country Fire Service truck outside trying to find a hydrant. I rushed inside, got a strong torch and found the hidden hydrant spot. By now the flames were up to the side of Emmett Road, threatening my property. However, it's amazing what a well-directed, full blast of fire-hose-water will do as they had doused the fire completely in about five minutes. Drama over.

The Productivity Production Council of Aust (PPCA) produced approximately 30 leaflets used to guide productivity groups and SPAP participants.

SPAP was an exceptional participative, experiential learning exercise. Over three weeks it involved 3 X 1 and ½ hours of observations of the participant and their manager. It concluded with a four-hour report back focusing on productivity and achievement.

I was so successful in selling SAPs that the D of P sent me to Melbourne to explain my successful methods to Head Office, and Vic Branch personnel. My formula was simple:

1. Find who is the relevant decision-maker retraining in the company,

2. Phone him/her and explain the fundamentals of SPAP,

3. Ask for the order – a supervisor to attend and manager,

4. Phone follow-up and repeat and repeat until I got the nominations

5. Ensure the fee was paid, and

6. Send reminders of times and dates of the particular course.

Simple, and it worked. I averaged one enrolment for each fourteen phone calls, so persistence produced results.

In all my contracts I defined a need for other Achievement Programs viz Manager PAP, Operator

PAP, "Small" Business PAP, Energy PAP, and Safety PAP. With Allan, we (mainly me) developed three new programs (for SPAP and MPAP Trainers' Manual). Three were unsuccessful and attracted insufficient participants, but the others were useful profit additions to SPAP. So we had now four good arrows to fire!

By 1980, I was married to Val (Esau). A big mistake! Again, "To yourself be true" and deep down I was not, just lonely. The boys had left home, and I was mainly alone. By the end of 1979, I had grown tired of the repetitive phone calls and follow ups of PAPs. I didn't mind the up-front training presentation part so I applied and was appointed State Manager SA Building and Construction Industry Training Committee (SAB & CITC for short).

In 1980, fourteen different tripartite – e.g. industry, union, Govt, ITCs – were formed. I accepted on the basis I would have a leave of absence for three weeks, as I had been nominated by IIE Fed: Council to attend IIE US Annual Conference and Productivity Day in Detroit, to which I was sponsored. I was able, at my expense, to travel on to Boston and attend the American Society of Training and Development Conference and Expos, again at my expense. I learnt a lot and bought back a heap of information from these conferences.

These leaflets were widely distributed in the Building and Construction Industries in SA.

I found there were unrealistic demands by the Commonwealth Dept Employment and Industries Relations that the ITC Managers should sell training and conduct the training at a profit, which would pay for the ITC Manager. Impossible! The SA B&CITC was quite unwieldy as every organisation wanted to have their six-penny worth into the ITC, hence, there were twenty-one persons with different axes to grind throwing their thoughts into the pot once a month. I found participating useful, taking the minutes, preparing and presenting the monthly financial statement, and keeping all twenty-one committee members happy far too much, but I soldiered on for nine years. The first thing I did on returning from the USA was to design a Training Needs Form and distribute it. Naturally, it took a lot of follow-ups to get the answers back, and even more effort to correlate the results, then print, bind and distribute them in a book form. This large and too comprehensive report was not understood, or accepted. I was told to simplify it. I was greatly deflated but went to a consultant who showed me how to present the bones of the findings and recommendations on one page. I had reduced thirty-seven detail data pages to twelve with "plenty of white" (consultant's advice) around the print. This report was accepted without fuss.

I further condensed my findings and held an industry seminar, which over 100 attended at the Australian Institute of Management to present "The Way Ahead" for the B&C Industries. It was received with acclaim, and several companies required training packages. Looking back, it's amazing how many of my forecasts have come about.

Maesbury Plumbers was one who requested a detailed training program, which I provided, quoted and carried out, with nineteen plumbers in due course.

To increase training resources available, the ITC became agents in SA for Power Human Resources and McGraw-Hill training materials. Tony Power presented several management participative training courses. I established a training materials bookshop at the old reception of the Master Builders. I enlisted my godson, Simon Barbour, to help set it up and made it part-time. He was finishing the last year of his Economics and Commerce Degree at the time. It was a happy relationship.

He has since established a major shell-buying and selling business and travels the world.

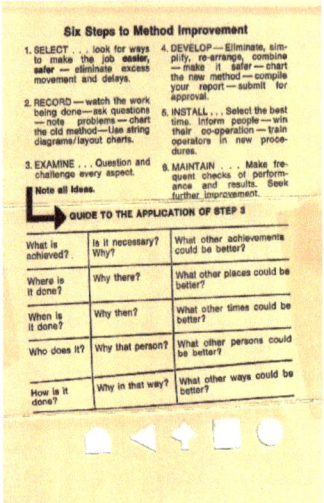

Simon Barbour in his shell shop.

I facilitated new fields of training within the Building and Construction industries with sustaining impact. It was in a time when traineeships and VET was being overhauled in Australia. I shortened a TAFE five-year bricklaying course to a more reasonable two-year course. I introduced roof tiler traineeships, reinforcing roof laying course, PAP and management courses. The "Big" significant one- and first in Australia- was the Earthworks Equipment traineeships! A lot of union and employee liaison and debate was required to set this up. But, now courses for traineeships in backhoe, bulldozer, scraper, and excavator still exist Australia-wide. A major effort each year was to get the finances segregated, then audited and the Annual Report printed and presented to ITC and distributed. Bi-annually. a national Station Managers meeting was organised by the Com Govt Dept E&IR which I attended in Canberra. Once stranded by an Ansett air strike, I had to bus it back to Adelaide.

Also, there was a National B&C ITC conference, usually in Melbourne to attend. A useful swap of ideas occurred at this.

By September 1989 I was worn out by the whole ITC set-up and getting little recognition and was told that I no longer had the ITC executive support, so I collected my long service pro-rata payment, plus Annual leave pay and resigned. I was again out of work at 59 years old. Things were difficult. And my marriage with Val was in trouble. I moved out to my apartment in Beaumont one Easter, then again to "Skye" for a year or so. It was an unlikely coincidence that the B&CITC hired a lady from WAWA to take my place. You'll see why in Chapter 9.

In 1983, I shortened the name to the Construction Training Committee SA.

Event at North Adelaide Country Club

SA Dep Premier Hon Jack Wright revealing the first sculpture award

In 1986, I was awarded my Fellowship in IIE. My post-notials are MIEAust, FIIE, MASTD.

I presented a 20-hour course in Engineer Management "C" at SA Institute of Technology School of Business Administration for six years at the Levels, now Uni of SA.

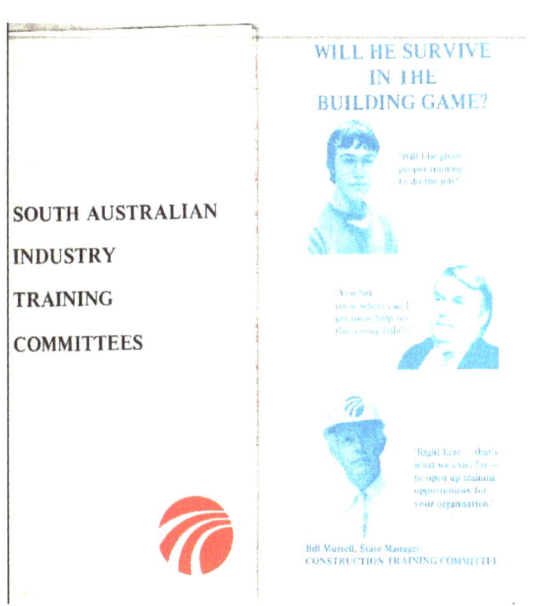

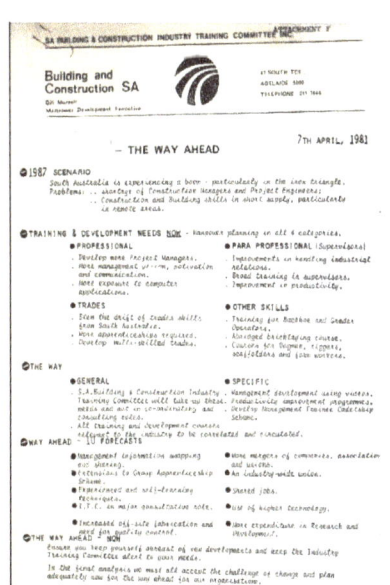

See syllabus, above right.

I enjoyed this challenge. It was an extension of my lectures at RMIT in 1961.

My friend Allen Gaze consulted on Training Achievement awards and brochure development. As the boys were staying away from Crafers – Jim went on an extensive US, UK and Europe tour – Val and I met up with him in Liverpool on our honeymoon. I nearly wrote 'honey-moan' as I had plenty of moans from Val. Marc was in a caravan (Julie's and Dave's) permanently parked in the Belair National caravan area. I decided to auction "Heathleigh". It did not sell well, but I gave $15k to Phil for her share and invested in two units in upper Beaumont.

Front

Back units 3 and 4. My 316 BMW outside.

In 1985, I sold the units and BMW and shares to buy "SKYE" a lovely big home in a sylvan setting as shown below.

Val Esau hated the place, and only slept there once. I was happy to be separated there.

Left: We had Christmas with Mum and Marc, Lucy and Jim.

"SKYE" Rostrevor Road, Stirling

Large Rhododendrons, see below.

Lounge room – Christmas at "SKYE", 1986.

Below: Picking Rhododendrons. I joined the Rhododendron Society at Aldgate.

Right: On return from overseas Jim organised a "T-shirts from all over" display.
It was good but poorly attended at the Burnside Town Hall, but showed his entrepreneurship.

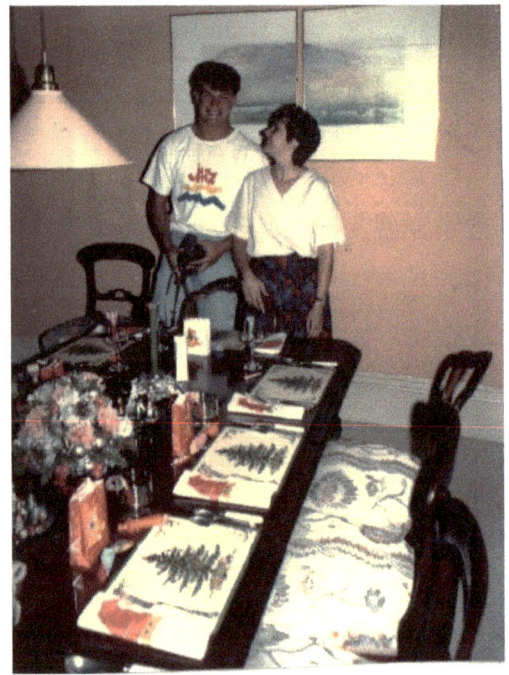

While overseas Jim took photos of many wooden toys. On his return, he and I went through them, and sorted out sixteen that were simple to make with basic carpentry tools – power saw, paint and gun etc. He produced them during the week, then took them to a stand at the Thebarton market on the weekend.

Above: Will and Lucy at Val's for
Xmas dinner.
My painting on wall, 1983.

Left: From the stand, about 6-8 toys were best sellers so he specialised in those.

Right: Jim at Burnside Town Hall.

Left: Jim's workshop at Strath.
"The Wall", now heritage-listed, that James built to enclose his property, Main Street, Strathalbyn.

A top event that Marc and I went to in Adelaide.

The noise of the motors revving at over 15,000 rpm is amazing. We could hear them easily at Walkerville.

Chapter 8

Fill-ins – Finding a Job at 60

I sighed as I gently sat down on the couch, leaning back before staring at the wall absent-mindedly. I idly tapped my fingers against my thigh, the sound resonating across the quiet room. Although the room was furnished with various fixtures and paintings adorned the walls, it felt desolate and empty.

It had been three weeks since I left CTC. Although the quietness of my routine felt blissful and serene, I was unnerved by a question that was constantly on the back of my mind.

"What's next?"

This was the first time I was confronted by this fear – fear of the unknown, fear of the uncertainty and fear of the future.

I smiled ruefully. At this age, people would be glad to be rid of the work. They'd be eager for the fishing trips, the cruises, the quiet mornings, and the lack of responsibility. I, on the other hand, was bothered by the lack of busyness and direction.

I had little assets aside from my equity in "SKYE" and my superannuation carried over from CAL to CTC.

So far, all the job applications I'd sent out had been rejected. I had even tried for Holden's again but unsurprisingly received a courteous "thank you, but we reject your application" letter.

Who ever claimed that ageism wasn't a thing?

Here I was, a 59-year-old man with a wealth of knowledge and experience in my field, struggling to find a job due to my "old" age.

After my 53rd attempt, Val excitedly informed me of an available IE position in Perth.

"It's a contract position for 12 months … you ought to give it a go," she told me encouragingly as she showed me the ad. It was for a company called the Water Authority of WA (WAWA).

I applied and was interviewed over the phone a week later.

A few days after, I found myself on the way to Perth via the East-West rail. I leaned back as I stared at a photo of Val.

"You'll come to visit me every three months … right, Val?" I remembered asking.

She gave me that bright, beautiful smile of hers before kissing me on the cheek. "It's a promise," she whispered.

She did keep her promise. She came over for a couple of months before her last visit in September 1991. Due to the distance, our marriage disintegrated. Not long after, Val became romantically involved with a guy she met.

I knew no one in Perth except for Bob Watson, who was the president of the WA IIE Division.

I'd known Bob for many years. He was kind enough to meet me at the train stop and offered to guide me in the Camry to my pre-booked apartment on Riverside Drive, Perth.

On the 15th of May 1990, I started my first day at WAWA.

Chapter 9

A New Career WAWA

Engineer takes on responsibility for our assets

With assets worth $7 billion, the Water Authority needs to be sure its asset management programme is spot on.

A lot of the responsibility for the way we look after our assets — everything from pipes and pumps to dams and buildings — now rests with South Australian industrial engineer, Bill Murrell.

Bill has taken up an appointment with the Water Authority to manage a multi-disciplinary team involved in the development of our operations and maintenance.

He will control the Systems Planning Section of the Asset Management Branch, conduct industrial engineering projects and develop and implement maintenance management systems policy.

In short, his job is to put in place within the next 12 months new maintenance policies and procedures that are good for the Authority and good for our customers.

"It's a matter of getting maintenance right and doing it better," Bill said.

One of his initial tasks is to visit all the regions as part of the planning phase.

"I want to meet the people involved and gain the co-operation of the regions," he said.

"I want to hear their ideas and

Bill Murrell . . . looking after our assets.

He matriculated in 1948 and went to work for GMH in South Australia for the next eight years.

During this time he was trained in the USA in Industrial Engineering and graduated in 1954 from GMIT, USA.

Since then he has held senior Industrial Engineering positions in large Australian organisations, including 16 years at Chrysler Australia Ltd.

Until September last year he was State Manager of the South Australian Construction Training Committee, a body established to develop and train personnel to higher competence at all levels from management through technical to trade levels in the building and construction

This article in "On Ta", WAWA's July issue announced my job. I spent a lot of time visiting the seven regions and Perth operations. A good start. Also being brought up as a child at the E&WS Depot at Thebarton SA until I was 21 years old when I lelft for training to the USA, helped.

This was my first desk at the John Tonkin Water Centre (shown below).

Enterprise Bargaining (EB) was all the go and they wanted to measure the WAWA's productivity and reward any increases. I applied to be EB Manager, missed out, but was seconded to the EB team. It was very absorbing presenting our progress each week to the top executive in the board room. I had a leave of absence temporarily from Asset Management for two years.

One day in late 1992 I received a dreadful phone call. My youngest son Will, who was working as a surveyor for the WAWA, had turned the Landcruiser end for end four times about fifty miles south of Menzies, WA and was seriously hurt – could I go to the emergency of Royal Perth Hospital immediately! When in the emergency theatre, a group of doctors said, "We think there's no brain damage, so over to the bone now."

I leave it to Will's letter to best describe the event, his injuries, and his feelings about recovery. One very brave man!

21/06/93
23 Colin St
Dalkeith. W.A 6009.
(09) 3891968

Thank you for your warmth and love that I received at a time when I needed it most.
I have indeed had a very trying time over the last seven months but I have also encountered lots of love and strength from people which has given me the motivation to make the best of my predicament. I am sorry that it has taken me so long to reply and I hope that this letter puts to rest any questions or at least tells what has happened and what is the current situation.

The accident happened on the 27/11/92 at about 3 a.m. travelling from Leonora to Kalgoorlie in a 4WD work car. I apparently, fell asleep, ran off the left side of the road - woke up - to see a cement culvert in front of me, over corrected and went over to the right side of the road and once meeting the dirt (on the side of the road) rolled about four times.
The car finally came to rest on the driver's side. I was in the middle of no-where and luckily before the dust could settle a bus passed and stopped. There were enough people to lift the car from me and (as a added bonus) there was a nurse on board who was to be my saviour. She carefully supervised people how they should get me out of the car and what to do when out. (She most probably saved me from being a quadriplegic because of her medical training). Two trucks stopped and radioed for the service of an Ambulance and it came within a hour.
I had massive internal bleeding and once they got me to the Kalgoorlie hospital had an operation on my hip and pelvis and then they decided to fly me to Perth (ie the Royal Flying Doctor service) so I could be treated at the Royal Perth hospital (RPH) where I underwent further surgery on my neck and knees.

This is a summary of the injuries that I acquired starting form the head down:

1) Dislocation and fracture of the # c7/c6 facet joint (R) (NND) Anterior subluxation # c6/c7 [no damage to spinal cord]
2) Broken 9th left rib
3) Dislocated right finger
4) Comminuted fracture (L) acetabulum with posterior dislocation of femoral head. [a dislocation and fractured hip joint]
5) Diastisis symphysis pubis and (R) sacro-iliac joint. [Fractures in my pelvis]
6) Mild urethra damage
7) Gross ligamentous disruption of (L) knee ACL/PCL/MCL posterior capsule and possible LCL. [dislocated left knee]
9) Ligament disruption of (R) knee ACL and MCL [dislocated right knee]
8) Sciatic nerve damage in (L) leg. [may take up to 18 months to 36 months to mend.]

P2 LibSup.

From the RPH I went to the Royal Perth Rehabiltation Hospital (RPRH) where I was to spend the next 4 months. Because I had dislocated my c6/c7 vertebrae I was put in what is known as a 'HALO'. This is a round piece of metal that is attached to the skull in four places. From the Halo is attached a triangular piece of metal which supports a pulley from which hangs a weight. i.e. the weight is suppose to pull your neck back into position. This meant being on my back and right side (moved every 2 hours to prevent bed sores) for the next 6 weeks. My legs were immobilised in splints so the ligaments could heal.

After six weeks I was put into what is known as a halo vest. This is a jacket that attaches to the Halo and immobilises the neck, however you are allowed to move around (in my case that meant a wheelchair) and the start of physiotherapy in a special spinal gym. I had to wear this for another 6 weeks and during this time I had another operation on my knees to induce their movement. My right knee recovered remarkably well but my left didn't and was told by the doctor to abandon phyiso on it because it would need another operation before it would improve. This mean the loss of a month in phyiso and while my right was coming along nicely the left dwindled away. I was able to walk on crutches in about the fourth week of phyiso, it was painful but I could do such things as go to the toilet for the first time by myself since the accident! The next big event was for the Halo to come off. It was simply a feeling of freedom to have it removed. To have a shower (and a haircut) for the first time since the accident was a tremendous feeling.

After the third operation on my knees, the left knee finally moved passed the 90 degree mark and I was able to at last go home. After 20 weeks in hospital it was quite a relief to say the least, although I still had to go to the Hospital outpatient gym 5 days a week for phyiso. I went to a different gym because my problem was a orthopedic one [bones and muscles] and not spinal.

I am now at a stage where I am going to Phyiso 3 days a week on Mon, Tues & Fri and working at the Water Authority (in Perth) for 3 hours after phyiso and on the Tues & Thurs work a 7 hour day. I am on a rehabilitation program and will have to return Kalgoorlie once I have a made suitable recovery. I am now walking on two walking sticks which is a progression from elbow crutches. From two sticks I hope to go to one and then to none! My left leg is coming on slowly and the nerve seems to be returning which is a major relief.

So things are looking bright but I know that this incident will take some time to get over, nevertheless I have the WILL-POWER to get on with life and make the best of it. That's about my story so far, I hope that it has, in the least, informed you on the saga thus far!
Stay tuned for the next adventure!

Thank you for your thoughts. And please write/ring and let me know how you are doing!

Left: Will and Valdean at spinal hospital

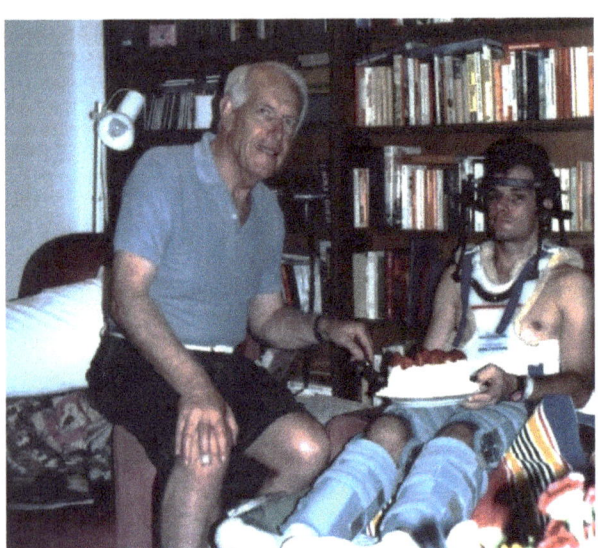

Me and Will recuperating at Tyrell Street

Above: Will in his halcyon days hitchhiking through the USA strumming his guitar in the snows of the Grand Canyon in 1988. He was 20 years old.

After the first temporary apartment, I leased a furnished upstairs one by the month, at Cambridge Street, Wembley, as shown below left.

A friend at St Edmunds Church was an Ansett pilot and had to go to Singapore for a long-term job. He offered me his home at Duncraig (below) to rent reasonably, so I moved there. It was fully furnished.

Rented home at Duncraig

In June 1990, one evening there was an IIE visit to the West Australian Newspaper Printing and Editorial facilities. I had lent Will, who was visiting from SA, where he was studying surveying, my Camry, so I wanted a ride back to Wembley after the tour. No one in our group volunteered but the tour guide for a group of lawyers overheard me and said she was going past. Her name was Valdean. What a blessed meeting of souls that was! We talked on the way home; I asked her if she would have coffee on a date in the future, and she said, "Sure but get in the queue." She had three other suitors. She had separated from her gallivanting husband, Rev Michael Dean, some four years earlier and was enjoying her freedom. She had a B.Ed and was highly intelligent. She retired from teaching to head the WAN telemarketing team. She had a very good sense of humour.

Right: Val Dean at Duncraig entrance.

As SA President of IIE, I was an invited guest of SA Railways to train to the SA-NT border to see the joining of the Ghan rails to Darwin. See photos below.

Last pictures of Dad, who died in July 1980, with Andrew my young "Scottish" brother.

Six weeks after starting at WAWA, Mum, 88 years, died.
This is my last picture of her with my friend from GMH and rugby days Wally Scott.

My yellow Hillman Hunter in drive.

Family saying and waving me goodbye in Adelaide.

Kerry Mahoney MD of Griffin Press phoned me to offer a 2-month contract to raise the output of the newly installed secondhand Kolbus Bookbinding line by 100%. I failed as I only increased the output by 50%. When reaching under the bench for a toolbox, my 2 x repaired RH inguinal hernia popped out. I was in agony until I had it repaired for the third time. I wrote my Xmas cards in 1989 in Calvary Hospital. The hernia has broken out again but doctors say it's too difficult to fix now.

As Valdean's birthday approached, she casually said that she'd never had a birthday party. So I said that I would remedy that, and asked for a list of her friends. I rang them all, and all of them came to Duncraig on 18/1/1992 and celebrated Valdean's birthday.

Valdean blowing out her candles

Valdean had been State Coordinator of Young Achievers in WA and VIC for six years. As you may have gleaned, Valdean and I clicked. She has continued to be very, very kind to me and spoiled me. We truly loved each other and as soon as my divorce was final from Val-ex, and after Will had recovered sufficiently to live on his own, we married on 6/8/1993. I was offered a rent-free, but pay the rates, taxes, phone, electricity deal on a friend's house at Tareena Street, Nedlands so I moved there, and so did Will when he was released from the hospital. He spotted an ad for a cheap house, mind at Colin Street, Nedlands, which we snapped up and moved there. Will and I had fun cooking for each other. When I came home on the 6/8 from work, got dressed in my hired tails, and said, "There's a bottle of "Hill of Grace", Will, will you get it, please?"

Will went all colours and produced the bottle full of water!

I said, "You have a big problem; I want to take a Hill of Grace on our honeymoon."

As luck would have it, at Steve's Cellar beneath where we had our wedding breakfast (actually a dinner), Will was able to buy a Henschke "Hill of Grace".

Murray's Mill where I proposed to Valdean on 25/3/1993 and she accepted.

Our wedding breakfast. Rachel Davis nee Barbour being playful, with a fertility wreath. She now has two beautiful children of her own and lives at Cribb Point in Victoria's Mornington Peninsular.

After returning from our honeymoon at Kalbarri, I bought a half share in Valdean's townhouse at 5/62 Onslow Road, Shenton Park (below right).

Left: Valdean and I cut our wedding cake.

Above: my birthday celebrations at 5/62. Behind me, Bob Watson, who'd met me at East Perth Railway Station 15/5/1990.

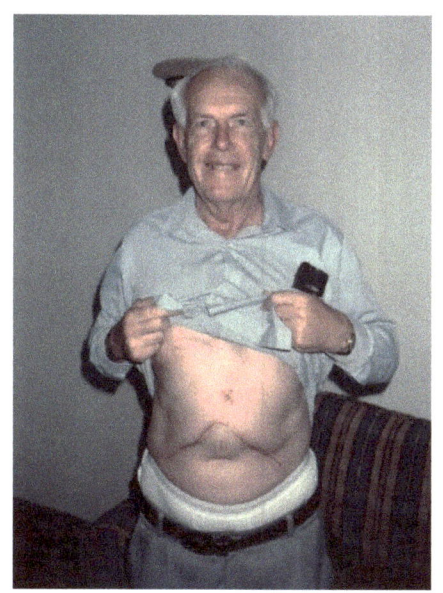

I had been unable to keep my food down for some months and Valdean said, "This is ridiculous, you must see a gastro doctor." I did and I had a serious 6 ½ Duo fundoplication operation. The surgeon said that I nearly died. I recovered in time to attend Alison and Tony's wedding on 4/2/1994.

* Alison is Valdean's only daughter and she married Tony Milne.

Left: Me showing off my "shark bite"

Above: Valdean's and my wedding.

Below: Mr & Mrs Murrell walk down the aisle.

Above: Valdean and I went on many trips together
e.g. Rottnest Island

Right: one of our many picnics at Somerville.

Left: The stairs at 5/62 I found hard to manage, and there was no carpet for two stairs, so we started to look for another one level home. We had just about given up when we saw 1/1 Kilpa Court and in one week sold 5/62 and bought it.

Right: We went on the paddle steamer "Decoy" on the Swan. Valdean was a WAN tourist trip guide and I went on four of her eight trips from Cairns to Sydney, Tasmania, Hong Kong, on the Arcadia and N & S NZ.

Left: Brian Stanton, ex-GMI and H, outside.

Valdean and I took away a carload for friends, including Will and Rachel, down to Ray Moss's Donnelly River Resort. Here we would have working bees all day Saturday, a gala dinner Saturday evening, then a fun time and return on Sunday. There were many ex-saw miller huts to do up. I went for a walk early one misty morning and got completely lost. I was retrieved five kilometres away.

In Christchurch NZ March 2000.

Left and Below: Rotto again – good times.

Left and Below: With friends at Donnelly Dam

Left: My head in "Jaws" Donnelly Saw Mill

General Manager Customer Service Drvn Colin Temby congratulating me on completing the Water Motor Project, 1993

Right: My follow up whiteboard of project tasks 1996.

After twelve months, I was asked to renew for another twelve at WAWA, then another twelve in 1995. I said that I wanted a permanent job, so my job as IE was advertised through the WA Government. Six applicants including me were interviewed and I eventually was appointed to my old job. This was repeated in 1995 when all jobs were spilled and again I was now IE Manager. I was actually a Program Manager in charge of six project managers; a very full-on job. One of the first that I was in charge of was the Water Meter project.

We boarded the *Arcadia* in Feb '98 at Hong Kong. Valdean was WAN tour leader. After leaving HK, sailing to Manilla, we both became sick on the way. I recovered enough to throw the welcome party on Val's behalf after two days. From there to Surbiton, Balthem on to Fremantle. It was my first long sea voyage and very enjoyable. It was part of *Arcadia's* maiden around-the-world voyage after a major refit.

Hong Kong

Indo Fleet Surabaya

"Dog Rock" – Albany.

I had four assignments at the Water Corporation's Great Southern Regional Office. I usually stayed at the Dog Rock Motel, opposite Dog Rock of course. Will, as Finance Manager Great Southern Region, now stays there too. 2012: issued a business model ex PPCA shown opposite effectively in my money cost reduction efforts at WAWA and Water Corp.

Holding a workshop at Water Corporation.

I presented a series of "Continuous Improvement" to sections of WAWA and also IIE WA Division. I was also instrumental in achieving "Work Programme Teams" in the regions. In 1996, I went to the UK with Valdean and visited the Leeds Waste Water Treatment Plan, plus reviewed Engineering and Maintenance procedures at several relevant places. I had this idea of a laser root cutter for sewer pipes and visited four CCTV and pipe travellers manufacturers. I later dropped the laser cutting idea as it was too likely to cause an explosion with sewer gas. The 1996 Tasks achieved small proposed 1997 plans, one outlined below.

Inspecting a country waste water settling pond.

The document starting on page 112 best summarise my qualifications, experiences and achievements in my work history.

Valdean and I do many things together such as:

Visiting art openings

Seeing Australia II trials

Visit sculptures at Margaret River

Visit Kal open pit.

Walk in the forests at Denmark

Right: Kalgoorlie Big Open Pit

Perth arrival.

150t dump truck on road trailer

**Will at Wave Rock Hyden on our way to his work
for WAWA as a surveyor (before his accident).**

Other pictures of my lovely Valdean.

On our wedding day.

By the way, I spelt her name "Valdene" until '93. I even had a special bowl with both of us on it engraved Valdene and Bill, 6 Aug '93 by Sharon Peters kin

'Tis 19th Jan 2014, 'Tis Valdean's 76th birthday. We'll celebrate at "Pregos" restaurant tonight.

In late 1998, in preparation for retirement, I bought a 1972 360cc 3-cylinder, water-cooled Suzuki Coupe GT "Fronte" model. It was in pieces, as this article by A. John Parker describes:

Automotive Engineer Bill Murrell and an Unusual Suzuki

Part One -
Starting off an Automotive Engineering career 1950-1960:-
Bill Murrell has been involved with motor cars for much of his career life, so when he retired he decided that it would be an interesting and rewarding pastime to take on putting back together one of Perth's most unusual little cars that Suzuki had brought to Perth in 1973 for evaluation - the Fronte.

His eyes misted over when I asked Bill where it had all started, "At Woodville in Adelaide. In 1950 I became a technical clerk at the Plant Engineering Department of the Woodville GM-H plant in South Australia. Very soon after I saw there was much more to life so in 1951 I applied for an Engineering Scholarship through General Motors Overseas Operations." It meant that he would be sent to Flint, Michigan, to attend the General Motors Institute of Technology (GMIT) to learn everything he wanted to know about automotive engineering. "However, "I was soon 'accosted' by top management who asked, 'If you knew that you had to be a clerk here for two years before applying, how come you did?'

Bill had obviously smiled to himself, drawing his trump card, "Because next year I will have been here 2 years and then you will select me!" Bill said, "I must have impressed someone there, for in the next year I was treated as a Cadet and given wide-ranging assignments in different tooling and manufacturing departments."

He was then given the task of designing a pencil 'schematic' plant layout for the proposed Elizabeth plant. Then, in exultation in 1952, Bill set out for Flint where he spent two years absorbing everything he could about metallurgy, processing, metals, foundry management, tool tryout and sidegate body assembly, while studying at GMIT and completing work assignments at Buick (1952-3) and Pontiac Fisher Body (1953-4).

After 3 years as supervisor in the Production Engineering Department at Woodville in 1957 Bill thought it time to leave GM-H, taking on the role of Director of a South Australian Management Consultancy.

He then worked at Australian Motor Industries (AMI) in Melbourne as Chief Production Engineer. At the time, AMI was assembling Mercedes-Benz, Rambler, Fiat tractors, the Triumph Herald and Vanguard cars. "In fact, I planned the assembly of the first 6-cylinder Vanguard car we built."

By the end of 1959 he could see that the writing was on the wall for AMI as sales were poor, and having a brochure on the then unknown Subaru car, showed it to the Managing Director of Standard Motor Co Australia explaining that it was front wheel drive, unusual, and had a 'boxer' engine in the front.

As the imported price of the Subaru was so low Bill suggested sending a team to Japan to Subaru to get the Australian distribution/assembly rights. Bill saw the potential and the low cost, stating, "At those prices you will sell hundreds! A team was quickly sent and came back with an assembly agreement for Toyota vehicles at AMI!"

He grinned proudly, "I believe because of this it was I who started Toyota sedans off in Australia!!"

A Move Away from the automotive world 1960-1962:-
In 1960 Bill Murrell left AMI and moved as Standards Manager, to New Holland in Dandenong. During this time he lectured part time in Industrial Engineering at Melbourne's Royal Industrial of Technology.

Part Two -
Back into the automotive world:-

In 1962 his wife's mother, who lived in Adelaide, became ill and Bill moved to Adelaide with Chrysler at Keswick (Tonsley Park had not been built at this stage) where the 'S' Model Valiant was the car of the moment. There, Bill supervised Methods and Processes. Bill reminisced. "I had to earn four times my own salary in new ideas which saved the company money. I got it up to six times!"

In 1963 Bill was promoted to Industrial Engineer at Chrysler.

"That was also the time of the Chrysler Royal and the first of the AP Series Valiants. "I well remember a marketing meeting on the model designations - we'd had the 'VC' Model and a 'VD' model loomed, putting a cloud over the heads of the planners. Suddenly, the Personnel Manager Harold Wallage cried out in a flash of brilliance, 'It doesn't matter if we don't have a 'VD' model!' - and so we never did!"

In 1966 Bill was at Chrysler and became Special Project Manager - he was asked to select 6 people and, in secret, to design a plant for Sydney. "But the plant was never built!"

In 1968-9 Bill was promoted to Chrysler International in Sydney which ran FEAO (the Far Eastern & African Operations) where he was Industrial Engineer and Quality Manager. The world was divided up - Mexico controlled Central and Latin America; Canada was controlled out of Detroit; London controlled Europe and North Africa, and FEAO controlled the rest. When things went sour for Chrysler two offices were slashed, with only London and Detroit being retained.

Before accepting this promotion Bill Murrell talked with Managing Director, David Brown, at Chrysler Australia whose forecast that Chrysler International was in trouble was proved correct.

During his time with Chrysler International Bill made 5 trips overseas (26 had been planned for the following year) to Karachi to check on quality of Valiants; to Canada regarding the boxing of trucks for overseas shipping; over to Hamtramck in Detroit; to the Philippines to check on Quality and to NZ where GM was wanting to buy out Todd Motors which assembled Chrysler models from CKD shipments.

In 1970 Bill was told by David Brown that there was a job for him with Chrysler in Adelaide - it was not known what he would do at that stage but David explained that Chrysler had a real problem with its service record being less than Ford's or GMH's, so he was appointed Chrysler's Australian Service Manager and was given 5 years to turn things around.

Bill smiled, "I knew little about service as such and put in an ex-Rolls-Royce engineer, the late Max Aspley. We launched the 'Chrysler Cares and Service Excellence' programme and the blue uniforms which you now see right through the industry. In fact, the material had a 'soil release' agent in it and once the mechanics' wives saw how well they laundered, within 2-3 weeks all the men were in them! Worn parts replaced during service were returned in special blue bags to the customer along with the car so that they could inspect them, and we provided loan cars. Service Awards became part of everyday life - I well recall presenting a service award to John Hughes at Skipper Chrysler in Perth as well as Lionel Sangster at Leederville Chrysler."

In 1973 Bill was delighted to find that his CAL SERVICE was independently rated ahead of Holden's and Ford's.

During that time Bill came to WA five times to assist the regional office at Kewdale. "The manager was followed by a much young manager who had been at FEAO with me. The Service Managers were Doug

McFall, then Peter Clark, assisted by Syd Breeden who did the service training for the Hemi engine."

The role was really to lower warranty costs with the Valiant and engineer out built-in problems. For instance the VG Valiant had a curl pin which held the gearstick in - once it wore the gearstick could come out in your hand which drivers found a bit disconcerting! I know how it felt, for I was in a taxi crossing Sydney Harbour Bridge once when it happened to my driver! It was all a matter of a few cents saved in cost during production - Chrysler saved in the short term but had ended up with a long-term problem.

On returning from Sydney, Bill sat on the Chief Engineer, Ian Webber's, table explaining what it was all about and then said, "I am not returning until you fix it Ian!' Ian took the fix drawing out of a drawer, signed it and it was soon fixed."

For a short time Bill was also involved in the recall of Chryslers because the wheels literally fell off! "Yes, a wheel nut runner on the assembly line did not work properly for a short time allowing the wheel nuts to loosen while on the road. Another time Bill had been at a barbecue with newspaper editor John Scales when urgent phone calls came for Bill about the brakes on the VG model failing. Without giving the game away, Bill was able to tell John Scales enough stories to head him off while sorting out the challenges they were having with a change-over from Girling to their Australian manufacturer.

"The dies were slightly inaccurate giving rise to the problem," Bill said, "and, we had already done our pre-release publicity! Such things make dealers very jittery and can make or break a model!" Bill had had a similar problem with a recirculating-ball steering system which had literally 'lost its balls!'

"The very first computer recall system Chrysler used, I set up about 1971, and I even gave evidence at a Senate Committee enquiry into Vehicle Safety Australian Manufacturers. At Chrysler around the World we were faced with 'lemon squeezers'- Lyn Townsend was Chairman. So, in 1976 some 750 people were laid off from Chrysler's SA factories.

Bill then moved into the Building and Construction Industries in South Australia before moving to Perth.

A denouement and an unusual Suzuki 1989-2004:-
In 1989 Bill decided it was time to use his skills by working in both government and private corporations and completely away from the world of automotive manufacturing. In 1990 he was appointed Industrial Engineer at the Water Corporation of WA from which he retired in 1999.

Now that I knew where Bill Murrell was coming from I was keen to see his cute Suzuki Fronte and so we repaired to the garage. What a sight! The most petite of Japanese cars stood in front of me. With my tall and bulky frame there was absolutely no way I could have got behind the steering wheel (or even in through the hole where the door shut!)

In 1973 Perth's car dealers, Mortlocks Sales & Service, had brought in three Suzuki Fronte 360 cars for evaluation purposes. A green LL20 sedan, a bronze L10 coupé and a maroon LC10W coupé. Two were later rolled over and destroyed after being stripped for parts, while the third, the LC10 coupé, is the one Bill Murrell acquired. He also has most of the mechanical parts from the other two cars for spares. This includes three engines.

The third car was then modified by having changes made -
1. Front suspension - disk brakes have been added;
2. Rear vision mirrors from the top of the front mudguards have been removed;

3. One-piece wheels (Mini Minor size) have been added;
4. Front air spoiler and roll bar added;
5. Rear demister and bronze-tinted windows added;
6. Body was stripped after an accident and the car was repaired and re-painted green but the quality of the workmanship is poor.

In 1990 the right-hand side of the car was damaged in an accident, and the power unit, radiator, heater, windows, interior, etc, were removed, the body was panelled and repainted in original colour with Dulux Two-Pack. On return from paint shop front guards and spoiler were removed, the car was covered with linen sheets and stored in a shed until March 1998. The car and parts are now in Bill's garage. Since 1991 the remaining coupé, up on its own wheels, has been stored under cover with all the spare parts.

The main difference between the LC10W and WGXCF model was front disc brakes, one-piece rims, front spoiler and rear demister. The LC10W was in effect converted to a WGXCF as all of these parts and other miscellaneous trim items were fitted to the LC10W.

There is a dismantled power unit (engine/gearbox/clutch/diff), the cylinder block has been re-bored, ports polished, crankshaft rebuilt plus there are new pistons, rings, gaskets, etc. The power unit removed from vehicle before it went to the paint shop is still complete and was working when removed. There is also another complete power unit from an LC20, this is basically the same except it has a single carburettor and different primary gear ratio.

There are numerous extra spare parts, windscreen, rear and side windows, left door, rear engine cover, bonnet, bumpers, grills, seats, dash, radiators, heater, hoses, cables, etc. There are some new gaskets, rear engine covers, bumpers, door rubber seals, etc - many of the parts from the vehicle that was wrecked are near new.

There are Parts Books for several versions of the Fronte (LC10W, WGXCF, LC20, SS10), plus Owners Manuals and an illustrated Factory Service Manual. The parts books are very well illustrated and the part numbers of bolts, etc, indicate thread diameter and length which will make re-assembly easier.

There is still a lot of work to do - quite a lot more than Bill had anticipated when he first took on the project. He has been slow on the uptake, mostly because ill health has dogged him in recent years.

Unsure if he really will finish his project Bill, particularly since his partner in the hobby died in 2003, Bill is currently thinking that he would enjoy it all a lot more if he could sit on the sidelines, help out where he could and watch the jig-saw puzzle he has in boxes all over the garage come to life in someone else's hands.

It's a quite unique little car, and Bill and Perth deserve to see it back on the road.

Our 2005 Suzuki Swift with Fronte

I joined "SIVA" Car Club and the members were very interested in my "Fronte" project.

I held several SIVA meetings at 1/1. At the first meeting, I showed my US-GM Motarama slides taken in Chicago 1953.

Fronte on way to SA Nov 2012.

This is a sample of the car photo albums that I've collected. I have about forty car books too! Now sold to Whiteman Park Motor Museum.

From 1996, I was going deaf in my right ear. So as not to be noticed I used a completely in-ear type of hearing aid. I also joined Better Hearing Aust (WA) Inc to attend Lip Reading classes. After I retired, I was elected to BHA WA's board, then later as President, we held the BHA Aust, national conference in Perth.

I'm addressing the dinner delegates here.

I was also elected to the BHA (Aust) Federal Council. For me, work on the computer at the Water Corporation was becoming increasingly onerous so I started to retire gradually, reducing to four days; then three days a week until actual retirement in April 1999. A one-year contract turned into an enjoyable nine-year journey. Fortunately, I pumped 12 per cent of my salary and extras into my superannuation accounts. On retirement, a financial advisor put all my four super accounts into a pre-1983 account and saved me $15 k in tax.

Hogmanay" celebrations in Jakarta with Tony and Alison Milne 1997/8.

Maypole dancers at Government House.

At Smiths Beach estuary I caught fish! (6)

Another favourite spot to visit with Valdean.

One of my best pictures.

Chapter 10

Retirement – The Story Continues!

Although I had retired, I returned to the Water Corp for a few mornings to tidy up loose ends on my projects. I forgot to say that in my last months I put in 29 written suggestions for significant improvements in the scheme that had just started. I was rewarded with golf balls, a water jug and a half dozen Water Corporation glasses.

We had planned to take a grey nomad's trip around half of Australia and set off in July. We had fortunately pre-booked as it turned out, accommodation at various caravan parks with the RAC WA. I'll list the places we stayed at.

1. Greenough West
2. Carnarvon
3. Yardie Creek inlet, west of Exmouth where I caught plenty of good sizes and a variety of fish on the Ningaloo Reef
4. Onslow
5. Karratha
6. Port Hedland where we saw an outdoor ballet on the Council lawns
7. Broome where we met Lucy, who had flown from Darwin to help us holiday
8. Derby along the Gibb River Road to Oscar Range and George to
9. Fitzroy Crossing – cruised Geikie George
10. Halls Creek – saw China Wall and got a puncture
11. Turkey Creek now Warnum took a helicopter ride over the Bungle Bungles
12. On the road to Wyndham, Lucy lost control of the car, skidded badly, nearly killing all of us and causing the front wheel rims to buckle
13. Back to Gibb River Road and El Questro, Zebedee Springs
14. To Kununurra where I had the Magna straightened and found two new front tyres, also had the car serviced
15. Victoria River
16. Leaking out to Katherine where I had the oil leak fixed (crossed thread during service) and

bought a set of four mag wheels (This insurance paid as less cost than two steel rims airfreight from Adelaide). Cruised Katherine George

17. To stay with Lucy in Darwin at Lucy's Palmerston townhouse. After two weeks down "the track" (Stuart Hwy) to Katherine again, and again soaked in nearby river pools to cool off
18. Mataranka
19. Tennant Creek
20. Into Alice Springs putting the Magna on the Ghan to Adelaide overnight plus
21. Stayed at Tim's for a week or so at his and Patricia's' home at Walkerville then set off for WA
22. Wilmington National Park
23. Wilpenda Pound for a week
24. Port Augusta
25. Tumby Bay
26. Port Lincoln
27. Coffin Bay where we had breakfast of delicious Coffin Bay oysters – the Best!
28. Streaky Bay – more oysters
29. Ceduna – more oysters
30. Yalata
31. Eucla WA
32. Cocklebiddy
33. Northampton
34. Esperance
35. Hyden to see the Wave Rock
36. Back to 1/1 and home, tired by happy

During the last month of this 3-month journey, I was not feeling well, just not myself. By the way, Valdean did 70 per cent of the driving on our trip.

Me in Hippo's Yawn, Wave Rock

In 2000, I went to the doctor and was referred to a urologist who did lots of tests and I had the big "C". Cancer of the prostate was a big shock. I was referred to Prof David Joseph at QEII hospital. He was very thorough and gave me very accurately aimed radiation doses plus two experimental hormone injections (basically chemical castration) which I agreed to.

I will not elaborate on this as I explained it all in this letter to my family with pictures.

I interrupted my treatment for three weeks while we attended the 2000 Sydney Olympic Games, staying with Keith and Marjorie Bashford at North Sydney with harbour views.

I attended eight out of nine events we had tickets for, but was in a wheelchair for several events to and from. We met up with Lucy there for the last event.

It took a bit of getting over the C, but I did. PSA is now 2.5 and I have a yearly check.

Because we prepaid both our funerals, this reduced our assets, so we both squeezed in for the part pension. Neither of us had huge superannuation nor assets or shares. But the pension enabled us to take yearly trips free on our Trans WA train or bus routes. So we've been to Bunbury three times, Busselton, Kalbarri twice, and Perth to Kalgoorlie to Esperance to Perth trips for far.

In 2001, Will and Jane were married. An excellent family gathering (below)).

In 2002, unfortunately, my brother Tim died of a massive heart attack while having a back operation in Adelaide. We occasionally see Patricia when she comes to Perth to see her son Tom, wife Aileen and two grandchildren, Georgia and Tim. In 2000, Jim and Jill made a big investment and bought a 100-acre farm with 40 acres of vines at Jupiter Creek Road, Echunga. Jim has planted another 40 acres of chardonnay grapes. He has a 6-year contract to supply Wolf Blass Wines (photo right).

Another event was the birth of Hugo to lovely Lucinda, 7/10/01.

We often twilight sailed at Freshwater Bay Yacht Club in *Apollo* or *Individual*. Earlier we sailed with Geoffrey (Valdean's son) with friends in *Two Dogs*, his catamaran.

I was lucky to win an Easter raffle – a basket of eggs.

Above: Tullie, Jim, baby Lily (her blessing ceremony), Will, Phillippa- all descendants of Arch Deacon JR Wollaston at the Wollaston Theological College and Conference Center, WA, 2002.

Right: Valdean and I went to Melbourne to attend Rachel Barbour's (now Davis) wedding in Malvern.

Below: One of my favourite shots.

Above: Alison Milne (Valdean's daughter) with children + Lily at a SIVA outing. Mischasmith 3-wheeler at back.

Right: Hannah on Jim's back was born 2/12/2002

Below: My step-grandchildren – Rachael Milne 29/8/1996 and Tara Milne 1/2/1999

Above: Again, I'm in my favourite place, Kalbarri

Kalbarri – rugged country

When I first drove to Kalbarri, I hired a Ford Falcon in Geraldton (I was there for a WAWA assignment) and on Saturday morning, the sun behind me on the straight flat good road into Kalbarri, I put my foot down until I was travelling at 200km/hr, only for two or so kilometres. Reckless, I know but I felt exhilarated!

In 2007, after Hans and Rachel Greenberg stayed with us at 1/1, we went to the USA.

First, we visited Gale and Joy Hagane in N.Chicago, Winnetka actually Glenview. Then to New York for a few days before taking a tour of Niagara Falls (photo above) shown here, next to Washington DC, then Philadelphia where Hans and Rachel picked us up in their M-B and drove us to their summer home at St Michaels, Maryland. After staying two weeks, they drove us to Dallas Airport and we caught a plane to Charaville then onto Myrtle Beach then a taxi to our motel at Murrells Inlet. Here, we explored for several days. Then caught a plane to Orlando, Florida, where we saw Disney World and the Epcot Centre. Valdean had to push me in a wheelchair as my right knee had given up (on return to Australia I had an arthroscopy operation but it is still not 100 per cent ok). Then we flew to Miami where Hans and Rachel picked us up and drove us to their winter apartment in Naples, Florida. After another two weeks with them, we flew the long flight from Miami home via Melbourne. A great trip!

Haystacks by Monet at Chicago Institute of Art we visited.

On 28 October 2002, I presented a paper to the International Federation on Ageing, 6th Global conference at the Burswood Convention Centre entitled "A Ding Dong sounding turning indicator may prevent more accidents than the existing click-clack indictor". I had done some research and found hard of hearing people, like me, could not hear the old click-clack indicator sound. I sent copies of my paper to GMH, Mitsubishi, Ford, Toyota and Suzuki and Dept of Transport and FCAI (Federal Chamber of Automotive Industries) for action. Now, in 2014, most car companies have changed to a different (better) sounding electronic type indicator.

During our visit to Norfolk Island 7-14 May 2003 I researched a convict relative on my mum's Calvert side named James Morrisby and his wife, also a convict, Ann Brooks. We went with my sister Ruth, her husband Dr Robert Barbour, and my cousin Dianne Marshall and celebrated the 200th birthday of Henry (James' son) Morrisby, whose daughter married a William Calvert in Tasmania. For more details, see Appendix 2.

On 10 August 2005, Valdean's mother Dorothy (Dot) Phelps died, aged 95.

Left: Me and "Dot" Phelps

Right: Picture of cat o' tails in Norfolk Island Museum.

Left: Thelma Murphy, Jenny Phelps, Valdean Murrell, Rodney Phelps, Roma Meers – All at Jenny and Rodney's wedding. Valdean's brother and sisters.

Chapter 11

Family and Friends

It was 2004 when Valdean and I decided to attend an ALFA course on Christianity at St. Christopher's.

I remember walking out of the room after my first class, my eyes wide and bright with astonishment.

"That was… something," Valdean remarked, breathless.

I only nodded in response. I felt spiritually enlivened.

It took a few months to set up, but after feeling inspired by the course, I decided to start a Men's Fellowship Group at St. Christopher's with Valdean. As the group got bigger with time, so did its influence and successes. We ran meetings, visited places, and even managed to invite a few guest speakers as well as an opera singer. We made certain that we had at least an activity per month for seven years straight.

Since I came from a family of five, and Valdean a family of four, we shared a large group of family and friends.

Since I believe that a person is best introduced visually rather than through words, this chapter will mainly consist of photographs rather than narratives. It's my hope that the images will give you an insight into the characters of those I hold dear in my life … and the stories and memories I've had with them.

Valdean gave me drinks at a party in Wollaston Centre for my 65th birthday. Frank and Jean Pound came from Melbourne to attend the event. We had another big breakfast in the new Wollaston dining room for my 75th, and for this celebration, Ruth and Bob Barbour came from Adelaide. For my 80th birthday, we had … surprise surprise … another big breakfast.

Valdean took photos of all who attended my 80th with me and I put together a DVD with music of it.

For Valdean's 70th birthday party, I organised a party on our back patio. I invited her mates and bought some drinks and finger foods.

A special card from our friend Judy Hartigan on my 75th.

Mum and Dad's 50th Wedding anniversary. I proposed the toast on 30th December 1976.

Dad's sister Christina Murrell outside "Teingrace", the Murrell family home at 265 Pakington Street, Geelong

Right: Mum's younger sister Mollie Maun Calvert.

Right: Bob Barbour, …… & Christobel Mattingly, me, Ruth Barbour (sister). Chris is an author of note. We in 1940's chased each other in the Brighton sand hills.

Left: Me, Lucinda and Hugo Nicolas Lindsay Murrell, dusk on the wharf in Darwin.

Lucy with Marc

Left: Lucy with her B.Ed, she now also has MAPPLI

Right: Jim and Marc on the steps of "Hathaway" at Stirling, approx. 1962.

Brother Andrew in his antiques shop, London House at Strathalbyn.

Marc more recently with his montage at back.

Above: Marc on stairway to his flat 4/58 The Esplanade, Semaphore.

Marc in a happy mood

Left: Brother Andrew and sister Ruth

Right: Sister Helen and I

Family shot of the gang at "Hathaway"

Joan Milson, Helen and us at Mandurah

Right: Christmas lunch at Aldgate Hotel

The family gathers after Dad's funeral 1980

Right: Ruth, Helen and Andrew

Another scrumptious meal at the Barbour's.
Rachel, Bob, Andrew, Ruth and Patricia

Cousins Deanne and Tony Calvert and Helen

Above: Tim, Tom, Ruth, Aileen, Georgia, Lily, Will

Right: Angela, Bob, Jill, Jim, Tullie, Ruth

Below: Will, Aileen, Tom Murrell,
Centre: Frank Dunn and Valdean and I
at our townhouse backyard in Shenton Park

Right: Me, Brian and Joan Colton (Jill's parents) and Jill Murrell

Left: Jill, Jim, Lucy and me

Right: Valdean, Sue Koo (Jane's Aunt), Jane, Lily and Will

Left: Quentin Wollaston, Phillippa's young brother, Valdean and I at Quent's nursery at Delamere SA

Two reindeer Tara and Lily decorate our tree

Right: Tullie Murrell

Fairy Lily dancing

Jane and Simon Barbour fooling. Simon is my godson

Lily in her room with my Christmas hat

Studio photos – us with Rachael and Tara

Studio photo – us with Lily

Geoffery and Alison in Bristol, UK

Left: Whenever I am in Melbourne I catch up with my ex GMI'ers. Valdean, Peter and June Green, me and Sam Harrobin at the GMH retirees luncheon.

Right: L to R: Frank Pound, me Nola Wylie, Faye Harrobin, Bruce and Dawn Black and Don Wylie all gathered around Frank's beautifully restored 1916 Doge in his garage after a GMI get together lunch

Left: Jean Pound in her laughter days with Don Wylie and Lindsay Mallen. I was Groomsman at Lindsay's wedding to Cynthia

Right: L to R: Bruce and Dawn Black, me and Frank Pound

Left: Frank Pound and Doug Cleary inspecting our original 48/215 Holden 1950 model I sold the "Beast" Essex to Doug in 1957.

Right: Frank Pound at the observation deck at Floreat Beach near 1/1. We usually take our visitors here to see the view and Indian Ocean

Left: Frank with Perth's black swans, the WA state emblem.

Right: Frank and Jean Pound in their front garden at 33 Parnell Street, Cheltenham

Left: One of my mates at GMH and Rugby days – Wally Scott at his 60th birthday celebrations in March 1989. Frank Pound handing him a GMH slogan of the day number plate

Right: Wal always sends Valdean and I a special Christmas card in rhyme and Wal in a different Father Christmas rig each year

Left: A "funny" that I pinned on the Customer Services Division's notice board at the Water Corporation

Right: Lily and "Buddy" (about 12 months)

Above: Bill (Frog), Debbie, Lily and Jane

Right: John, Andrewatha, Ian Wallace at Saints WA Old Scholars Dinner

Left: Valdean, Aileen, Tony, Will, Tom, and Dedee in Tom's backyard.

Below: John and Margaret Kemp (UK), Valdean and Marc

Below: Simon Barbour's family

Photo: Lily practising her trumpet

Above: Toby and Dawn Metcalf

Right: Me with "EMU" at the Duncraig house I rented 1991/2

Left and Below: 'Mo'vember for me. It turned out ginger and I quickly shaved it off

Left: 1980 eating Boston Lobster in Boston

Right: Going crabbing with John Dean (Vald's B-I-L)

Below: Old cars fascinate me. This 1925 FLINT car is unusual

Above: I've always liked this photo of me. Taken for the 1954 GMI Year Book

Me leaning on my chest of drawers

Left: Going fishing. I never caught much except at Smith's Beach – the Ningaloo Reef

Right: Yet another one of guess who?

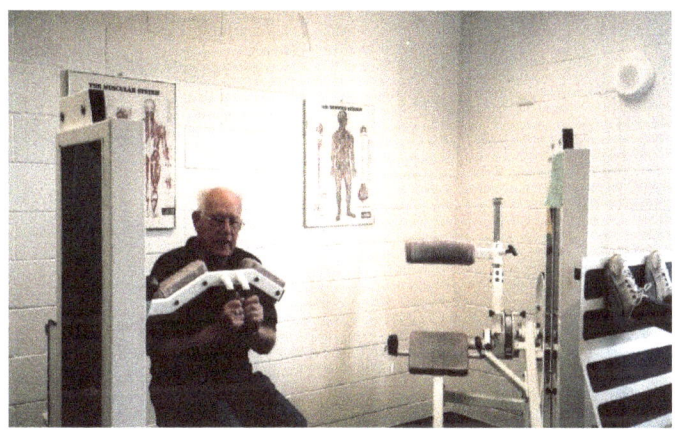

Above: I go to gym two days per week and aquarobics two days at the UWA Health and Rehabilitation Centre. It, with pills (9 per day) and Valdean's immense help, keeps me alive

Above: Me with the late Robert Juniper in his studio

Me fooling again

Above: I've always enjoyed merry-go-rounds

Me in front of SF Mark's Picton WA Church.
Built by Archdean John Ramdsen Wollaston

Above: Reflection at Walkaway pool – on our honeymoon

Taken from our dinner table at Cable Beach Broome

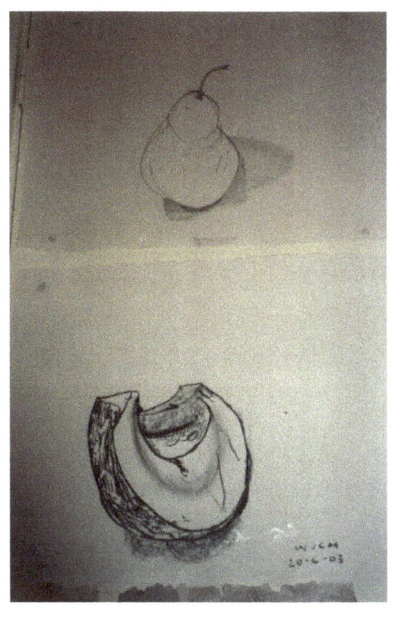

Left: I went to a drawing class at USA, this was my first attempt at a pear and slice of pumpkin

Above: A cheeky Quokka at Rottnest Island

Above: A collection of Colin Gardiner's paintings in his studio; 25 Merrion Terrace, Stirling

Above: Jim and Marc have their names on the benefactors engraved tablet at the entrance here.

Above: Our seat high in the stands Sept 2000 Olympics.
Valdean on stairs returning with snacks.

Left: A walk in the tall forest timbers of S-E WA.

The pinnacles about 300 kms N of Perth are worth visiting. Best effect is early morning or at dusk.
A haematrolites pool is nearby.

A croc in the aquarium at Litchfield NT

Randell dock at Mannum. Both the Randell and
Kinmont families are ancestors/relatives of Phil.

Left: I'm a big fan of Bradman. Fielded a ball he hit at Saints in 1948.

Above: Postcard: The Ghan was an adventure. Left late, arrived very late

L to R: Valdean, Tom, Yvonne Farrow, me, Aileen

Right: L to R Lee Davis, Colin Ross, me, Brian Davis, Jenni Ross

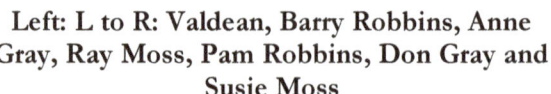

Left: L to R: Valdean, Barry Robbins, Anne Gray, Ray Moss, Pam Robbins, Don Gray and Susie Moss

Right: Mum and Helen at entrance of Holy Trinity Church, North Terrace, Adelaide. Where I was baptised and confirmed.

Above: L to R: Frank Dunn, Helen Dunn, Judy Hartigan, John Hinton and Lorna Hinton and Helen Sandercock

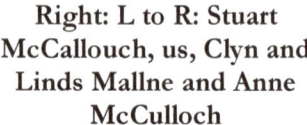

Right: L to R: Stuart McCallouch, us, Clyn and Linds Mallne and Anne McCulloch

Above: Col Gardiner shows me his art

Right: Stuart McCulloch and I set out for the Melbourne Cup

Above: Valdean and Iris Vodanovich

Right: Helen and Frank Dunn; Lyn Driscoll in the middle

Above: Sunset at Kalbarri with Eric and Margaret Fleay

Left: L to R: Don Gray, Clem and Charlie Hammond, Pam and Barry Robbins and Ray Moss

Below: Me, Allen Gaze, Mary and John Scales

Below: L to R: Me, Ivan Vodanovich, Valdean, Iris and Carol Wood (now Reid)

Right: L to R: Yvonne Farrow (UK), Helen Murrell, Betina (UK) and Frieda (UK)

Above: Valdean, Me, Rev David Bradbury. David claims I influenced him to take up the Ministry

Above: Valdean, Jenni and Colin Ross. The Ross' are my gym pals.

Above: Valdean John Dean (V's BIL), Margo Dean and me

Us again

Above: Our great American friends Hans and Rachel Greunberg with Valdean viewing Freshwater Bay

Left: L to R: Colin Gardiner, me, Valdean, Mary and John Scales

Below: Our dinner group and wives L to R: Don Gray, Susie Moss, Anne Gray, Ray Moss

Below: Dressed up on the Arcadia 1998

Right: Harry and Phyl Billinghurst

Left: St Nic's flower festival

Right: Tullie, Hannah and Valdean

Left: Jim's sheep and vineyard in autumn

Right: We used our pool a lot. 38°C this day

Left: In North Carolina USA

Below: Will, George and Tom Murrell

Above: Gov Lord Calvert formed the new settlement of Maryland in early 1600's in USA

Right: Tony and Marget Reiger at Saints over 70's lunch. I used to play trains with Tony in the 1940s

Above: Mr and Mrs Ian Wall and Malcolm Bear at Saints.

Right: We attended the "Sculpture by the Sea" at Cottesloe Beach each year.

Above: Panda posing at the Adelaide Zoo

Right: Valdean sampling John S Trellen Wines

Left: All set to go at Christmas at Will's place

Below: St Christopher's Men's Fellowship

Below: Bruce Chappel, Milton Rundle and Andre Scotford

Right: Windy and Richard Cornfield

Left: SIVA luncheon under our patio

Below: **Bernadette (V's previous boss at Bethesda Hospital) and Ron Lloyd**

Below: **50th celebrations of IIE in Melbourne**

Right: **Valdean with Ian and Chris Webber at Saints**

Right: Dann Van Banton and Valdean in Melbourne. Danny worked for me at CAL

Left: Me, Garth and Helen Polkinghorne and Son Sarah at Saints over 70's (I took Helen, new Angowin to the Blue White Ball in May 1948).

Right: Valdean and Jill Phillips from Holy Trinity at Reabold Hill Lookout (Perth city in background)

Above: L to R: Jim, Valdean, Tullie and Helen (85 years)

Above: L to R: Helen, Angela Barbour, me, Deanne Marshall, and Ruth Barbour (80 years).

Above: I planted these liquidambars in 1955 in the main street of Stirling.

Above: Lucy, Hugo and Valdean in front of Perth's new Arena before seeing the Hopman Cup 2013.

Above: At a St Christopher's breakfast
L to R: Me, Elaine, and Brian Embleton, Isobel and Jim Jones, Margaret King at edge

Above: Valdean with "the cows" at Cowaramup, WA

Left: Joe and Gale Hagen with Valdean at our farewell dinner 2007 in Northfield USA

Right: Geoffrey with his new love Clementina at Valdean's 75th Birthday party

Left: Len and Shelia Eckerman at my 80th Birthday breakfast on the 8th of November 2010.

As I celebrate my 80th birthday, I would like to reflect on the achievements of my siblings. They are all high achievers and my parents were very proud to have produced an engineer, an artist and art dealer, a nurse and two doctors.

**Portrait of Helen Calvert Murrell
born 21/5/1928.**

She gained science and medical degrees at the University of Adelaide and became an obstetrician and gynaecologist, was a missionary with the Bible and Medical Missionary Fellowship (BMMF) and worked in the Department of Obstetrics and Gynaecology at the Christian Medical College Ludhiana from 1963 to 1971. She later lived and worked in England in General Practice and Public Health and was the long-term partner of Joan Milson.

Auntie Chris, with Helen and myself (L to R) pictured at Apollo Bay in 1944.

Belle Hughes nee Murrell (another sister of my father Jack) ran *The Falls Guest House* at Apollo Bay where we stayed and I learnt how to bodyboard and body surf. Helen is holding the board which says something about her love of the outdoors.

My oldest sister, Helen was a pioneer in her field. She was one of the first women to graduate from Medicine at the University of Adelaide and was very close to my own daughter. I will let Lucy tell Helen's inspiring story.

"This amazing queer woman identified herself as a gay lesbian woman to me and gave her life to Christ. Women's health has improved because of her. As an Anglican she worked for Interserve as a missionary in India in the 1960s and 70s based at Ludhiana for 10 years, often going into Iran. She became mentally unwell due to men not following her authority and was rescued by her lifelong friend and significant other, Fellow Interserve missionary and English as a Second Language teacher, Ms Joan Milson.

Helen and Joan loved their life in India. I have fond memories of dressing in silk saris as a child. Afterwards, Helen and Joan lived in Slough, UK where they hosted many of their Australian nieces and nephews. They were dedicated to their churches, the ordination of women movement and were progressive in their views about LBGIQ+ Christians marrying. They worked with and helped many migrant families from Iran and India.

Helen told me stories about eyebrows being raised when they arrived at hotels they had booked under Dr H. Murrell and Milson only for the hoteliers to find two women had made the booking for the room on arrival. They had their revolutionary fun! Helen had a twinkle in her eye as she told me this story as they travelled throughout the world and enjoyed their timeshare apartment at Lanzarote, the easternmost of the Spanish Canary Islands in the Atlantic Ocean.

Dr Helen worked for the UK public health system seeing too many pierced and mangled vaginas and uteruses. She worked for the UN in women's health too. Aunty Helen gave me strength, direction, and care throughout my life. She loved that Fi and I had Hugo via sperm donation. She was one of the first to see him and visited us here in Darwin when I became unwell when he was three years old. She was always interested in our lives and I feel deeply indebted, grateful and thankful for her. She encouraged my studies in Theology, my service to the Anglican church and in my identity as a queer woman and teacher. She had to remain in the closet for many years but loved the open movement. She told me of the care she had given to HIV patients – one man in particular, in the early times – and in her early retirement when it wasn't trendy to do so. She loved her family, her strong Christian faith and many others."

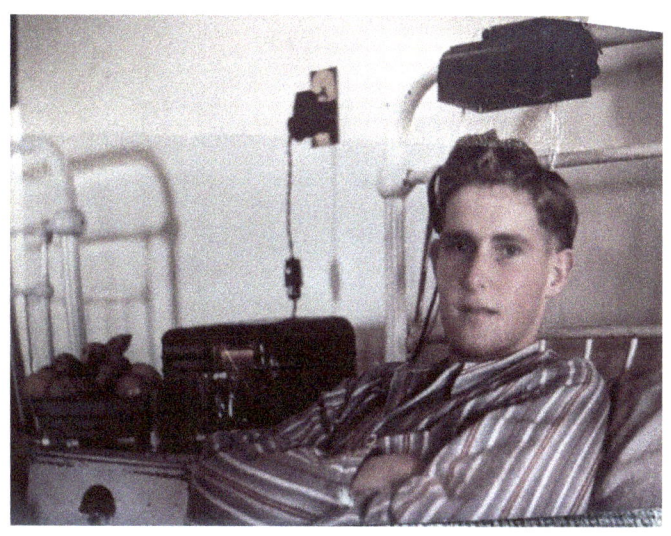

Tim Murrell in hospital recovering from polio in 1951.

Professor Tim Murrell at work in 1992.

He became the first professor in the new Department of Community Medicine at the University of Adelaide in 1975 and established teaching health centres in Adelaide. In June 2002 he was awarded a Member of the Order of Australia (AM) for service to medicine.

My younger brother Tim, who was a twin, had a very fascinating career in medicine also. He died way too young at 69 years of age. I miss him. My nephew and his son, Thomas wrote a moving obituary that was published in *The Australian*, *The Advertiser* in Adelaide and London *Times* newspapers after his death.

Obituary - Timothy George Calvert Murrell AM
Born: April 8, 1933, Adelaide
Died: August 15, 2002, Adelaide

Medical Educator Challenged Norms

A brush with the paralysing effects of polio as a first-year medical student and experiencing the indignity of the ward round during a long convalescence motivated one of Australia's leading medical educators to be a teacher in the community rather than in a hospital.

Tim Murrell was a product of the Adelaide establishment who continually challenged the norms and conservative attitudes within Australia's health profession.

He was captain of the Anglican collegiate school, St Peter's, in Adelaide, leading the First XV111 Football team and winning the medal for Best and Fairest player. Following a serious knee injury, he took up rowing, becoming Captain of Adelaide University's Rowing Club and winning a University Blue.

One of the highlights of his undergraduate years was to spend a voluntary elective with Dr Cliff Jungfer at Lobethal in the Adelaide Hills early in 1957.

Jungfer had a major impact on the young medical student who would later become the Foundation Professor of Community Medicine at the University of Adelaide.

This experience ignited a lifetime passion in studying the interaction of human beings with themselves; with living organisms; and within their shared environments.

Murrell's observations as District Medical Officer in the highlands of Papua New Guinea in the early 1960s led to the discovery of the disease 'pigbel'. Known as 'Belly on Fire' and associated with sporadic pig feasting, it killed thousands, especially children. It is now controlled by vaccination.

This gave him a real insight into how the GP is the gatekeeper of the Health-Care system and why doctors need to understand their role in the human ecosystem.

He completed a Diploma in Tropical Health and Medicine at Sydney University in 1963 and an Australian Nuffield Dominion Travelling Fellowship in Medicine in 1966 allowed him to study developments in general practice in Britain for two years at Guy's Hospital in London.

Returning to Australia in 1968, he pioneered Australia's first health care centre in the outer Adelaide suburb of St Agnes.

A World Health Organisation Fellow on two occasions in Iran and Nepal, his most outstanding career achievement was being awarded a Visiting Fellowship to Corpus Christi College, Cambridge in 1992.

Always a lateral thinker inspired by observations around him, Professor Murrell's research interests moved to the prevention of breast cancer, the sociology of sudden infant death syndrome and insights into the cause of multiple sclerosis.

He believed a good GP takes a holistic approach to health care – diagnosis, long term care, disease prevention, acting as an advocate for the patient and importantly a role as human ecologist.

He put this into practice with another innovation: The Family Practice Unit at suburban Highbury in Adelaide provided a mutually satisfying teaching environment where academics and students could mix professionally with 'hands on GPs' out of hospitals.

It was the forerunner of community general practice, a new era in medicine. The Highbury example set a standard for medical teaching that has been adopted by programs around the world.

At a time when more than 90 per cent of the health budget was directed to curative medicine and institutional care, Professor Murrell began challenging the conventional wisdom and was the catalyst for a new role of practitioners – preventative medicine.

As part of a reassessment of cherished values, he believed that somewhere between raising life expectancy and reducing mortality, medicine had forgotten to consider the quality of life in the debate about health.

His patients held him in high esteem and his 'Recipe for Living' hung on his wall in his surgery for years, with many patients asking for a copy.

He urged patients to find a reason to believe, to believe in themselves and to set limits. He advised them to tackle one thing at a time and include a daily lifestyle regime of relaxation, exercise, diet and meditation.

It was his own recipe for how he lived life -full of courage, compassion, enthusiasm, insight and intellect. He believed very strongly in the importance of self-identity, family, spiritual bonds, community involvement, sporting achievement, and finding a balance between recreation and work.

The theme of guiding and developing ran throughout his life and he went out of the way to help the physically disabled. For example, he established facilities for disabled bowlers and worked with a team of engineers to design a method to allow blind people to play lawn bowls.

In June of this year, he was awarded an AM for his service to medicine, especially developing innovative courses in general practice and medicine.

He retired to Sydney in 1998 to be closer to his grandchildren and is survived by his wife of 43 years Patricia, three sons, one daughter and eleven grandchildren.

Thomas Murrell, son, August 2002

My younger sister Ruth Calvert Barbour, nee Murrell (8/4/1933 - 17/2/2019) was the twin of Tim. She married on 19/5/1956 Robert Angus Barbour (29/7/1931 - 20/8/2017). Ruth trained as a nurse and midwife before marrying. Robert did medicine and worked in the Department of Anatomy and Histology at the University of Adelaide. She was a very caring and loving woman who raised a wonderful family of four children. Her eldest son, Simon, was my godchild. Her legacy lives on at St Peter's College Chapel where she was responsible for the decorative needlework and embroidery of the kneelers in the school chapel.

Ruth and Tim pictured far left in a photograph promoting the benefits of milk at Thebarton Primary School in 1938.

My youngest brother, Andrew Douglas Ambrose Murrell, was born 22/7/1945 and was the most creative and colourful member of our family. He was a favourite and you can read his extensive biography in the Appendix section of this book about my art collection, written by my nephew. Andrew went to St Peter's College and left after completing the leaving certificate. He starred in school theatre productions taking a more creative approach to life rather than the sporting careers of his other siblings. He went to Melbourne in 1961 and worked for Channel 9. He did a variety of other jobs including working for Trans Australia Airlines and Ansett and dealing in antiques and art. He was very interested in acting and the arts, writing a musical about Monarto and is an avid stamp collector. He and his long-term partner, Les Bailey, live near Mannum in South Australia.

My youngest brother Andrew was always the centre of attention in our family. Pictured from L to R with Ruth, Mum, Tim, Andrew, Helen and myself in 1948.

I've done my dash and been through fifteen years of photo albums and have writer's cramp, so I'll only add a few more words and photos.

Right: A final photo of the Murrell Family at Port Road, Thebarton. Taken the day I left for USA and GMIT. L to R (Back): Dad (51), Mum (49), me (21), Helen (23); L to R (Front): Ruth (19); Andrew (7); and Tim (19) – 3rd September 1952

I'll finish off this chapter with some of my favourite quotes. Firstly, words of wisdom from a motivational talk by Walter Dickman in 1970. "Life is a gift on a daily basis: you have to grab it and enjoy it".

Finally, I want to finish with the words of French writer Voltaire. "God gave us the gift of life; it is up to us to give ourselves the gift of living well." This quote summarises the values instilled in me and my siblings by my parents.

Chapter 12

Introducing Me

I feel like I haven't been able to talk about my interests much in the previous chapters.

I'll start off by sharing with you my most favoured hobby, photography. I used to borrow Helen's Baby Brownie to my mum's 120 Bellows Type just so I'd be able to practice taking photos. I made a black mask for the Baby Brownie so I could take sixteen naps in lieu of eight on a 120-roll.

I bought a 3.5 F 120 *Voigtlander* to take with me to America. I also joined a photography club where I learnt to process several rolls of *excitacbrne trans parencises*, which was very difficult to achieve as it used thirteen different solutions.

When I came back to Australia from the US, I bought a *Voightlander* 35 mm which lasted until the digital age took over. Now, I have a compact Canon 70 IXUS with a 2 – 8G chip that stores thousands of photos.

I should mention some health problems which persist. Since a teenager, I've suffered scales of my eyelids (Bufritis). I wash the scale off under the shower. About ten years ago the stitching of my rolled-up stomach came adrift so now I have a protruding tum. Perhaps you have seen this in some recent photos. Also, I have very narrow ear canals, which easily get blocked with wax and causes itching. I have Dr Geof Emergy syringe them out about every six months.

In 2005, I experienced severe chest pains and was rushed to St John of God Emergency Chest clinic, where I had an angiogram, then an angioplast, and had two stents inserted in a. LAD and b. Diagonal arteries. Since then I've been in hospital three times with chest pains but NO heart attack symptoms. I have to have a Nitro Liquid spray always in my pocket. One or two puffs usually relieves the chest ache. If after nine minutes and three puffs the pain hasn't gone, I must ring 000.

> "To laugh often and much;
> to win the respect of intelligent
> people and affection of children;
> to earn the appreciation of honest
> critics and endure the betrayal of
> false friends; to appreciate beauty,
> to find the best in others, to leave
> the world a bit better, whether by
> a healthy child, a garden patch,
> or a redeemed social condition;
> to know even one life has breathed
> easier because you have lived,
> this is to have succeeded."
>
> Ralph Waldo Emerson (1803-1882)

> "missa-bulla" Fijian for 'hello
> and also means..., 'I respect the
> life-breath in you...'
>
> So, missa-bulla Dad,
>   thankyou for succeeding
> ... with love from your healthy
>   daughter, Lucinda xx

> "Count what is countable,
> Measure what is measurable,
> And what is not measurable,
> Make Measurable."
>
> Galileo Galilei.
>
> W.J.Hurrell,
> Manager - Industrial Engineering.

Lucy's card and letter quote by Emerson sent to me from Fiji for my 62nd birthday is worth reading.

And remember: "To yourself be true".

In 1985, at a seminar, we had to write at least ten words to describe one's self. I wrote 13. Valdean has just reviewed them (21/1/14) and ticked each one and added the last two to which I agree. So here is what I think is my make up:

1. Caring
2. Loving
3. Sincere
4. Kind
5. Good looking (was)
6. Smiling
7. Hardworking
8. Intellectual
9. Likes a joke
10. Serious
11. Christian
12. Engineer (industrial)
13. Interesting
14. Persistent
15. Imaginative

So reading this narrative and seeing the photographs, my dear grandchildren, you can tick off which attribute you think embraces me.

Grandpa Bill

Chapter 13

Convicts, Norfolk Island Family Trees

Before I start on the Calvert's convict side, I should bring the article below to your attention. Mum said she was related to Rev John Fawcett of Headon Bridge, UK.

The connection is through the Wrights. Mum's mother was Winifred Wright. The Wrights had a foundry at Circular Quay, Sydney and they produced a lot of the cast iron fretwork that is still seen in Paddington, Sydney, today.

Eleven generations after Rev John Fawcett we have John Skirrow Wright, Mayor of Birmingham. See the photo of my mum in front of his plaque in the Birmingham Town Hall on page 269, top right.

Then several generations on to Winifred Wright who married my grandfather William Henry Fairfax Calvert, who then had three children, Douglas, Mollie and Beatrice (my mother) – also known as "Trixie". Dedee Murrell has traced the Morresbys of Cumberland back to the Earl of Gospatric (1040-82). A direct line is traced back to Morrisby in Cawood, Yorkshire 23/1/1756, James Morrisby's birthday, and his descendants are shown on the chart on page 170.

Valdean and I, plus sister Ruth and her husband Dr Bob Barbour, and my cousin Dianne Marshall (nee Calvert) went to Norfolk Island 7th – 14th May 2003, and have researched and commented on convict James Morrisby, Ann Brooks (his convict wife), Calvert slaver, Murrell a sealer and Norfolk Island in Appendix 2.

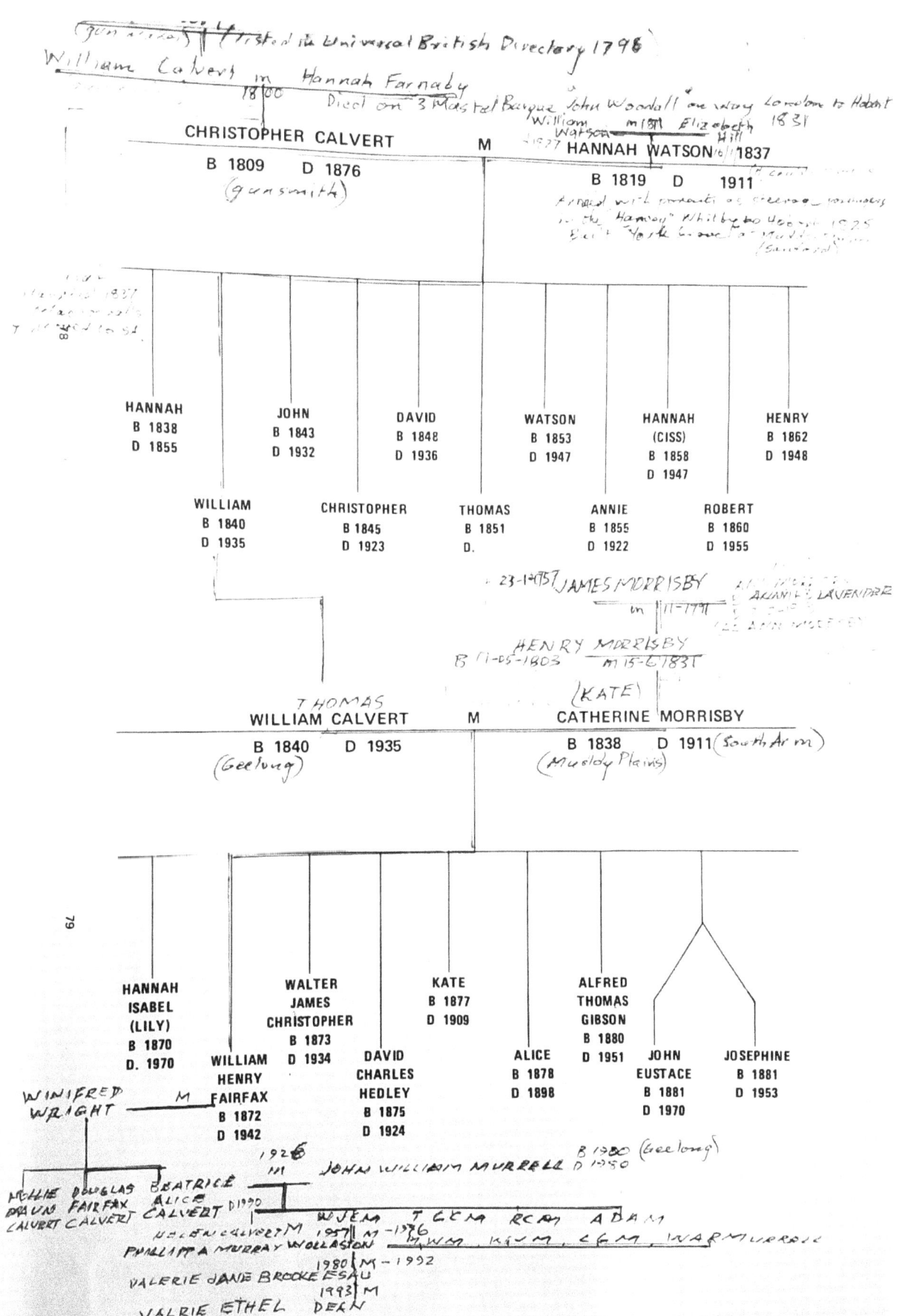

We celebrated the birth of Henry Morrisby, born 11 May 1803 – 200 years to the day, later with a "Happy 200th Birthday" cake. Henry was baptised on 26 June 1803 by Bishop Henry Fulton on Norfolk Island.

From this chart you can trace Henry born 4/5/1803 Norfolk Island; died 25/3/1853 in Tasmania.

They were shipped to Van Diemen's Land in 1806 when the Norfolk Island colony was closed down.

James was given 80 acres of uncleared land at South Arm, which many Calverts live on today. Anyway, Henry married Elizabeth Mary Mack 20/10/1824; they had two children.

Elizabeth died and Henry married Christiana Smith on 15/6/31; they had thirteen children of which the fifth was Katherine Morrisby born 1/8/1838.

Kate married William Thomas Calvert of Geelong, B 1840; D 1935; Kate had nine children, one being my grandfather, William Henry Fairfax Calvert, B 1872; D 1942.

Below is a photo of the patch that James Morrisby had to walk from his plot and home (near the end of Godary's, Norfolk Island, runaway) down the hill behind Helen Reddy's home to the goal muster area near the wharf, each Friday and Sunday mornings.

The lineage of the Calverts from 1798 is charted here as is the lineage of the Murrells from 1805.

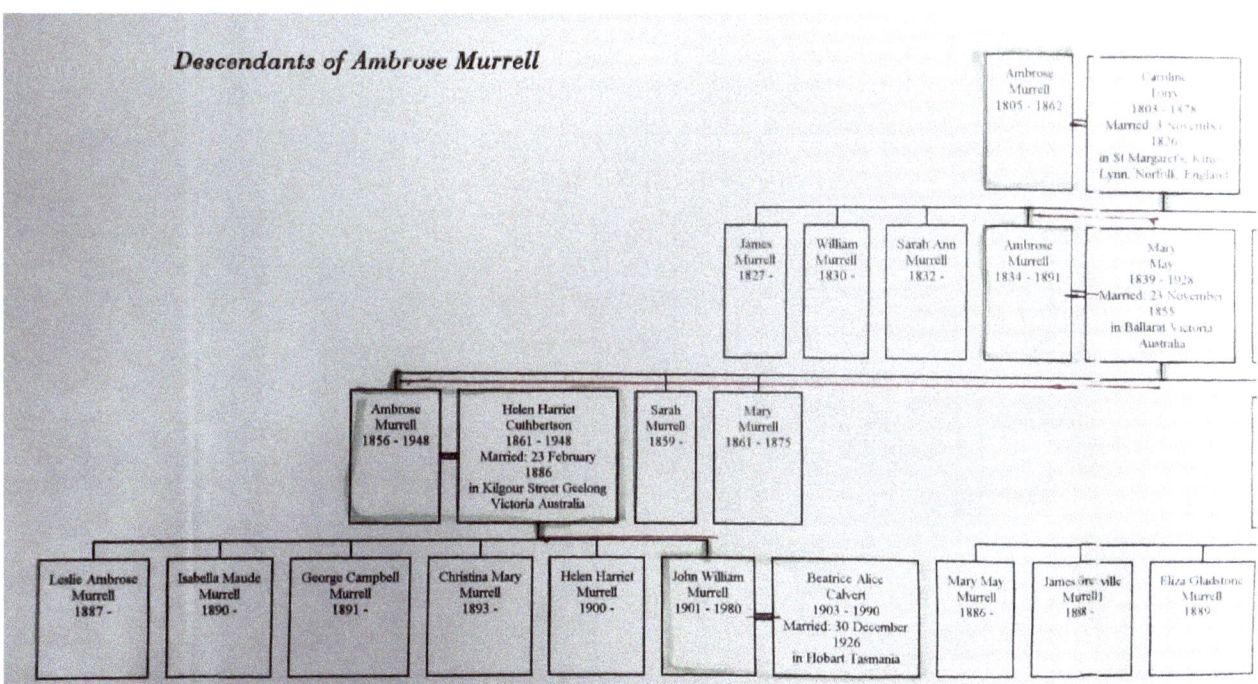

BEATRICE ALICE (TRIXIE) NEE CALVERT BORN 2.3.1901 HUONVILLE, TASMANIA
DIED 4.6.1990 ADELAIDE STH, AUST
MARRIED IN 1926 AT ST. JOHN'S ANGLICAN CHURCH, NEWTOWN, HOBART TO
JOHN WILLIAM (JACK) MURRELL BORN 23.6.1901 GEELONG VICTORIA
DIED 3.6.1980 ADELAIDE STH. AUSTRALIA

AFTER THEIR MARRIAGE TRIXIE AND JACK CAME TO ADELAIDE, WHERE JACK WORKED AS AN ENGINEER WITH THE E. & W.S. DEPARTMENT. THEY HAD A FAMILY OF 5 CHILDREN : HELEN, BILL, TIMOTHY & RUTH (TWINS) AND ANDREW.

THEY WERE INVITED TO WORSHIP AT HOLY TRINITY CHURCH, WHERE THEY WERE CONFIRMED AND JACK WAS A TRUSTEE, FROM 1947 - 1978. AS A THANKSGIVING FOR THE LIFE AND WORK OF TRIXIE AND JACK, PEW CUSHIONS WERE PLACED THROUGHOUT HOLY TRINITY AND AT VICTOR HARBOR A NEW MOTHERS' UNION BANNER WAS MADE IN MEMORY OF TRIXIE'S LIFE AND DEDICATION TO CHRISTIAN WORK. TRIXIE WAS A FOUNDING MEMBER OF MOTHERS' UNION AT HOLY TRINITY IN 1950. DURING HER MEMBERSHIP SHE SERVED AS TREASURER AND VICE-PRESIDENT.

TRIXIE JOINED THE DIOCESAN MOTHERS' UNION EXECUTIVE WHEN SHE WAS APPOINTED CONVENOR FOR HOSPITAL VISITING AT THE ROYAL ADELAIDE HOSPITAL BETWEEN 1960 - 1969. SHE WAS ALSO A VISITOR TO PATIENTS AT GLENSIDE HOSPITAL.

IN 1980 TRIXIE & JACK RETIRED TO VICTOR HARBOR, AND JACK DIED SHORTLY AFTER. TRIXIE BECAME AN ACTIVE MEMBER OF MU AT ST. AUGUSTINE'S THERE FOR 10 YEARS UNTIL HER PASSING.

AN OBITUARY TO TRIXIE APPEARED IN THE MOTHERS' UNION MAGAZINE, 'THE LINK' , VOL. 27 NO.3 JULY/AUG. 1990

"IN MEMORIUM – ON MONDAY JUNE 4TH, MRS. BEATRICE A. MURRELL DIED, AGED 87 YEARS. FROM 1960 - 1969 MRS. MURRELL WAS THE MOTHERS' UNION DIOCESAN CONVENOR OF HOSPITAL VISITING AT THE ROYAL ADELAIDE HOSPITAL. DURING THIS TIME SHE GAVE FREELY OF HER TIME AND TALENTS AND IT WAS SAID OF HER "...SHE IS AN INSPIRATION AND GUIDING LIGHT TO US ALL". PERHAPS IF YOU WERE A PATIENT DURING THAT TIME YOU MAY EVEN HAVE RECEIVED ONE OF THE MANY GIFTS WHICH SHE FREQUENTLY ORGANISED TO BE DISTRIBUTED TO PATIENTS AND NURSING STAFF. WE EXTEND OUR LOVING SYMPATHY TO HER FAMILY AND UPHOLD THEM IN OUR PRAYERS."

DONOR: MRS. RUTH BARBOUR
DAUGHTER

A citation by my sister Ruth, re Mum's involvement in Mother's Union.

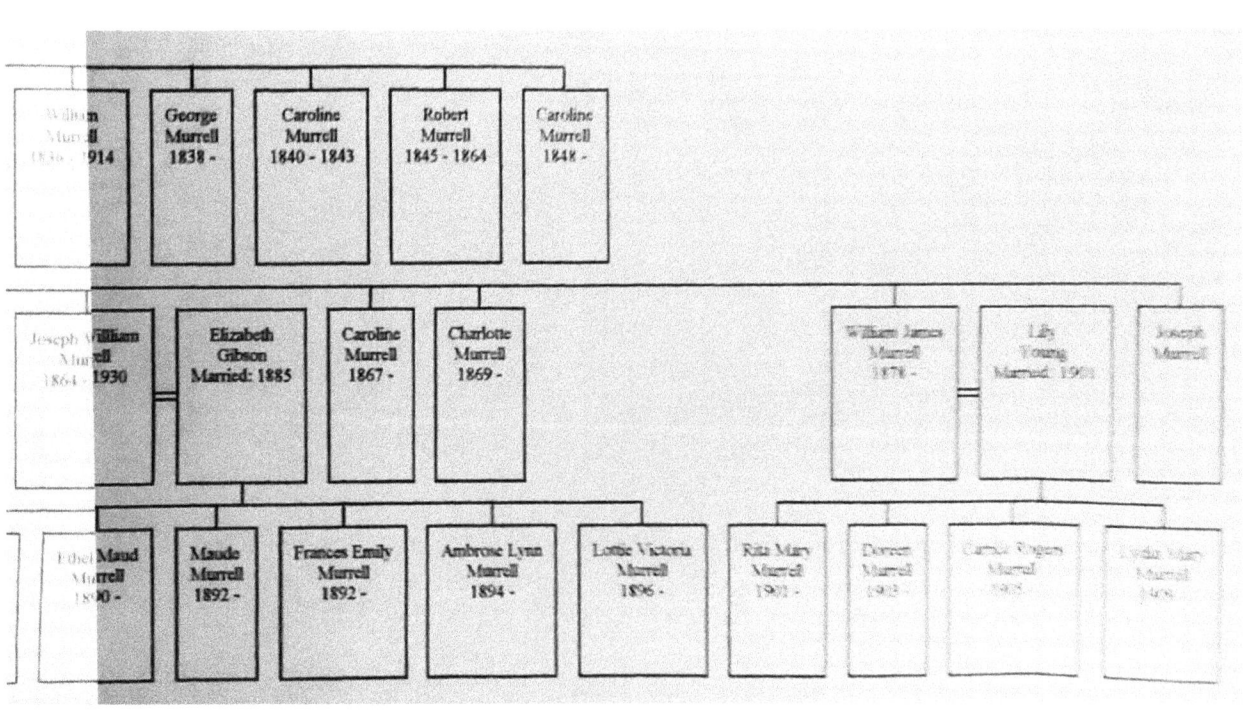

CERTIFICATE OF MARRIAGE.

DISTRICT, Hobart   Register No. 375

on (¹) Dec. 30, 1926 at St. John's Church New Town

Marriage by (²) Licence was celebrated between us according to the (³) rites & ceremonies of the Church of England

BRIDEGROOM
- Name (in full): John William Murrell
- Residence, Present: Adelaide, S. Australia   Usual: Adelaide, S.A.
- Age (last Birthday): 25
- Profession or Occupation: Civil Engineer
- Condition (Bachelor or Widower): Bachelor
- If Widower: Former Wife deceased in year 1 _____; Children living, _____; dead _____
- Birth-place: Geelong, Victoria
- Father's Name (in full): Ambrose Murrell
- Occupation: Retired
- Mother's Name (in full): Helen Harriet Murrell (nee Cuthbertson)

BRIDE
- Name in full: Beatrice Alice Calvert
- Residence, Present: New Town   Usual: New Town
- Age (last Birthday): 23
- Profession or Occupation: Household duties
- Condition (Spinster or Widow): Spinster
- If Widow: Former Husband deceased in year 1 _____; Children living, _____; dead, _____
- Birth-place: Ranelagh
- Father's Name (in full): William Henry Calvert
- Occupation: Orchardist
- Mother's Name (in full): Winifred Calvert (nee Wright)

This Marriage was celebrated between us
John W. Murrell
Beatrice A. Calvert

In presence of us Witnesses—
E. S. Cuthbertson   Address Heathfield St. Elsternwick
M. Calvert   Address Swan St. New Town

The above Marriage was duly celebrated by me at the time and place above named, and in the presence of the Witnesses whose Signatures are above written.

Witness my hand this thirtieth day of December 1926

(Signature) F. N. Whyting Esq.
(Designation) Vicar General Diocese of

I CERTIFY THIS TO BE A COPY OF AN ENTRY IN A REGISTER OR RECORD KEPT BY ME, GIVEN IN PURSUANCE OF THE ACTS OF PARLIAMENT OF THE STATE OF TASMANIA THIS 21ST DAY OF NOVEMBER 1973.

DEPUTY REGISTRAR GENERAL

DAUGHTER

A copy of Mum and Dad's marriage Certificate

The Murrell's lineage has been traced back to Ambrose Murrell 1804 in NKK 002. Sheets 1 and 2 also details the Murrell's Family History Society by Donavan Murrell. Another history is depicted below from Jeffrey Murrell 1525 viz SKF 026 sheet 2 and NFK 002, Sheet 1 and 2.

Murrells Family History Society

Telephone 081-310-6773

428 Bedonwell Road
Abbey Wood, London
SE2 0SE

NFK 002.

19th October 1994

Dr Helen Calvert Murrell,
8 Lawkland,
Farnham Royal SL2 3AN

Dear Helen,

A Mrs Betty Stewart of Caulfield South, Victoria, whose Great Grandmother was Charlotte Catherine Murrell, who emigrated to Australia from Kent in 1862 has transcribed much of the early Victoria State Indicies for me in the name of Murrell(s) and she has kindly sent the results to me.

I am consequently able to make several changes to your family group. The most interesting being that the surname of Ambrose's 1834 wife was May not Rogers as we had thought. Her parents were James May and Mary (Rogers). Their sons Joseph William 1864 and William James 1878 both had families which are now shown in NFK002/2. It is a delight to see that Joseph William named his younger son Ambrose Lynn Murrell in 1894. Hopefully he and his elder brother, James Greville both married and had a family but I have no other details at the moment.

During an all too short holiday in Norfolk this year I spent an hour or so in Kings Lynn and aquired a descriptive map of the town plus a post card and pamphlet on St Margarets Church, thought you might like to have a copy.

Hopefully an eleventh issue of Murrell(s) Miscellany will be published in time for Christmas.

Kindest regards.
Yours sincerely
Don Murrells.

Enclosures. NFK002/1 Rev 5
NFK002/2
Kings Lynn map
Post card & description
St Margarets' church.

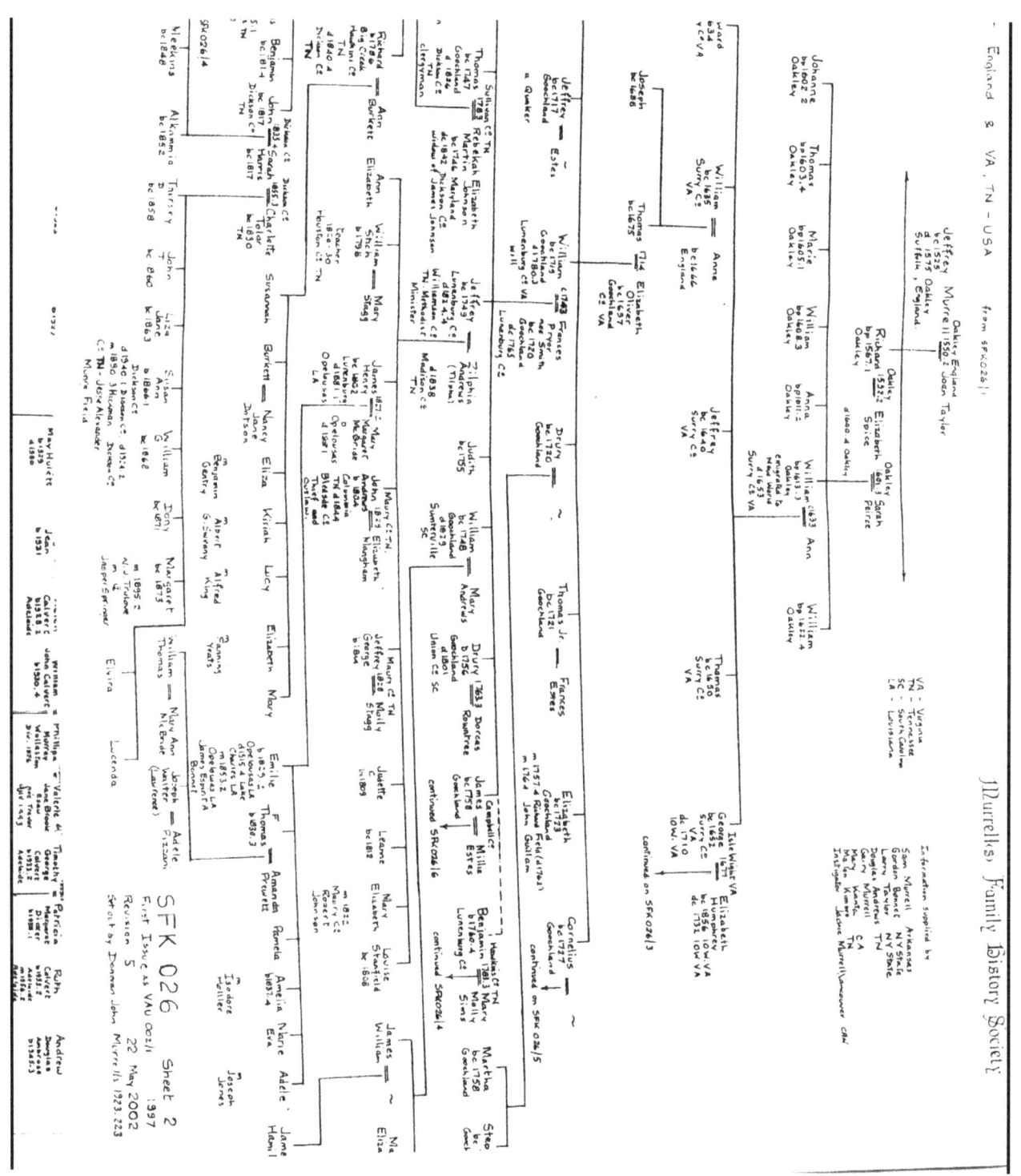

Below is a Murrell's Miscellany No 27 and has Tim's (my brother) obituary and information on Joseph Murrell and Robert Murrell.

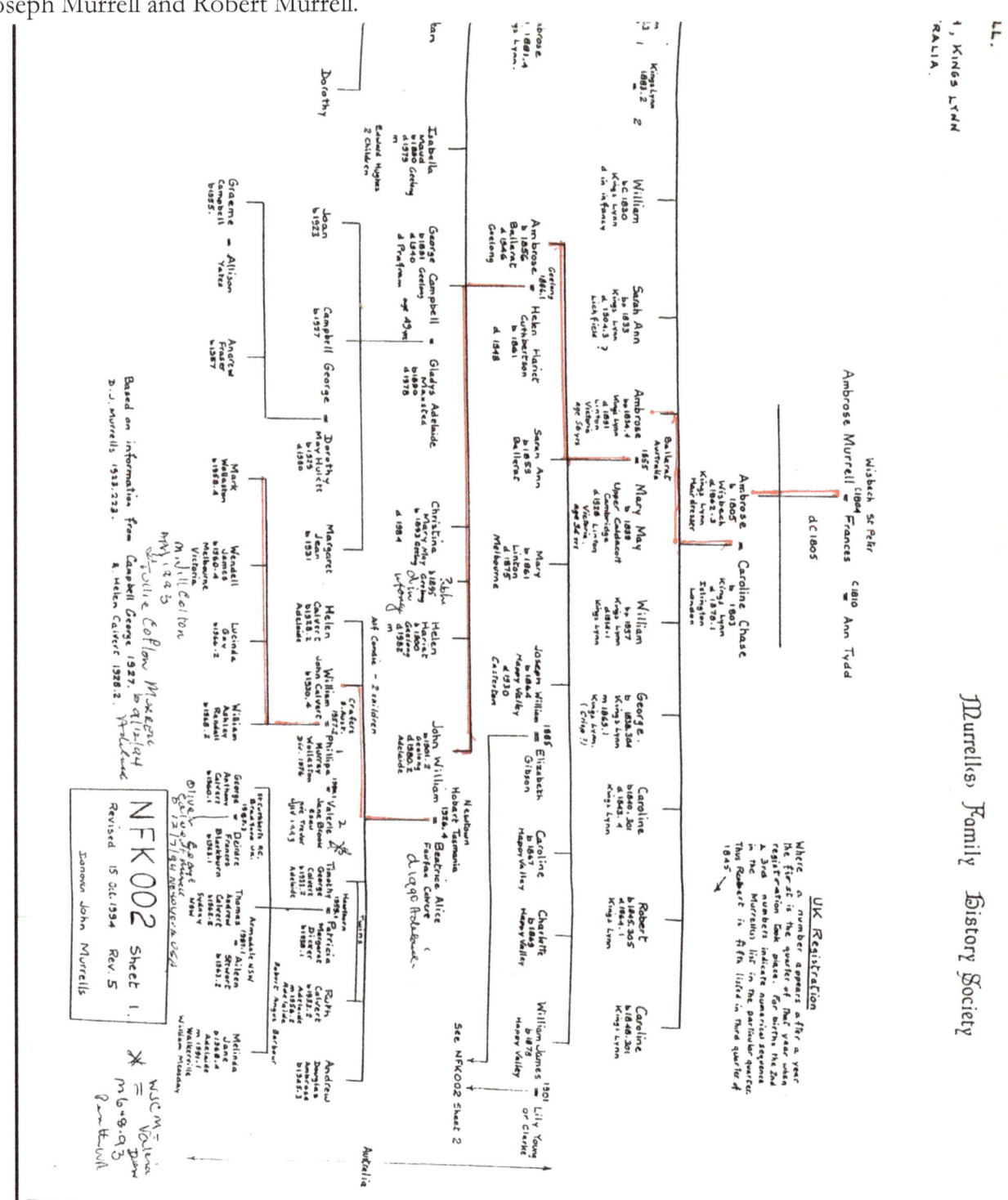

George Cutherberson (19 years) sailed from Liverpool on the *Chance* on 28 July 1852. He arrived in Melbourne 26 October 1852 and was released from ship 11/11/52.

Christina Andrews (18 years) departed Liverpool on 28 July 1853 on the *Bankers Daughter*. She was from Fife, Scotland. With her were two sisters, Elizabeth (16) and Mary (14).

Murrell and Cuthertson

John William Murrell's parents were Ambrose Murrell and Helen Harriet Cuthbertson.

Murrell

There were possibly 'Murrells' in Norman times in Norfolk. Alternate spellings: Morrell, Morrel, Morel, Morrall, and Murrill from centuries ago when the name was just written as it sounded.

Ambrose Murrell married in Kings Lynn, England on 3/11/1826 Caroline Torry (Chase). They had nine children born in Kings Lynn.

Right: Ambrose and Helen Cuthbertson circa 1870s

The 4th child, Ambrose (1834- 3/12/1891) migrated to Australia. He married in Ballarat on 22/11/1855 Mary May (1834 (1839 - 1928), born in Bedfordshire, UK (parents James May and Mary Rogers). They had seven children: Ambrose, Sarah Ann, Mary, Joseph William, Caroline, Charlotte, William James.

Left: Ambrose and Helen Cuthbertson circa 1870s

Right: Ambrose and Helen Cuthbertson circa 1860s

Left: Ambrose and Helen Cuthbertson circa 1887

The eldest, Ambrose Murrell (5/10/1856 – 26/9/1946), born in Ballarat, married in Geelong on 23/2/1886 Helen Harriet Cuthbertson (8/3/1861 – 14/1/1948) from Geelong. He was a blacksmith. Ambrose and Helen lived at 'Teigngrace', 256 Pakington St, Geelong West in Victoria which has since been demolished. Children:

- Ambrose Leslie (11/2/1887 – 23/3/1928) married in 1922 Jean Montgomery Brown (1901 - 1971). Children: Beatrice, Robert, Dorothy.

- Isabella (Belle) Maude (1890 - 1979) married in 1913 Edward Hughes. Isabella and Edward Hughes ran a guest house at Apollo Bay where Trixie and Jack's family used to stay (e.g. in 1938). They later moved to Ivanhoe. Two children: George Campbell (Flying Officer in the RAAF, died in an air training accident in 1941 in Queensland), Jean (married name Smith). (*Andrew Murrell said Belle loved flowers and grew dahlias*).

- George Campbell (14/7/1891 – 15/12/1940) married in 1923 Gladys Adelaide Maxstead (27/9/1890 – 19/6/1978). Children: Joan, Campbell George, Margaret (Margaret's married name was Guy). Campbell George married Dorothy in 1951. They had Graeme (a doctor) and Andrew who live in Victoria

- Christina Mary May (3/12/1893 - 4/12/1984). Unmarried. Chris continued to live at 256 Pakington St, Geelong.

- Helen (Nell) Harriet (1/4/1900 - 1982) on 15/9/1926 married Alfred William Condie. Nell and Alf lived in Pakington St along the road from Chris. Children: Margaret and Max. Max lived in Geelong, wife Gwen. They had 2 sons. Max worked at Dalgetys. Nell married again to George, they moved to Fitzroy.

Helen's Childhood Memories of the Twins- Timothy and Ruth

In my Christmas Letter of December 2002, following Tim's sudden death on August 15th 2002, I wrote: " I have so many memories of our childhood, of out smooth haired Irish terrier, Paddy, standing guard beside the twins' large swinging canvas cot on the front verandah at 'Port Road', of the specially made long basket to hold the babies- Tim& Ruth, on the floor in the back of the maroon Fiat car, later the navy Morris, on long country and interstate trips; of family trips in the caravan to spend Christmas in Geelong, and summer holidays on a 'block' between Townsend House and the sand dunes at Brighton S.A. during school days. And so on..." Unfortunately I cannot find the photos I had of some of these occasions, although I have found a few others even from my little Baby Brownie camera my pride and joy from about 8 years old.

I was almost 5years old when the twins were born at the Memorial Hospital, North Adelaide. Soon after Mother went up to the Mount Barker Rest/nursing Home with them to convalesce and establish a good breast feeding pattern. Later, they must have changed to bottle feeding with a Vi-Lactogen mixture, as I vividly remember the red labelled tins which, when emptied were subsequently painted cream and blue to provide storage tins for flour, dried fruit, rice, tapioca, semolina etc. Whilst the twins were small, I was taken to visit Mother's relatives in Tasmania by her sister, Aunt Mollie. We had a good time, but that is another story. How ever I do remember visiting great grandfather William Thomas Calvert and Auntie Emm, his second wife at 'Clifton' South Arm or was it on Bruny Island?. WTC's first wife was Catherine Morrisby, daughter of Henry Morrisby, whose birth on 11th May 1803 on Norfolk Island some of the Calvert/Marshall/Murrell/Barbour families are about to celebrate by a visit to Norfolk Island next month-May,2003.

There is a lovely portrait photograph of Mother with the twins sitting on a table in front of her, Ruth looking up into her face, but Tim looking firmly ahead. I guess Ruth or Tim had the original. There were two other 'Rembrandt' photographs of the four of us one about 1936, coloured and sepia (b&w copy enclosed) and one later in our school uniforms about 1943, of which I do not have a print.

I remember 'the twins' often being dressed in similar colour combinations. I particularly liked them in their similar yellow jumpers with a fruit-like motif and brown short pants for Tim, and skirt for Ruth.

We had many animals at 'Port Road': hens, roosters, chickens, pet possums, pet lambs, Jersey cows-Buttercup and Strawberry, a horse *Prince* or two as well as cats and dogs. I have mentioned Paddy, very patient with us all and most long-lived; Pete a black& white Pomeranian/Pekinese cross, who followed Paddy everywhere; Terry the wire-haired terrier and an Airdale all had shorter lives, a consequence of living beside a very busy main road from Port Adelaide to the city. The Police Training College was opposite, quite useful for providing boyfriends for the different maids we had; I can remember three, Dorothy, Nancy and Dorrie. There were several trained nurses to care for |Mother at different times; Sister Burns when Bill was born at home, Grace Roberts, who married John Cornelius, a mining engineer, with whom the family kept in touch through their children Elizabeth and Robert.

Descriptions of Photos   *Prince*

The photo of Helen, Tim and Ruth on the horse at Port Rd. must be about 1935; the one of Helen, Bill, Ruth, Tim, Gertie Green and her daughter Cynthia, was taken at Victor Harbor in May 1936. Mother used to stay with her friend Gertie in the Midlands of Tasmania when both were boarders at Collegiate School, Hobart.

There are a couple of photos taken at 'The Falls', Apollo Bay where we stayed at Aunt Belle's Guest House (Isabella & Edward Hughes); the smaller one is about 1938 and the larger one with Marie Smith is dated 1940. The paddlers at Portland include Aunt Chris, on an overnight stop in the caravan on the earlier visit.

The small square photo on the sand dune at Brighton includes Margaret and Christine Shepley. Margaret married John Carey who appears in the photo taken in front of the grape vine alongside the tennis court at 'Port Road'. The other two taken at 'Port Road' in 1945 after Andrew's birth and christening with Aunt Belle in the first and Aunt Mollie in the later one. Finally there's one of us all on the steps in the front garden of Hathaway, Mt. Lofty, Bill was probably in the USA then.

There is much more I could tell, but you all have your own memories too. Sometimes I wonder how my parents, Jack and Trixie put up with us all, the scrapes, pranks we got up to, not to mention Mother nursing us each at various times through serious illnesses and accidents. We had our arguments and fights:- boys versus the girls or twins versus the oldies, or Helen & Tim versus Bill & Ruth, but I expect we all learnt the early lessons of life from each other, living together and sharing in a loving family, which has stood us all in good stead through our lives.

Helen Murrell   at 8 Lawkland, Farnham Royal . Buck SL2 3AN
9/04/03

I would like to add some thoughts about a) my parents and b) my grandparents.

Mum and Dad tried to be good parents to us five children.

Andrew was spoilt. Dad opposed Helen being a doctor as "girls got married".

Mum opposed Helen's engagement to Peter W. Helen then never married. Dad nearly always came to watch Tim or me play footy or row. He was a firm but good disciplinarian and loved us all. Mum was often unfair and lost her temper. Once she hit Tim across the side of his face several times with a piece of wood in a wild rage. Tim took off on his bike to Port Adelaide. He went missing for several hours. Mum coped surprisingly well for the ten years alone after Dad died. She loved us too. Looking back, I have much more kind feelings and admiration for Dad than for my mother. See over the page Dad, E&WS colleagues.

Grandparents: Granddad, as I knew William H F Calvert, was a big, stern man who found it hard to relate to us kids. I don't remember him telling me any stories or jokes. He did give me an R Hobbs large, heavy cricket bat that he had used. I was too small to use it, did not oil it and eventually it cracked.

Mum was only young when her mother Winifred Calvert died. Granddad married Gwen, the Mayor of Hobart's daughter. I found Auntie Gwen okay, but Mum could not abide her.

On the Murrell's side, Grandma, Helen Murrell (nee Cutherberson) was a stout, about 5ft tall, very kind, able cook and always had a good word to say. She had three boys (Les, George and Dad) and three girls (Isabelle Hughes, Nell Candie and Christiana – never married).

There was always lemonade in the pantry when we all arrived at Geelong for Christmas.

My Grandpa Ambrose was a short wiry man, who often smoked a cigar with a crabs claw holder. He always wore a waistcoat with a gold chain, a gold watch on one end and a gold sovereign case full of sovereigns on the other. He gave me one and I wished I had kept it. I would sit on his knee and he would tell me stories. He was born on the Ballarat goldfield on 5/10/1856 and died 26/9/1946 – 90 years later. He was a blacksmith, first on the Ballarat Goldfields, then moved to Geelong. He was an ardent Freemason and so got Dad involved too. One of the goldfields stories I remember was: One day a bushranger held him up, and at the point of his gun demanded Grandpa to remove his horse's shoes and put them on backwards. The bushranger thought the troopers would follow his tracks in the opposite direction. That obviously failed as the bushranger was caught and Grandpa received an invitation to his hanging, but he didn't go! Grandpa was a great smallish man, whom I loved.

This you might find interesting: you Murrell's are descended from a Celtic Tribe in old England.

EXTRACT FROM BIRTH ENTRY

SOUTH AUSTRALIA № 320555

Name: William John Calvert MURRELL Sex: MALE
Date of Birth: 8th November, 1930
Place of Birth: Thebarton, S.A.
Registration No.: 256A/106

I hereby certify that the above particulars are extracts from an entry in a register kept in the Office of the Principal Registrar, Adelaide.

E.D. BYERLEE
Principal Registrar

Date: 16 OCT 1986

A bit more about me. My Birth Certificate (copy).

S.A. NEWS

1987 - S.A. Division IIE Calendar

Aug: Applied Ergonomics Seminar Materials Handling concepts.

Sept: ROH Automotive Components Plant Visit.

Oct: JIT/TQC Presentation/Seminar Evaluation of installed systems in S.A.

Nov: Office Automation Modern concepts for IEs in the Office environment.

Dec: Bridgestone Factory tour.

Profile.

William J. C. Murrell, FIIE, MAIIE, MIE Aus, AAIM, AAIB.

Mr Murrell, affectionately known as Bill, joined the SA Division IIE in 1976 with Member grading and since that time has been a leading effective senior member of both the SA Council and the Federal Council. In 1978 he was elected President of the SA Division. After serving as President for 2 years, he served as Vice President from 1980-85. From 1981 to 1984 he held the dual roles of Vice President and Treasurer. After serving two years on Federal Council as SA Delegate and as acting Federal Secretary for a period of about six months, he was elected Federal President in 1982.

In addition to serving in those capacities he has been a significant driving force on the SA Council. He has initiated and arranged Plant and Site tours, conducted some highly successful IE oriented film evenings and addresses for the SA Division. He continues to provide innovative ideas and stimulus to the SA Council.

Mr Murrell was educated at St Peter's College and obtained Matriculation in 1948. He commenced employment at General Motors Holden in the field of Industrial Engineering where he served for some 8 years, during which period he was trained in the USA in Industrial Engineering. In 1954 he obtained his Diploma Industrial Engineering at G.M.I.T, USA.

Since that time Mr Murrell has successfully held Senior Industrial Engineering type positions in large Australian organisations including some 16 years at Chrysler Aust. Ltd in senior positions such as Manager Industrial Engineering.

In total, Mr Murrell has contributed to date some 38 years to the field of Industrial Engineering and is known and respected for his competence and effectiveness in the private and public sectors of the South Australian industrial and educational scenes.

Bill is currently the State Manager South Australian Construction Training Committee which is established to develop and train personnel to higher competence at all levels from management through technical to trade levels in the Building and Construction industry.

He has membership and contributes his knowledge and talent to the following professional organisations:

Member Institute of Engineers Aust.
Member Institute Training and Development
Member Institute Personnel Management Aust.
Member American Institute Industrial Engineers
Associate Aust. Institute of Management
Associate Aust. Institute of Building
Member Building Science Forum

In the field of Industrial Engineering training outside of his occupational activities, Mr Murrell developed and presented a course of training in Industrial Engineering to Diploma Engineering students for RMIT. From 1978 to the present time he lectures SAIT BE Students (4th year) in Engineering Management C and Industrial Engineering subjects.

He has conducted numerous adult training programs on behalf of PPCA and has published **several training manuals** relating **to productivity improvement and** related **subjects.**

In 1981 Mr Murrell attended functions in the USA and officially represented IIE Aust. at: American IIE Conference Detroit, International IE Leadership Conference and World Productivity Conference.

Bill has wholeheartedly devoted some 38 years to the effective study, implementation, training and practice of Industrial Engineering both during the hours of his employment and during a large proportion of his private life in a most unselfish and cheerful manner.

In 1986 Bill was rightly honoured with the status of Fellow of the IIE Australia in recognition of his achievements, efforts and contributions to Industrial Engineering.

Whereabouts Unknown.

Mail has been returned from the following member. If any member knows the new address of the member listed, could they please contact the S.A. Division Secretary.

Thanks, Paul McGurk (08) 268 5262

Mr P. Macoun MIIE, last known address: PO Box 1318 Nhulunbuy, N.T. 5797

An article written about me in 1985. I'm standing in front of a CTC Training Achievement Award.

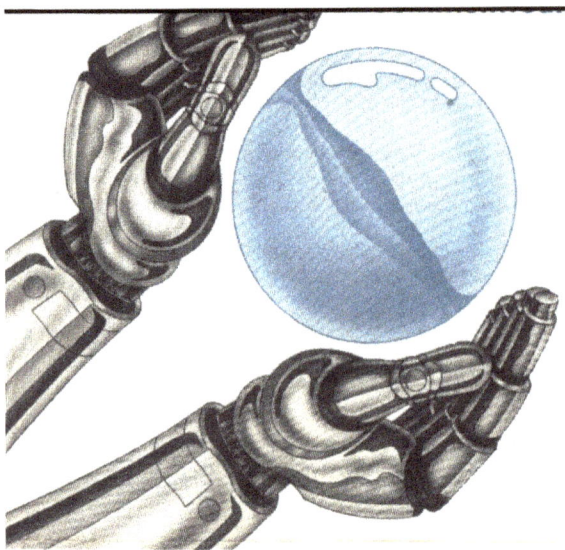

INDUSTRIAL ENGINEER CFOTPS 1

Industrial engineering is concerned with the design, improvement and installation of integrated systems of people, materials and equipment in industry and commerce in the public and private sectors.

Although 'Industrial Engineer' is the most commonly used title, some organisations use other titles to describe the field including methods engineer, production engineer, organisation and methods officer, systems officer (administrative) and management services officer.

The industrial engineer may initially be employed in any of the following major areas of industrial activity:

1. Industrial Economic Analysis — One of the principal functions of industrial engineering is to analyse a product, project or process from the economic point of view to ensure that an adequate profit can be obtained from it. A general working knowledge of economics and management skill has to be directed towards the making of decisions on how to operate an enterprise most efficiently. The basis for such decisions is furnished largely by the logical application of mathematics and statistics.

2. Production and Manufacturing Engineering — Manufacturing processes and operations must be planned in detail throughout an enterprise to ensure that they proceed smoothly and economically. Functions in this field include the establishment of production standards, the setting of production targets and, finally, control of quality.

The ultimate responsibility of those in charge of the planning and control of production is to ensure that the goods, as originally specified, perform satisfactorily and are produced when required at an optimum cost. Computers are an integral part of the system to achieve this.

3. Product and Process Design — The design interest of the industrial engineer goes beyond normal mechanical design to develop a product that will not only function effectively but will also have a pleasing appearance.

The product also has to be adapted to suit existing manufacturing equipment or a manufacturing process has to be developed so that an existing product can be manufactured at the right price and of the right quality. The design work of the Industrial Engineer also incorporates problems of equipment selection and application for both economy and performance. Fundamental scientific studies of manufacturing processes are continually being made to improve their efficiency. Industrial Engineers play an active part in the ergonomics of workplace design and layout and contribute greatly to minimising work injuries.

4. Methods Engineering — Methods engineering is particularly concerned with the coordination of personnel, materials and machines so that an enterprise will run at maximum efficiency. A considerable knowledge of engineering in general, as well as an understanding of human factors and materials science, is necessary for methods engineering.

In case you have been wondering "what is an Industrial Engineer?" Here is the Commonwealth Government's answer.

management services officer.

The industrial engineer may initially be employed in any of the following major areas of industrial activity:

1. Industrial Economic Analysis — One of the principal functions of industrial engineering is to analyse a product, project or process from the economic point of view to ensure that an adequate profit can be obtained from it. A general working knowledge of economics and management skill has to be directed towards the making of decisions on how to operate an enterprise most efficiently. The basis for such decisions is furnished largely by the logical application of mathematics and statistics.

2. Production and Manufacturing Engineering — Manufacturing processes and operations must be planned in detail throughout an enterprise to ensure that they proceed smoothly and economically. Functions in this field include the establishment of production standards, the setting of production targets and, finally, control of quality.

The ultimate responsibility of those in charge of the planning and control of production is to ensure that the goods, as originally specified, perform satisfactorily and are produced when required at an optimum cost. Computers are an integral part of the system to achieve this.

3. Product and Process Design — The design interest of the industrial engineer goes beyond normal mechanical design to develop a product that will not only function effectively but will also have a pleasing appearance.

The product also has to be adapted to suit existing manufacturing equipment or a manufacturing process has to be developed so that an existing product can be manufactured at the right price and of the right quality. The design work of the Industrial Engineer also incorporates problems of equipment selection and application for both economy and performance. Fundamental scientific studies of manufacturing processes are continually being made to improve their efficiency. Industrial Engineers play an active part in the ergonomics of workplace design and layout and contribute greatly to minimising work injuries.

4. Methods Engineering — Methods engineering is particularly concerned with the coordination of personnel, materials and machines so that an enterprise will run at maximum efficiency. A considerable knowledge of engineering in general, as well as an understanding of human factors and materials science, is necessary for methods engineering work. Time and motion study is part of methods engineering. In many cases the methods engineer works in close cooperation with the design department and executives engaged in industrial economic analysis.

5. Operations Research — This is the application of modern science to complex problems arising in the direction and management of large systems of people, machines, materials and money in areas such as industry, business, government and defence. The industrial engineer develops a scientific model of the system (incorporating measurements of factors such as chance and risk) with which to predict and compare the outcomes of alternative decisions, strategies or controls. This model helps management determine its policy and actions scientifically.

Personal Requirements

Industrial engineers should have the ability to work closely with all levels of staff in a problem solving environment, be able to initiate new ideas, to work with and lead groups, have an interest in cost benefit analysis methods and a statistical aptitude. A working knowledge of the use of computers in all aspects of the profession is becoming an essential requirement.

> We are happy to announce that on Friday
> 6 August, in the presence of members of our
> immediate families who were able to attend,
> we celebrated our marriage at St Andrew's
> Anglican Church, 257 Barker Road, Subiaco.
> The ceremony was conducted by the
> Right Reverend Brian Macdonald at 6 pm.
>
> On Sunday 15 August, during the usual 10 am
> Holy Eucharist service, at St Andrew's, prayers
> will be offered for our marriage, and we would
> be delighted to have you share in this service.
>
> Immediately following the service, refreshments
> will be available in the Church Hall, next-door
> to the church. To assist with catering
> arrangements, if you are able to attend,
> please ring either:
>
> Geoffrey or Carol Dean 457 8638 (H)
>
> or Will Murrell 389 1968 (H)
>
> Val Dean and Bill Murrell
>
> We are looking forward to seeing you on 15 August.
>
>
> By request, no gifts, please.
>
> *Vald   Bill*

And you are all invited to celebrate Valdean and my wedding!

And for those who love tripe (me) the National Tripe Anthem. I belonged to the Perth Tripe Club for many years until my doctor suggested I drop tripe from my diet as it is very high in cholesterol. Unfortunate!

NATIONAL TRIPE ANTHEM
Music from Tripe Prince (Student)

TRIPE, TRIPE, TRIPE,
FIT FOOD FOR A KING
NUTRITIOUS WITH EVERYTHING,
TRIPE, TRIPE, TRIPE
COME JOIN IN THE FUN
THERE'S PLENTY FOR EVERYONE.

TRIPE IS ALWAYS FIRST ON OUR MENU
THIS WAY AND THAT WAY, FOR ME AND FOR YOU
LET THE NATION, HAIL THIS FOOD
FOR BRUNCH OR TEA, FOR ANY MOOD.

TRIPE, TRIPE, LET THE TRIPE START,
TRIPE, TRIPE, FIRST IN MY HEART
TRIPE, TRIPE, TRIPE
LET EVERYONE STAND AND DRINK TO THE TRIPE.

TO TRIPE.

TRIPE, TRIPE, TRIPE,
FOOD FIT FOR A KING, NUTRITIOUS WITH EVERYTHING,
TRIPE, TRIPE, TRIPE, COME JOIN IN THE FUN
THERE'S PLENTY FOR EVERYONE.

TRIPE, LET'S STAND AND DRINK IN UNITY
TRIPE IS THE BEST FOOD FOR OUR GREAT COUNTRY,
LET THE NATIONS HAIL THIS FOOD
FOR BRUNCH OR TEA, FOR ANY MOOD.

TRIPE, TRIPE, LET THE TRIPE START,
TRIPE, TRIPE, FIRST IN MY HEART,
TRIPE, TRIPE, TRIPE
LET EVERYONE STAND AND DRINK TO THE TRIPE.

TO TRIPE.

Another bit of nonsense for you to read.

Alphabet spells out the ailments

A IS for apple, and
B is for boat,
That used to be right, but now it won't float.
Age before beauty is what we once said,
But let's be a bit more realistic instead...

Now A's for arthritis;
B's the bad back,
C is the chest pains, perhaps car-d-iac?
D is for dental decay and decline,
E is for eyesight, can't read that top line.
F is for fissures and fluid retention,
G is for gas which I'd rather not mention.
H is high blood pressure – I'd rather it low;
I for incisions with scars you can show.
J is for joints, out of socket, won't mend,
K is for knees that crack when they bend.
L for libido, what happened to sex?
M is for memory; I forget what comes next.
N is neuralgia, in nerves way down low,
O is for osteo, the bones that don't grow.
P for prescriptions, I have quite a few,
just give me a pill and I'll be good as new.
Q is for queasy, is it fatal or flu?
R for reflux, one meal turns to two.
S for sleepless nights, counting my fears,
T for Tinnitus; there's bells in my ears.
U is for urinary; big troubles with flow;
V is for vertigo, that's "dizzy" you know.
W is for worry, now what's going round?
X is for X-ray, and what might be found.
Y is another year I'm left here behind,
Z is for zest that I still have – in my mind.
I've survived all the symptoms, my body's deployed,
And I've kept 26 "doctors" fully employed.

Western View Eddy Joyce,
Post 26/8/07 Armadale.

And some sense by Dwight Eisenhower.

"A THOUGHT FOR THIS ERA"

Every gun that is made, every warship launched, every rocket fired signifies, in the final sense, a theft from those who hunger and are not fed, those who are cold and are not clothed. This world in arms is not spending money alone. It is spending the sweat of it's labourers, the genius of it's scientists, the hopes of it's children.

Dwight D. Eisenhower 1890-1969
34th President of the United States

(Speech in Washington, 16 April 1953, in *Public Papers of Presidents 1953* (1960) p.182)

DESIDERATA

GO PLACIDLY AMID THE NOISE & HASTE & REMEMBER WHAT PEACE there may be in silence. As far as possible without surrender be on good terms with all persons. Speak your truth quietly & clearly; and listen to others, even the dull & ignorant; they too have their story. Avoid loud & aggressive persons, they are vexations to the spirit. If you compare yourself with others, you may become vain & bitter; for always there will be greater & lesser persons than yourself. Enjoy your achievements as well as your plans. Keep interested in your own career, however humble; it is a real possession in the changing fortunes of time. Exercise caution in your business affairs; for the world is full of trickery. But let not this blind you to what virtue there is; many people strive for high ideals; and everywhere life is full of heroism. Be yourself. Especially, do not feign affection. Neither be cynical about love; for in the face of all aridity & disenchantment it is perennial as the grass. Take kindly the counsel of the years, gracefully surrendering the things of youth. Nurture strength of spirit to shield you in sudden misfortune. But do not distress yourself with imaginings. Many fears are born of fatigue & loneliness. Beyond a wholesome discipline, be gentle with yourself. You are a child of the universe, no less than the trees & the stars; you have a right to be here. And whether or not it is clear to you, no doubt the universe is unfolding as it should. Therefore be at peace with God, whatever you conceive Him to be, and whatever your labours & aspirations, in the noisy confusion of life keep peace with your soul. With all its sham, drudgery & broken dreams, it is still a beautiful world. Be careful. Strive to be happy.

FOUND IN OLD SAINT PAUL'S CHURCH, BALTIMORE, DATED 1692.

Worth reading quietly.

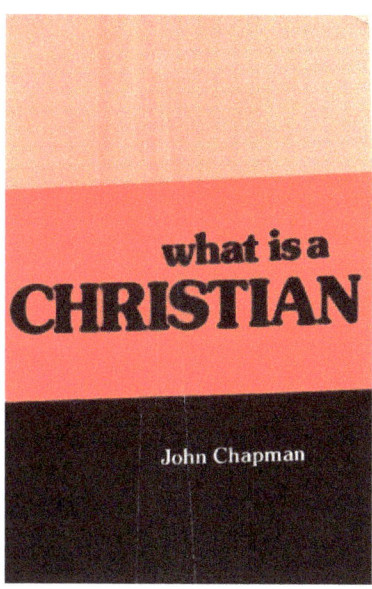

This too.

Calla

> To Bill, & all who've eyes to see
> & hands to feel
>
> In the sweat of your face
> You've eaten bread ---
> But look!
> The sword is cold and still,
> The cherubim asleep;
> Put forth your hands
> And take from the tree of life:
> Then time is nothing,
> And Eden everywhere.
>
> Was this His secret?
> Poor Adam! – And Eve!
> Fancy not thinking
> of it!
>
> John

Card: Interesting card from my school friend and Rugby mate, John Callaghan (lawyer).

And so my dearest grandchildren and step-grandchildren, as we near the end of this epistle, I leave you this blessing.

And I leave you one word: "Integrity".

And one slogan: "To thy self be true", which I consider the most important in the Bible.

The gospel of St John Chapter 3 verse 16, "For God so loved the world that he gave his one and only Son, that whoever believes in him shall not perish but have eternal life".

So, as the sun sets at the end of a beautiful day, so "My Story" by Grandad Bill ends, 21/1/14

One last photograph of a very happy couple at the Saints over 70's luncheon in the Memorial Hall, October 15, 2011

And may my story continue for a long time yet.

PS. Valdean and I often go on visits followed by lunch with the Retired Engineers and a group of the Institution of Engineers, Australia (IE Aust). Also, I like listening to classical music and we go about four times a year to the WA Symphony Concerts. I have built up a large CD collection.

Nicknames

I forgot to mention my four nicknames.

When at Primary School I brought a Bugum Worm to "Show and tell" one morning. I was christened "Buganz" by my friend Adrian Bates.

While at Saints, the Advertiser newspaper published a photo of Hitler's doctor "der Herr Doktor Murel". Malcolm Beaven Bill Hollis called me "der Herr Document" which was soon shortened to "Doc". If I meet even today a long term Saints friend, I am greeted with "Hello Doc".

When at Holden's, I was always inquisitive and Don Wylie and his father Tom dubbed me "The Enquiring Mind". I quite liked this kudos.

I led various teams at the Water Corporation. One day one of my team members presented me with a real plastic mug with "Skipper" on it. So from then on, I was "Skipper".

"Every man's life ends the same way. It is only the detail of how he lived and how he died that distinguish one man from another". *Ernest Hemingway*

Roar, sea, and every creature in you;

Sing, earth, and all who live on you!

Clap your hands, you rivers

You hills, sing together with joy before the Lord;

Because he comes to rule the earth.

He will rule the peoples of the world with justice and fairness.

Psalm 98

Another apt quote: "Life is not what one lived, but what one remembers and how one remembers it in order to recount it." *Gabriel Garcia Marquez*

And another: "Events of our past, shape the people we are today" *Janis Harrieson*

And "The quality of life is determined by its activities": *Arishok*

Chapter 14

Life Through the Lens

I will continue "My Story" in rough diary form.

9 June 2014: I had chest pains, plus under my jaw and in both upper arms. After four puffs with Nitro Lingual spray and no abatement, I rang St John of God's Heart Emergency Dr, who after discussion, suggested I be driven to the ECU (Emergency Cardiac Unit) ward straight away. The next morning Prof Merhe Hands examined me and ordered an angiogram to see what my heart trouble was. During this procedure, he discovered an 80% blockage of my RCA (Right Coronary Artery) and then unblocked it with an inserted stent. Thus I now have three stents viz LAD, DIAGONAL and RCA arteries. Prof Hands said afterwards "It was a good call for you to come into hospital."

As a follow up he ordered me to have a Perfusion radioactive thallium MRI. This showed no definite results, so Prof Hands ordered an Angiogram the following week. This showed that the three stents were working okay and had no function problems. Chest pains have vanished since Hands increased the dosage of Nexium 4x to prevent reflux.

On 14/01/2015 I had a Gastroscopy examination of my gut and stomach. Result – no indication of cancer – good! Next check-up in two years!

January 2017: I had another endoscope. Results are also good. No need for another endoscope until 2020.

28/8/2018: but still good!

20/1/2020: but still good!

Valdean thought it was a good idea to have a group of recent (July 2014) photos of our families, so here they are taken on our recent holiday in Melbourne and Adelaide.

Valdean and me

Above: Rachel, Alex and Tim Davis

Above: Angela Barbour and Tim

Right: Barry and Alex Davis

Left: Ruth and Bob Barbour

Above: L to R: James, Hannah and Jill Murrell

Right: L to R: Jane, Tim Barbour, Me, Olivia, Zac Barbour

Above: L to R: Sebastian, Jayne, Sophie, James Barbour

Left: Clementinia van de Grift and Geofry Dean

Right: Hugo Nicolas Lindsay Murrell (age 12 years)

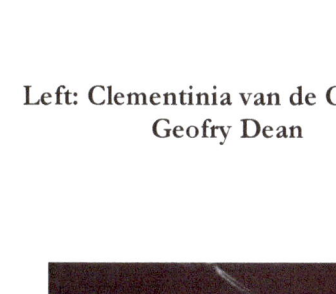

Above: Marc (18 months) at "Whitewoods", Heathmont, Vic

Left: 6th – 7th and 8th generation of Archdeacon Wollaston at Wollaston College with Archbishop Carnley. Phillippa Nynam (nee Wollaston). Baby Lily Grace Murrell and William Ashleigh Randell Murrell

Right: Auntie Chris, Grandpa Ambrose Murrell, Dad John William Murrell, Grandma Helen Murrell and Auntie Nell.

Left: My Dad's sisters (L to R) and Grandma: Auntie Belle, Grandma Helen Murrell, Auntie Chris and Auntie Nell.

Right: Phillippa Murray Wollaston/Murrell Nyman

Above: Four times a year three couples meet and the husbands cook – entrée, main and dessert. My turn at the Gray's place for dessert – a raspberry/strawberry trifle. Me opening the Muscat wine to match. Showing off my new birthday (84) shirt. November 2014

Above: Two of our dear friends Margot and John Dean. Taken on the occasion of John's 80th birthday. June 2014

Above Other friends in Melbourne, Ann and Stuart McCullough. We minded their home at Templestowe while they holidayed in Vietnam and Cambodia. June 2014.

We visited the Victorian National Gallery where I was greeted by this bear!

Right: We visited the Shrine of Remembrance. Most hallowed and inspiring inside. All the men who enrolled in WWI are listed in calligraphy books. Ten Murrells are listed. Uncle George; Uncle Leslie, both Dad's brothers. Both left Albany in the 1st fleet to Egypt.

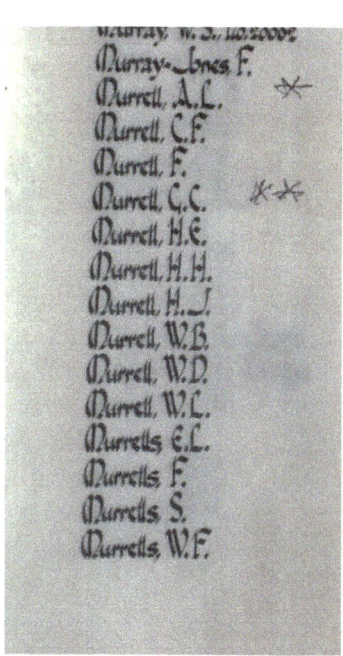

Above: We were able to arrange an ex GMI/GMH reunion at the Yarra Glen Country Club. L to R: Frank Pound, Korla and Danny Van Benton (ex-Chrysler and Nissan), Don Wylie and (Hidden) Sam Harrobin and Gene Twining. A good get together. June 2014

Above: Valdean's special spread for my 84th
L to R: Tara, Alison, Tony Milne, Valdean, Will, Lily and Jane Murrell

Left: Will dressed to kill 60's style for Jane's 50th birthday

Right: Father and son 60's style

Above: A delayed celebration of Rachael's 18th at the Fish Pub
L to R: Rachael, Alison, me, Valdean, Tara, Tony Milne

In December 2014 we experienced a very luxurious 3 day escape to Margaret River region, staying at the sumptuous "Cape Lodge" (pictured)

Helen and Joan, John and Margaret Kemp often send us postcards of their travels. This 3D one from the Canary Islands from John and Margaret Kenny is one of the best we have ever received.

Above: Feb 17, 2015 we went to Perth Pier St and saw the little girl giant puppet. We were mesmerized. For further pictures of their 3 day journey around Perth refer Appendix 31 for WAN's senior edition. Little Girl with her father puppet "Diver Dan".

Above: During March 2015 Valdean and I spent 3 days at Seafront Resort at Dunsborough. Here's Valdean contemplating on a bench in the adjacent stand hills which looks out on Dunsborough Eastern beach as pictured.

Left: Geoffery took Clementide, Valdean and myself to a friend's holiday cabin on Malloy Island for a few days in May. Here we all are having a meal at the refurbished Pub at Augusta. 5 kilometres by Blackwood River, 20 kilometres by away road.

Occasionally we go to the Heath Ledger Theatre to see a show – here on 26/7/2011 we were snapped in the foyer attending a ballet.

We had fourteen for 2014 Christmas lunch e.g. Lucy and Hugo, Tony, Alison, Rachael and Tara Milne, and Tom Murrell and us of course – and Jane, Will, Lily. A great spread each bringing major parts eg Milne's roast turkey, Tom prawns, Lucy trifle, Jan ham, and Valdean worked hard on extras and special ice cream pudding.

Our Christmas present from Lucy were tickets to *Les Misérables* – an excellent show which we all enjoyed immensely. Our Christmas present to Jane and Lucy were two tickets to the Hopman Cup.

Also to Geoffry and Clementina. So we had two rows of four enjoying Czechoslovakia beat Canada in men's and women's singles and also the mixed doubles.

I bought a slick-pic in the special $30-million lotto and was lucky enough to draw five numbers hence the $1,160 payout. One more number and the payout was over $2 million!

Another excellent outing to "The Lion King"

During January 2015 Valdean suddenly lost 15kg in weight which has not been replaced. In May she had neurological tests (6 hours) as she was sometimes confused.

Left: Me, representing SA in Under 19 State Rugby Union 1949

Below: Auntie Mollie's house at Belair Road where we were all evacuated during the war in 1941.

Dear Marc
Thanks for all the kind acts you've done for people you've met through out your life. Thanks for being my brother and Uncle.
Love Lucy, Fiona and Hugo.

Above: Marc on his travels near Mylor.

Left: Kind words from Lucy to Marc.

Left: Marc loved fishing. This was at Robe SA that he loved staying at.

Below: Marc with some of his artistry

In Loving Memory of

Marc Murrell

10-10-1958 ~ 19-12-2015

Poet

Artist

Writer

Left: A bookmark tribute to Marc given to all at his funeral 23/12/2015

On Thursday 17th December 2015 I received a phone call from a doctor at Queen Elizabeth Hospital (Woodville, SA) to inform me Marc was very ill, with both kidney and liver failures. Valdean and I flew to Adelaide next day and saw Marc about midnight. He was breathing heavily but unconscious. We left after an hour or so and returned to stay at Ruth and Bob Barbour's. At 3:15am on 19/12 they had a call from the hospital suggesting I should see Marc as soon as possible. Valdean and I quickly dressed and reached the QEH. We arrived just after Marc had passed away at 4:00am, 19/12/2015.

A very hectic time followed for me. Arranging Marc's death certificate, funeral at Berry's Function Home on 23/1/2015 **(see Marc's casket below)**, arranging disposal of all Marc's belongings and finally handing over the keys to the Real Estate office, then paying for his funeral, and all his outstanding accounts (there were many).

His friend Mona Khizharn Norberg was a great help and intends to make a video/film of Marc's life. She has most of Marc's artworks and all of his poems and writings. Friendly Street Poets have said they will publish his poems.

Berry's handled the funeral arrangements exceptionally well, I thought. Afterwards, they gave me a presentation carry bag containing: DVD of the funeral service, DVD of Marc, a special commemorative candle, which was alight on his coffin during the service, and a memorial book containing attendees names and addresses.

I always visited Marc when in Adelaide and he visited us at 1/1 Kilpa City Beach on two occasions. Our visits with him to the SA Art Gallery with a meal at their restaurant were a highlight of many visits. He had many friends and will be greatly missed.

Marc and I spoke on the phone at least fortnightly.

Marc was christened Mark Wollaston Murrell, but about fifteen years ago he changed Mark to Marc by deed poll, as he thought Marc suited an artist better.

Marc originally trained as a Chef and gained a Certificate at TAFE. However, he never worked as a Chef (I think the regime of fixed and long hour's never suited him). He once cooked me a five-course Japanese meal at his flat at Semaphore.

2016 – In April, Lucy and Hugo visited. Hugo and I visited the Lego exhibition which was fascinating and very clever.

We all visited Penguin Island which was on my bucket list.

We had an excellent day together.

Unfortunately further testing of Valdean's cognitive, memory and manipulative skills showed further decline in July 2016, and possibly the onset of dementia.

In August, she fell on the pavement while walking. Grazes on her knee took a long time to heal, and when examined by her GP, a lump at the side of her left knee was detected. Very unfortunate x-ray and biopsy revealed spindle cell carcinoma – a very aggressive cancer of the soft tissue and bone. Further MRI's and PET scans revealed the extent of the cancer right up her left leg into her groin. She is currently undergoing Radiation Therapy (25 treatments).

2017 – The radiation has eradicated the lumps on Val's leg. We await further MRI and CT scans in April to see how the cancer has been arrested.

3/6/2017 – Unfortunately, the sarcoma spread to Valdean's bowel, stomach and chest.

She went to Charlie Gardiner's Hospital on Tuesday after Easter then, after ten days there, she was transferred to the Palliative Care Ward at Bethesda Hospital. After four weeks there, she died peacefully at 7:35pm on Sunday 28/5/2017. Fortunately, I had decided to sleep in her room that night, and noticed that Valdean had quietly stopped breathing so I alerted the nurses, who confirmed her death.

Valdean's funeral service on 7/6/2017 is shown on the following pages.

City Beach
Wednesday 7th June 2017

A Service of Thanksgiving for the life of
VALRIE DEAN MURRELL
18.1.1938 — 28.5.2017
79 joyous years

Love does not waste, but lives forever in our hearts.

OPENING PRAYER
The Revd Debbie May

EULOGY
Alison Milne

HYMN: Love Divine, all Loves Excelling

Love Divine, all loves excelling,
Joy of Heaven, to earth come down,
Fix in us Thy humble dwelling,
All Thy faithful mercies crown.
Jesu Thou art all compassion,
Pure unbounded love thou art;
Visit us with Thy salvation,
Enter every trembling heart.

Come, Almighty to deliver,
Let us all Thy life receive,
Suddenly return, and never,
Never more Thy temples leave.
Thee we would be always blessing,
Serve Thee as Thy hosts above,
Pray, and praise Thee, without ceasing,
Glory in Thy perfect love.

Finish then Thy new creation,
Pure and spotless let us be;
Let us see Thy great salvation
Perfectly restored in Thee.
Changed from glory into glory,
Till in Heaven we take our place.
Till we cast our crowns before Thee,
Lost in wonder, love and praise!

WELCOME & INTRODUCTION
The Revd Debbie May

HYMN: Lord of the Dance

I danced in the morning when the world was begun,
And I danced in the moon and the stars and the sun,
And I came down from Heaven and I danced on the earth,
At Bethlehem I had my birth.

Dance then wherever you may be,
I am the Lord of the Dance, said he,
And I'll lead you all, wherever you may be,
And I'll lead you all in the dance said he

I danced for the scribe and the Pharisee,
But they would not dance and they wouldn't follow me.
I danced for the fishermen, for James and John,
They came with me and the dance went on.

Chorus

I danced on the Sabbath and I cured the lame;
The holy people said it was a shame.
They whipped and they stripped and they hung me high,
And they left me there on a Cross to die.

Chorus

I danced on a Friday when the sky turned black.
Its hard to dance with the devil on your back.
They buried my body and they thought I'd gone,
But I am the Dance and I still go on.

Chorus

They cut me down and I leapt up high;
I am the life that'll never, never die;
I'll live in you if you'll live in me-
I am the Lord of the Dance, said He.

Chorus

READING
John 14:1-6
By Rachael Milne

WORDS OF COMFORT
The Revd Debbie May

PRAYERS

THE LORDS PRAYER
Our Father, who art in Heaven
Hallowed be Thy name
Thy kingdom come
Thy will be done
On earth as it is in Heaven
Give us this day our daily bread
And forgive us our trespasses
As we forgive those who trespass against us
And lead us not into temptation
But deliver us from evil
For thine is the kingdom
The power and the glory
For ever and ever
Amen

PHOTO TRIBUTE

TIME OF REFLECTION AND FAREWELL
The congregation is invited to come forward and place a sprig of Rosemary on Valrie's coffin.

HYMN- Mine eyes have seen the glory of the coming of

Mine eyes have seen the glory of the coming of the Lord;
He is trampling out the vintage where the grapes of wrath are stored;
He has loosed the fateful lightening of His terrible swift sword;
His truth is marching on.

Glory! Glory! Hallelujah! Glory! Glory! Hallelujah!
Glory! Glory! Hallelujah! His truth is marching on

He has sounded forth the trumpet that shall never call retreat; He is sifting out the hearts of men before His judgement seat;
Oh, be swift, my soul, to answer Him! Be jubilant, my feet;
Our God is marching on.

Chorus

In the beauty of the lilies Christ was born across the sea,
With a glory in his bosom that transfigures you and me:
As He died to make men holy, let us live to make men free;
While God is marching on.

Chorus

He is coming like the glory of the morning on the wave, He is wisdom to the mighty, He is honour to the brave;
So the world shall be His footstool, and the soul of wrong His slave,
Our God is marching on.

Chorus

COMMENDATION

COMMITTAL

BLESSING

PROCESSION OUT
Music: Edelweiss

Thank you.

It is comforting to know that we are surrounded by so many people
who loved and supported Valdean throughout her life
and that you are here today to pay tribute
and share the beautiful memories of her.

*"Those we love can never be more than a thought away…
For as long as there's a memory, they live in our hearts to stay".*
Author unknown

You are warmly invited for refreshments in the Church Hall
immediately following the service.

In Loving Memory

VALRIE MURRELL

18.1.1938
—
28.5.2017

Valdean

She was always unselfish,
helpful and kind,
What beautiful memories
she has left behind.

Hebrew Proverb

MURRELL (Valrie Dean): Died peacefully on Sunday 28th May 2017. Loving wife of Bill and mother of Peter, Geoffrey and Alison. Grandmother of Rachael and Tara. Greatly loved by all family and step-families. Rest in Peace Valdean. The family requests donations in lieu of flowers to Cancer Council WA, 420 Bagot Road, Subiaco WA 6007 or call 1300 65 65 85.

WAN 3/6/2017

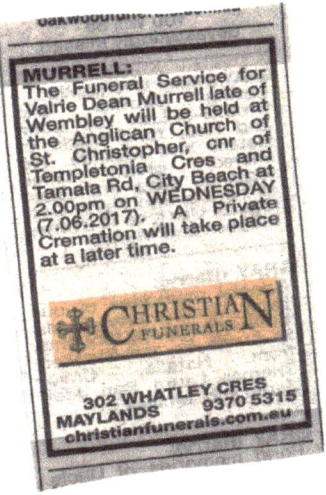

MURRELL: The Funeral Service for Valrie Dean Murrell late of Wembley will be held at the Anglican Church of St. Christopher, cnr of Templetonia Cres and Tamala Rd, City Beach at 2.00pm on WEDNESDAY (7.06.2017). A Private Cremation will take place at a later time.

CHRISTIAN FUNERALS
302 WHATLEY CRES MAYLANDS 9370 5315
christianfunerals.com.au

MURRELL (Valdean): To our dearest Valdean, thank you for the joy you brought to our lives. May you rest in peace. Our deepest sympathies to your family. Love always, Will, Jane, Ben and Lily

MURRELL (Valrie): In loving memory of Valdean, a gracious, gentle lady. Deepest sympathy to Bill and all the families. Treasured memories of our friendship. Rest in Peace. Gerry and Diana.

8/6/17

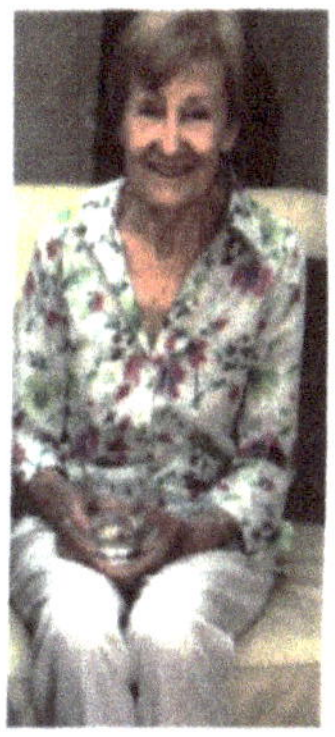

Death is the gateway to the promise of eternal life as we shed our earthly bodies to enter the presence of God

This is a quote I found one day when I was sitting by mum's bedside in Bethesda. It has helped me get through some of the really difficult moments and neatly summarieses my mother's relationship with her faith and her outlook on life.

In September 2015 we saw a suitable place to downsize. One less bathroom, and extra room, less garden and no pool. We put in a subject to bid, but found another buyer had outbid us by $5,000.

We saw CBA and they agreed to lend the whole of the purchase price for 85 Marlow Street. We went ahead blithely thinking that 1/1 Kilpa, City Beach would sell within two months – Wrong! It took five months and a reduction of the initial advertised price of $100,000! A very costly move. Hence, there was hardly any $ difference when all commissions, stamp duties and large interest were accounted. Still, we are now happily ensconced in our eight-year-old home and left a 38-year-old strata title with large garden and pool to maintain.

I thought the above depiction of past and future ages the best I have seen. I have included it for your contemplation. I hope you enjoy this, and "My Story" written 23/10/2016 on the first day of the rest of my life.

Below: This sarcoma cancer is the type of which Valdean died. The oncology surgeon specialist suggested to us in October 2016 that he remove V's left leg at the hip (a 6 hour op), but he could not guarantee that this would remove all the cancer cells. Of course, we declined, as V's quality of life hopping on one leg would be hopeless. Valdean died peacefully 7:35pm 28/5/2017.

Curtin University student Matilda Gorce lost the finger on her left hand to sarcoma. Picture: Nic Ellis

Aggressive cancer led to amputation

Cathy O'Leary
Medical Editor

When Perth university student Matilda Gorce noticed a small lump on her left ring finger almost three years ago, she barely gave it a second thought.

But after it persisted and became annoying, she went to see a doctor, triggering tests that confirmed she had the rare and aggressive cancer, sarcoma.

Ms Gorce was stunned to learn that the only way to treat it was to have her finger amputated.

"When I found out that was the only option, to lose my finger entirely, I was completely distraught," the 21-year-old said.

While the cancer is rare, the number of cases has risen 50 per cent in the past decade.

Research funding and awareness group Sock it to Sarcoma wants people to recognise early warning signs such as a lump that changes in size or unexplained pain in the back or a limb.

Co-ordinator Mandy Basson, who lost her 20-year-old daughter Abbie to sarcoma, said there were often delays in diagnosis.

"Sarcoma is highly aggressive and the symptoms can be hard to spot as they can be easily put down to other things," she said.

Jordan Hay-Hendry of Golden Bay recently lost his battle with sarcoma at 23.

His family is running a season of Theatresports this month to raise funds for the support group, ahead of WA Sarcoma Awareness Week starting on June 19.

Details at justimprovise.com.au

Although a lot of work went into arranging the funeral by Alison, myself and others the result was (I think) excellent. Over 100 (117) attendees. Christian funerals performed very well. Tara prepared an excellent Powerpoint depiction of Valdean's life.

Alison's eulogy covered Valdean's life events very very well, See next pages.

Eulogy: This eulogy gives a very good picture of Valdean's "dash".

"Death is the gateway to the promise of eternal life as we shed our earthly bodies to enter the presence of God."

This is a quote I found one day when I was sitting by mum's bedside in Bethesda. It has helped me get through some of the really difficult moments and neatly summarises my mother's relationship with her faith and her outlook on life.

Thank you all for coming and sharing this celebration of her life now she has embarked on a new journey.

Mum was born Valrie Ethel Phelps on 18th Jan 1938 in Nannup.

Second child to George & Dorothy Phelps. After she was born, George drove Dot and baby Valrie home on their horse and cart. Valrie, tucked away safely in a wooden crate was stowed behind George's legs for safety.

It was a humble beginning for Valrie with George and Dot doing it tough on the land in Nannup. They moved to Perth several years later.

Valrie had 2 sisters, older sister Roma & younger sister Thelma, and younger brother Rodney.

Valrie worked as a secretary after she left school. She had a full time job, but she was also very actively involved in church and sporting activities.

We all know that Valrie was a very active member and a great volunteer within the Anglican Church for many years. What you may not know is that her volunteering and community involvement started at a very early age.

Lets talk about CEGS. That woke up a few of you.... I did not say Sex. C.E.G.S. The Church of England Girls Society. For those that don't know...It's a very worthy Anglican church based Girl Guides movement.

CEGS, VERY often misheard as SEX. So, going forward when I say CEGS, I know some of you might be a bit hard of hearing, but please be assured that I am talking about the Church of England Girls Society.

At 12 years old Valrie joined CEGS, for something to do. At 14 years old, she became a Junior Leader at the Palmyra CEGS branch. At 16 years old she started a new branch in Willagee.

By the time she was 18, she was Secretary to 2 CEGS branches and 1 CEBS branch (the boy version). She would take about 70 girls each week for branch meetings, attend various CEGS & CEBS council meetings & executive meetings. She would fit in all her club typing into odd moments before and after work and during lunch breaks. She was also an enthusiastic member of the Fremantle Police Boys' and Women's Athletic Club and trained about 4 nights per week. When she was 17 she won a trophy for the ½ mile. She was a runner and ran at state level. She also played Basketball in the winter with the St Johns Association.

At the age of 20 in 1958 she was the Diocesan Secretary of CEGS and the Diocesan Commissioner managing 5 branches. She instructed CEGS Leaders in branch control and management. She visited every branch about once every month, travelling BY BUS after work to her branches – Rockingham, Bicton, Floreat Park, Bassendean and Mundaring. She also taught in Sunday School, did all the CEGS Society secretarial work and studied Theology part time. At this point she was also engaged to Michael Horace Dean, a Theology student and they were subsequently married in 1959 and had 3 children, Peter, Geoffrey and me!

Her activities and work with CEGS laid the foundation for a lifetime of selfless volunteer work. And this makes me most proud of my mother…. Apart from the way she lookied after her loved ones……her selfless giving to others.

Valrie made many friends during her volunteering work with CEGS and I know she was highly regarded with in the CEGS family for many years after she had to give up her CEGS life... and still is. But marriage, 3 small children and with Michael being posted to country towns, this didn't stop her from being a valuable community member and volunteer. As a Rector's wife, she was always heavily involved on the Parish side lines in Wyalkatchem and Bruce Rock. Rosters, Admin, Flowers, Raffles etc. Again, more people and friends left behind who have very fond memories and a great respect for Valrie.

Apart from being a devoted wife and a loving mother raising 3 children, there was one other important aspect in the way she lead her life…. In the service of others. By the time she was 20 years old, there had been several articles in various WA Newspapers about Valrie and the volunteer work she undertook. I can only assume they were writing about her and trying to highlight her as the good role model that she was. I remember her ALWAYS being very involved with the Anglican Church and also giving her time and service volunteering to many charities and organisations during her life.

In no particular order ....St Phillips in Cottesloe, St Lukes in Mosman Park, St Andrews in Shenton Park, Friends of Wollaston, The Cancer Council, The Joint Doorknock, The Heart Foundation, Young Achievers Australia, Bethesda Social Work Department.

I am sure I have probably missed off many entities that have benefitted from her involvement and her commitment to serving others. Any ommissions or complaints about this list can be sent me, after you have written it out in shorthand, typed it up in triplicate on a typewriter with carbon paper, with correct spelling and grammer ......because this is how Valrie would have done it!

Valrie discovered a new career when we were living in Bruce Rock back in the late 1960's. Teaching. She was offered a job at the local high school teaching Secretarial studies. She had no formal qualifications to be a teacher, but in a small country town where you are the only person who knows how to type, that isn't already in full-time employment... then you get the job! Whether you want it or not!

When we moved back to Perth in 196? 197? well I was in grade 2, she went to Teachers College to get her teaching qualifications. With plans to send all 3 children to private schools, a second income was needed. Teaching vs Secretarial work was a practical solution as it was a good salary and very family friendly hours, especially at school holiday times.

Following the kids all leaving home and a divorce from Michael, and after she had had enough of teaching, she worked at other places including about 10 years at The West Australian Newspapers where she worked in the Telesales Dept, conducted the site tours for groups, and even helped out the Travel Dept by being The West's representative on several package tours, i.e. taking a heap of strangers on overseas package holidays and travelling on someone else's dollar!

It was during one of The West's site tours in 1990 that she met Bill Murrell. Bill had recently arrived to work and live in Perth and did not know a lot of people. Valrie in her usual hospitable way thought Bill was OK and started inviting him to join in at social events to help him meet people and develop a network of friends. Love blossomed and they were married in 1993.

Mum has been a devoted wife to Bill for 24 years, looking after him during many years of challenging health. She was still trying to look after him when she was in hospital the past few months. One day, when Bill and I were visiting her in hospital and she wasn't having a good day, lying in bed in pain and half asleep, the tea lady popped into the room to see if anyone wanted a cuppa. Bill asked for a cup of coffee with milk. And in an instant, mum with eyes still closed and head on pillow, says rather loudly.... "with NO sugar!" She was still trying to look after Bill from her hospital bed.

Luckily Bill's health improved a few years ago but sadly Valdean's health started to decline and the table was eventually turned. Bill was now looking after Valdean. And he looked after her to the very end. Thank you Bill for loving my mum so completely and being such a dedicated husband. You were her rock.

Valdean and Bill have enjoyed bringing their families together to create their own special extended family. The Murrells, Milnes and Deans have enjoyed many good times together and we hope we will continue to do so. Val would want that too.

Valdean & Bill have also spent many years worshipping here, in the Parish of St Christopher. As usual, Valdean has been an enthusiastic volunteer with many years of service within the St Christopher parish family. It is an honour to be able to share this celebration of Valdean with them. I just want to very quickly thank all the wonderful people of St Christophers who have helped to pull this funeral together. They have made a very daunting task of organising a funeral and a wake so much easier. Another example of how loved and respected Valdean is.

There is always a common thread that wove through her life. Family. Family was one of the most important aspects of her life. Her own family, Bill's family, her volunteering family, her parish family, her social family. She made friends, lots of friends, many who are here today. Many who have already moved on to heaven above. Val has been a wonderful friend to many people. She was kind, polite, thoughtful, loving, helpful, compassionate, witty, very organised and threw great dinner parties! Her friends were part of her family.

She was a wonderful mother, always there when needed, always loving and supporting us in our endeavours, making the sacrifices most mothers do to give their kids a decent upbringing, guiding us to become decent human beings, and always on hand to help with anything.

As a Stepmother to Mark, James, Will & Lucy, she always regarded them as part of her family and loved spending time with them and their families.

She managed to do quite a bit of travelling overseas. A lot of that was following Peter, Geoffrey and I to various parts of the world where we would be living.. England, Scotland, Jakarta. I was away for about 15 years, but have treasured memories of the past 15 years having returned to Perth with Tony, Rachael & Tara. It was wonderful for the kids to grow up with "Gran" in their lives and I wouldn't change it for the world.

She was a wonderful grandmother, not just to my Rachael & Tara, but also to her step grandkids, Lily, Hugo, Tully & Hannah. As our kids were growing up in Perth, Gran was always on hand to help out with babysitting, school runs, she would take them to concerts, museums etc,. Gran would also always host our special family birthday dinners for whoevers birthday it was…. And with an extended family over the past 20 something years. ….This was quite frequent. Mum's dining table is probably one of the most photographed tables on this planet… with thanks to Bill and his enthusiasm for keeping Kodak in business, latterly Officeworks print shop.

I have spent the past week trawling through about eleventy thousand photos (thanks Bill!) looking for photos of mum. There were so many photos of so many friends and not enough room for all of them in the Photo Tribute. Also, so many photos of many people who have been a part of her life that I never knew or met.

But on behalf of all of us here and absent friends who knew and loved Val,

You might be gone…. But not forgotten… a volunteering stalwart, a giving and generous person and a wonderful family matriarch.

So many happy memories to keep in our hearts until we see you again.

Au Revoir & Rest In Peace.

Above: Easter day lunch at Milne's. This is the last photo of Valdean before she was admitted to hospital on 18 April 2017.

Above: I received 53 cards of "Get Wells" and sympathy, some depicted here above TV. They are still arriving as of 12/6/2017

Above: People gathered after the service of thanksgiving.

My daughter Lucy (pictured below) flew down from Darwin to be with me for a few days. She was a great help and comfort for me.

The flowers on the left are from my sister Ruth and brother-in-law Bob Barbour. The red roses sheath on the dining table was on Valdean's coffin.

13/7/2017: I am coping along reasonably well but find 86 quite lonely at times. I'm keeping up gym and aqua-aerobics, each twice a week. Also trying to keep in touch with our many friends.

I miss Valdean heaps. I still do 18/10/2017

"Invictus"

Out of the night that covers me,
Black as the pit from pole to pole.
I thank whatever gods may be
For my unconquerable soul.

In the fell clutch of circumstance
I have not winced nor cried aloud.
Under the bludgeonings of chance
My head is bloody, but unbowed.

Beyond this place of wrath and tears
Looms but the Horror of the shade,
And yet the menace of the years
Finds and shall find me unafraid.

It matters not how strait the gate,
How charged with punishments the scroll,
I am the master of my fate,
I am the captain of my soul.

"Invictus" is Latin for "unconquerable".
Poem by William Ernest Henley (1849-1903)
Worth reading, I think. What do you think?

"Twenty years from now you will be more disappointed by the things that you didn't do than by the ones you did do. So throw off the bowlines, sail away from the safe harbour. Catch the trade winds in your sails, Explore. Dream. Discover."

Mark Twain (1835-1910)

Since Valdean's death, I've wondered how I could contribute more to St Christopher's.
a) I'm restoring the Men's Fellowship Group on a quarterly meeting.
b) I'm donating a new overhead projector in memory of Valdean.

Many readers have asked me how I compiled "My Story". Well, first I asked Will and Jane for a large scrapbook. This was my Christmas present in 2010. I kept it for five years, while I gathered and sorted old photos and put some thoughts about my life on 5" x 4" cards which I stored in a small box. Then, as a 2015 New Year's Resolution, I started:

a) the Chapter Indexes

b) dot points which I governed from my thought cards under chapter headings. This took up ten pages.

c) started writing: The Prologue was going to start with Alphabet chapters but I changed my mind and launched into this story full-on chronologically. I got really rapped with writing, getting up at 4 am and writing until about 8 pm – minus meals, of course. Twenty-two days later, I finished to page 168. It was the same month, Jan 15, that Valdean suddenly lost 15kgs. Looking back, I think this was when she contracted her sarcoma cancer. It was diagnosed by Dr Koek twenty-two months later. Sometime in the future, I'm going to check off which of the dot points I've included in "My Story".

Five rolls of Sellotape and seven biros were used 3/8/2017

"Life is not measured by the number of breaths we take; but by the moments that take our breath away" *Brenda.*

25/9/2017 – I will add bits and pieces of my life as might interest various readers progressively as they occur to me. I'm finding it very lonely without Valdean. I miss her greatly and I will have to try and be more sociable and meet more people.

"We are what we repeatedly do.
Excellence, then, is not an act, but a habit"
Aristotle 384-322 B.C

Editors Postscript:

Bill lived on his own for another couple of years with some hired home help and help from Will, Jane, Alison, Tony and Tom. Bill's dementia worsened.

He did however, have a few more adventures and did in fact, sail away. Bill went on another two or three cruises. One, The Diamond Princess was around Australia. He stopped in Darwin to visit Lucy, Hugo and Fiona and went 4WD ing and toured NT Govt House.

Also, Lucy and Hugo visited Bill and stayed with him at Christmas and New Year school holidays in 2018/19. At this time she and he investigated some nursing homes together. Approximately six weeks after Lucy and Hugo left, Bill developed a fast-growing large lump on his neck. He was hospitalised, operated on but, the recovery and ongoing treatment weakened him. Additionally, his dementia was worsening. Bill never returned home as a good room at his preferred Nursing home came up. He commenced his nursing home journey about mid-way through 2019. Will, Tom and Alison were regular visitors. In 2020, due to the pandemic Covid 19, it was closed and restricted to visitors and WA closed off from the world. Bill told Lucy by Facetime that he used to wave to people as they went passed from his 2nd floor balcony - he had friends in the neighbourhood. He and Will used to enjoy a Sunday afternoon whiskey.

Bill was determined to reach 90 years old. He did! Will arranged a wonderful party with a host of family and friends allowed in the Nursing home in November 2020 for the celebration.

Six weeks later, the cancer that had started as a sarcoma freckle on his head took his life. It was a peaceful death and last rights were given. Will stayed by his side throughout and Lucy had talked with him earlier via Facetime.

Bill's funeral and estate wishes were carried. His lovely St Christopher Church community held a memorable funeral. He had us all go to his burial in a black stretch limo!

And his dear Valdean's ashes buried with him … He used to say "Kangaroos will be able to jump over us in a beautiful park setting" in WA.

Robyn Camerer
Jack Murrell Geelong Football Player,
2023, oil on board, 60 x 50 cm.

Appendix

Appendix 1

Bill Murrell, The Art Collector

by Thomas A.C. Murrell

T.G.B. (Theo) Hendricks,
Back Valley McLaren Vale,
1984, oil on canvas, 32 x 26 cm.

Early Life

Despite having an acute and sharp mechanical engineering mind, Bill Murrell loved the visual arts and was a keen art collector and patron. His love of collecting started early in life at the large house in Adelaide at Sewers Yard, an Engineering and Water Supply (E&WS) property provided to his water engineer father in the inner-city suburb of Thebarton. Jack Murrell held many senior professional positions, including Engineer for Sewerage and Deputy Engineer in Chief for the South Australian Government and, as was the custom of the day, lived at his workplace.

"I was always interested in collecting things, that's for sure! I had a museum out the back at Port Road, Thebarton. It was the foreman's shed that dad let me have. It was an interesting situation where I charged a penny each to go in," Bill cheekily told me in an audio podcast recorded just prior to his passing in November 2020.[1]

"People went in and had a look and they found it interesting. The top row had a lot of pennies and coins. The second row, a whole lot of badges. I gathered it up myself. I was horrified when Mum gave it away while I was away in America!"

Jana Della-Noce,
Still-life Flowers Milan Style,
1986, Oil on Board, 27.5 x 22 cm.

Bill credits his father's philanthropic efforts for getting him interested in collecting when his father swapped tools for money with unemployed people when the Australian economy collapsed and unemployment reached a peak of 32 per cent in the 1932 Great Depression.

---

[1] William John Calvert Murrell - Art Collector and Industrial Engineer 1930 – 2020, *Hidden Talent: Untold Stories of The Fairview Art Collection* podcast, June 2 2021, www. https://8mmedia.libsyn.com/william-john-calvert-murrell-art-collector-and-industrial-engineer-1930-2020

Jack Murrell 1925

"He collected old tools and gave money to people over the period of the Depression. He ended up with quite a lot of tools, which covered the whole one side of the shed. He had a run in the Stawell Gift, he tried but he didn't win it."

Jack Murrell Geelong Team. He played 36 games for Geelong in the Victorian Football League between 1920 and 1922 on the wing and was paid £5 a match which helped fund his diploma course in civil engineering and surveying at the Gordon Institute of Technology, Geelong.

He was 175 cm (5 ft 9 in) tall and weighed 74 kg (163 lb). He later played in 1925 for New Town in Hobart, Tasmania and then played eight games in 1926 for Norwood in the South Australian National Football League.

Bill Murrell had great affection for his father Jack, who played Australian Rules Football for Geelong, New Town, Hobart, the Tasmanian State team and Norwood. After his parent's marriage in 1926, it took them 27 years to save enough money and buy their first home together.

After Thebarton Road, for 17 years his parents lived at the beautiful and historic Adelaide Hills property "Hathaway" at 43 Ayers Hill Road, Stirling, which they owned from 6 May 1953 to 9 July 1970. It had a magnificent cool climate garden, and a fine watercolour of the house and garden by E.M. Hodge in 1960 is one of Bill's favourites.

E.M. Hodge

Hathaway,

1960, watercolour on paper, 28 x 33 cm.

"It was due to dad that Adelaide is sewered. He put out the plans in the early days, got them approved and mainly paid for by the State Government, which was a big thing. That was a good thing that everybody got sewered eventually. It took a while but that's what happened. It goes back from the 1930s to the present day."

John William "Jack" Murrell (23 June 1901 – 3 June 1980) was one of 750 South Australians awarded the Coronation medal in 1953; was president of the South Australian Division of the Australian Institution of Engineers and also of the Town Planning Institute. There is a street named in his honour in the Adelaide suburb of Para Hills.

John C. Goodchild,
St Peter's College Main Oval,
1955, limited edition etching, 22 x 34 cm.

Jack Murrell valued education and sport. He sent all his five children to private schools in Adelaide. Bill Murrell especially enjoyed his time at St Peter's College.

An etching of the Main Oval by South Australian artist John C. Goodchild was one of his favourite works.

The Influence of Two-Time Archibald Portrait Prize Finalist Eric Wright

Jack Murrell married Beatrice "Trixie" Alice Calvert at St John's Church, New Town, Hobart on the 30th December 1926.

Jack Murrell and Beatrice "Trixie" Alice Calvert outside St John's Church, New Town, Hobart on the 30th of December in 1926 on the wedding day

The large society wedding was reported in the local Hobart press at the time.
"The ceremony was performed by Archdeacon Whittington, assisted by the Rev. Hughes. The church was beautifully decorated by friends and the service was fully choral. As the bride entered the church with her father, the hymn, *Lead Us Heavenly Father, Lead Us* was sung, the choir ably assisting. The bride looked lovely in a beautiful silver brocaded gown made in old-fashioned style, with a tight bodice, and full skirt, the latter being wired at the hips and forming an uneven hem, long tight sleeves finished with a pointed cuff; her long veil was of plain cut tulle, with a tiny wreath of orange buds finished with clusters at either side. Her only ornament was a diamond and platinum wristlet watch, gift of the bridegroom. She carried a bunch of white roses. The bride was followed by two bridesmaids, Miss Mollie Calvert, sister of the bride, and Miss Iris Cuthbertson (Melbourne) cousin of the bridegroom, who were frocked alike in delphinium blue georgette frocks over silver lace, finished with diamante trimming and buckle, and wore silver turbans. They carried sheafs of delphiniums and wore long crystal bead necklets, gifts of the bridegroom. Mr. Eric Cuthbertson (Melbourne) was best man, and Mr. Gordon Simmons (Hobart) groomsman. Messrs Les. Shield and Marcus Calvert acted as ushers. About 90 guests were entertained at a reception in the ballroom of the Continental, where the Hon. and Mrs. W. H. Calvert received and the usual toasts were honored. Mrs W. H. Calvert wore a navy crepe de chine frock with a smart crinoline hat, Mrs A. Murrell (Geelong) wore a black ensemble, with smart black hat. The bride travelled in a cherry crepe de chine frock under a smart navy crepe de chine coat, with navy hat. Their honeymoon will be spent in Sydney and Melbourne before leaving for their home in Adelaide."

Eric Wright,
Huon River Tasmania,
1926, oil on board, 26 x 41 cm.

Trixie's favourite uncle was Eric John Joseph Wright, who was born in Sydney in 1899 to Albert G. and Victoria Wright and died in 1972 at Burwood and is buried at the Northern Suburbs Cemetery. He was one of nine children and a finalist in the Archibald prize in both 1946 and 1947, and he exhibited with the Royal Art Society in 1946. He painted a beautiful oil painting of a river scene near "Forest Home", the award-winning orchard in Judbury in the Huon Valley where Trixie grew up, and presented this to them as a wedding gift. This work is now held in the Fairview Private Art Collection.

"I liked art right from grade school. I collected bits and pieces and put them aside. Then my younger brother Andrew took it on. He was a dealer in art and painted a few himself. He did a good job of it actually," said Bill in his 2020 interview.

Andrew Douglas Ambrose Murrell,

Mrs Brewster Jones' Garden in Victor Harbor,

1988, oil on board, 34 x 44 cm.

Andrew Douglas Ambrose Murrell was born 15 years after Bill Murrell, as a war boom baby.

"I remember very clearly the feeling of Ryan, the last person hanged at the Adelaide Gaol, which was opposite our family home at Port Road, Thebarton. I remember the quietness," Andrew Murrell told me in a podcast recorded in April 2022.

Ronald Ryan was the last man hanged in Australia, on 3 February 1967. Ryan and his accomplice Peter Walker escaped from Pentridge Prison on 19 December 1965. The escape set in motion a chain of events that would lead to Ryan's execution and, eventually, to the abolition of the death penalty in Australia.

"Other memories include sitting at the dining table at Port Road and hearing the news of the death of King George VI in 1952," he said.

So how did Andrew Murrell get into art dealing?

"Opposite my home in Stirling was a wonderful, eccentric lady, Lob Robson, who ran a guest house and a lot of the elderly aristocracy of Adelaide used to summer up at Olivet House and eventually live there. The owner was an amazing art philanthropist, and she used to support people like Colin Gardiner and artists of the local Adelaide Hills. She took me to art auctions in Adelaide and I started buying," Andrew explained.

Queen Anne Federation style and South Australian State heritage listed "Olivet House", was built in 1900 by pastoralist Edward Hawker in 1900 and then called 'Wachenappee' after a group of First Nations people by whom Hawker was received in his youth at their East Bungaree estate. It is a magnificent mansion sitting on about 6,600 square metres of beautifully landscaped grounds in Stirling.

**Wachenappee, Mt Lofty, 1901 showing house and early landscaping.
Source: State Library of South Australia. B46647. Used with permission.**

"I think it's definitely a gift to know what's good and not. It's instinct. I had everything from traditional to modern and I didn't like losing my money. So, if I bought a painting, I wanted to know to resell. I had one stipulation, they all had to be dead because the market was already there with limited supply!" Andrew explained of his skill in buying and selling art.

"I never bought from a gallery. I never bought from an artist. I just bought at auctions."

A wonderful portrait of Andrew in his Scottish tam o'shanter and scarf was painted when he was forty-two years old by Archibald Prize finalist Timothy Messack. Messack was a finalist in the 1953 Archibald Prize with a self-portrait.

So how did Andrew Murrell transition from art dealer to oil painter?

"I was coming out of alcoholic rehabilitation and it was really a discipline. That's what the art was about because I was painting the Holy Family, Angels and Saints. It had a profound spirituality about it. I always felt taken over by painting. I never felt in control of it. I love the impressionists."

"Art has been part of the collectibles in my life. Ever since a child, I went to an aunt, Belle Hughes, Dad's sister, in Melbourne who had a massive and incredibly valuable Australian stamp collection. I couldn't believe the art in the engraving with each stamp."

"What I've learnt is with art, you own it for sometime, and then you pass it on. Never get attached to a painting."

"It always moves. The more it moves, the more you see. And the more you learn."

Wise advice from art dealer, oil painter and younger brother of Bill Murrell, Andrew Murrell.

Artist, Neighbour and Friend - Mary M. Wigg

Bill lived next door to South Australian artist Mary Millicent Wigg (nee Lamphee) (8 October 1904 – April 21 2009) at Frederick Street, Gilberton in Adelaide.

"I used to go in and talk to her about art and art collections and she gave me several paintings of hers, including the first one she ever did, a nude of her, the first painting she ever did! Very good work, I thought, especially for a first off nude!" Bill said of his relationship with her.

Mary M. Wigg,
Nude Self Portrait,
1960, oil on board, 32 x 26 cm.

"She kind of downplayed her paintings. I used to climb over the fence because we were next door at the back and admire her paintings which were often in the shed. She and I got on well, and we talked about art a lot."

Mary M. Wigg,

Milang,

1963, oil on board, 28 x 33 cm.

Mary M. Wigg,

Mt Difficult - Grampians,

1963, oil on board, 32 x 26 cm.

Mary M. Wigg,

Grampians,

1963, oil on board, 27 x 23 cm.

"She travelled down to Milang and Victor Harbor and lots of country areas."

BBC Radio Connections – Joe Latham

Bill also had artist friends who lived overseas. Joe Latham of the London suburb of Ruislip in the United Kingdom was one such example.

"He was a very good friend of mine who worked for the BBC," Bill said.

Joe joined the BBC at the Droitwich Transmitting Station on 24th May 1943 when he was just 17 years old and still had his Higher School Certificate to cope with later in the year.

As a Youth in Training, the first five weeks were taken up with courses run by On-Station Instructors. Joe often cycled from Worcester for nightshift, which started at midnight until 9.30am, and sometimes was accompanied by a few German bombers flying overhead.

"They never stopped at Droitwich I was pleased to say! It was a wonderful station, with its 700ft masts, and I really enjoyed my first taste of the BBC," Joe said in his life memoirs.

Next, he was promoted to Technical Assistant Grade II and posted to Washford in Somerset, a couple of miles from Watchet where he lived. It had two 50kW medium wave transmitters and a directional aerial aimed at South Wales.

Joe Latham,

Chichester Cathedral, 1991

watercolour on paper, 25 x 35 cm.

"The masts were a mere 500ft high! It had wonderful views of the Quantocks from the rest room, which also had a splendid snooker table! The shift system was interesting and followed this Sunday to Saturday pattern: seven evenings (1400 - 2200), with a quick change-over to seven days (0700 - 1400), then seven nights (2200 - 0700) and back to another seven evenings - and so on."

"Holidays were two weeks in the Summer and one in the Winter."

In October 1944, a young lady arrived from Weymouth H-Group transmitter and was posted to Joe's shift - Sylvia Beechey by name. Years later, in 1949, they met again at 200 Oxford Street. She became Sylvia Latham on November 25th 1950.

Washford was in a group of three medium wave stations all on the same frequency so that German aircraft could not use the carriers for direction finding. If any one of the transmitters in the group was off the air for more than three minutes the others had to close down. This gave plenty of incentive to get a move on when a fault occurred and to get back on the air. Mains failures were fairly frequent, and this meant the inevitable shut-down for the whole group.

"I well remember rushing down the corridor to the engine room to get three out of the four diesels started up to cope with the station load - five minutes at least! Incidentally, the station mains were DC and mercury arc rectifiers were used to convert the incoming 415 volt AC into 220 volts DC. The two control rooms were powered by batteries. There were three sets of batteries, one on each Control room and one on charge. These had to be changed over from time to time by using three banks of knife switches - plenty of scope for the odd error there!"

"Round about D-day, the frequency of one of the transmitters was changed. Rumour had it that we were on the same frequency as Calais so that German aircraft could not use it for direction finding. The transmitter was 'switched on' from somewhere in London and the whole thing was called Operation Bareback - I never did find out too much about it - hush hush, you know!"

Before the war ended, Joe served as a Radio Mechanic in the Royal Signals - his National Service lasted for two years and eight months. On de-mob, he re-joined the BBC in Radio Outside Broadcasts for the period of the Olympic Games. Shortly after, he retrained as a Programme Engineer and worked as a Studio Manager at 200 Oxford Street for more than six years before becoming an Instructor with Staff Training for more than seven years.

In 1962, he got the job as Senior Station Manager Central Unit at Broadcast House and later as Operations Staff Organiser, Chief Production Services Manager and eventually Head of Programme Operations, Radio. He retired at the end of December 1983 - over forty years since joining.

"The two jobs I enjoyed most in the BBC were being a Transmitter Assistant at Washford and working as a Station Manager at 200 Oxford Street."

On retirement, Joe was able to concentrate more on watercolour painting and sold more than 550 pictures since then. He was elected a full Member of the Guild of Aviation Artists a couple of years ago and, in 1997, won the award for best watercolour.

"Who says there's not life after work?" he quipped.

"Joe was a very important and highly thought-of member and joined in any event we took part in," said Society of Ruislip Artists (SRA) Exhibition secretary Joyce Carpenter.

"Everyone loved his paintings, mainly of aeroplanes in watercolour, and our exhibitions won't be the same without them," she said.

"He came to our rescue recently when we needed a heavy-duty easel for one of our demonstrations."

Just like Bill Murrell, Joe Latham had a technically sharp and practical mind combined with a creative eye.

Landscaper, Electrician, Abstract Artist and Friend Colin Gardiner

Colin Russell Gardiner,
Teddy Bears Picnic,
1989, oil on board, 60 x 90 cm

Bill developed a lifelong friendship with Adelaide Hills abstract artist, Colin Russell Gardiner.

"He and I used to talk over his paintings and I used to tell him what I thought was wrong with them! He'd tell me off, of course. That went very well. Colin Gardiner became a very good friend."

"Colin was good fun, good company. I certainly saw a lot of his work."

Bill opened one of Colin Gardiner's exhibitions in Stirling in the early 1980s.

"It was a great honour for me and Colin was pleased with what I said."

"Art has meant a lot to me. I was always interested in going to art exhibitions and I was particularly interested in promoting Colin Gardiner, who was a new artist around town at the time."

Colin Russell Gardiner,

Warm Love,

1989, oil on board, 25 x 30 cm

Advice For Other Collectors

Bill always enjoyed talking about his collection and showing it to his family and friends.

It gave him great joy over his life. That passion has been passed down to his family, especially daughter Lucinda Murrell, who is an emerging abstract artist based at 'Birdsong Cottage', a beautiful artists' studio set in bushland on the outskirts of Darwin near Humpty Doo.

"I'd say start off slowly. Get the art you like, a gut liking. Stay with it. Satisfaction in what you buy," Bill concludes.

Bill Murrell's collection lives on and is now an important part of the Fairview Art Collection, a nationally significant collection of women artists from South Australia and Western Australia.

Colin Russell Gardiner,
Centre Point,
1989, oil on board, 46 x 62 cm

Selected Biographies of Artists in the Bill Murrell Art Collection

Jana Della-Noce, Gold Coast oil painter active 1980s.

Jana Della-Noce was of Italian background and trained in the Milan style. She ran a gallery on the Gold Coast in the 1980s. She is best known for her still life's.

Colin Russell Gardiner – South Australian Abstract Oil Painter active 1970s to 2010s

Born in Adelaide, South Australia in 1937, Colin Gardiner is a mostly self-taught impressionist and abstract landscape painter. He has exhibited his work in Adelaide since 1972. He passed away on 12 October 2015, aged 77 years, in Stirling, South Australia. Gardiner started painting at eight years old and, at 17 years, started at the South Australian School of Art but left to qualify as an electrician. In 1972, he took up full-time painting and worked under Polish/Australian artist Stan Ostoja-Kotkowski, including working on a giant mural *Spacescope 1970* installed at the Adelaide airport in 1970 and now in storage at the Art Gallery of South Australia. He has produced more than 600 works of art.

John Charles Goodchild – South Australian etching, pen and watercolour artist active 1920s to 1970s

John C. Goodchild was born 30 March 1898 and died 9 February 1980. He was a painter and art educator in South Australia who mastered the mediums of pen drawing, etching and watercolours. His wife, Doreen Goodchild (8 March 1900 – 28 February 1998), was also a significant South

Australian artist.

Goodchild was born in Southwark, London, the fourth son of John Goodchild (ca.1873 – 13 March 1939) and his wife Jessie Mary, née White (ca.1874 – 13 November 1948), and was educated at the Strand School, London. In 1913 the family emigrated to South Australia, where young John worked as a signwriter before enlisting in the First AIF in 1917, and served as a stretcher bearer with the 9th Field Ambulance in France, where he was wounded in 1918. While recuperating in hospital, he made a series of sketches for the Army field paper *Digger*. After the war, he was commissioned by the Australian Government to produce a series of thirty-six pen drawings of war graves for the book *Where Australians Rest*, published in Melbourne in 1920. Returning to Adelaide, he resumed studies with the South Australian School of Arts and Crafts, and produced a book of drawings of Adelaide landmarks and taught etching at the School of Arts and Crafts. In 1923, he held a one-man exhibition of his etchings in Adelaide and participated in an exhibition in Sydney.

In 1926, he married fellow South Australian artist Doreen Rowley. They studied at the Central School of Arts and Crafts in London for two years.

In 1929, they established a studio in Adelaide and John began exhibiting his watercolours with the South Australian Society of Arts of which he was a prominent member and its president 1937-1940. Around 1935, he and F. Millward Grey were commissioned by the South Australian Tourist Bureau to produce a series of posters, which were extensively used on railway station billboards and elsewhere. He was gazetted to the board of the Public Library, Museum and Art Gallery in 1938, and served in that capacity for much of the next thirty years. He served as principal of the School of Arts and Crafts from 1941 to 1945.

In March 1945, he and Max Ragless were commissioned by the Australian War Memorial board as South Australia's official war artists. He painted several watercolours of RAAF aircraft in flight. He was present at the signing of the Japanese surrender aboard the USS *Missouri* on 2 September 1945.

In 1946, he worked for the Adelaide *News* as staff cartoonist. He produced several works for commercial houses such as F. H. Faulding & Co, on the occasion of their centenary. He produced a series of oil paintings for Elder, Smith & Co. Ltd. depicting landmarks associated with the company's history.

He held several exhibitions, including in 1934 at the Newman Gallery. This group show was with sixteen other exhibitors, including John Shirlow, Victor Cobb, Oscar Binder, J. C. Goodhart, Sydney Ure Smith, Jessie C. Traill, Harold Herbert, Allan Jordan, Cyril Dillon and Charles Nuttall. Goodchild also designed the distinctive lamps and standards that grace the Adelaide City Bridge, King William Road, which opened in 1931.

T.G.B. (Theo) Hendricks, South Australian landscape oil painter active in the 1980s and 1990s.

T.G.B. (Theo) Hendricks was a South Australian landscape oil painter who was active in the McLaren Vale and Willunga regions south of Adelaide. He trained under David Driden and sold his works through Driden's McLaren Vale studio and Gallery, called "The Barn".

He signed his name TGBH. David Clyde Dridan (born 15 December 1932) was educated at St Peter's College and an Order of Australia was awarded in the 2007 New Year's awards, citing service to the arts and to the community. Driden's painting *Hills Landscape* (1969) is held at "Carrick Hill" as he was a great friend of Sir Edward 'Bill' Hayward and his wife Ursula, the original owners who built the historic residence in the suburb of Springfield, in Adelaide's foothills. Driden was later a member of the Carrick Hill Interim Committee, and founding member of the Carrick Hill Trust.

E. M. Hodge

E. M. Hodge, South Australian watercolourist active in the 1950s, 1960s and 1970s. Very little is known about this artist.

Joe Latham – Watercolourist from Ruislip in the United Kingdom, active 1980s to 2010s

The former BBC Radio Executive from Ruislip in the United Kingdom passed away on Friday 10th 2012 in Hillingdon, London, UK.

He was a watercolourist whose paintings of planes, trains and ships adorned galleries in Ruislip for more than a quarter of a century. His 'trade mark' scenes are of BBC Broadcast House and religious buildings. He was honoured at an exhibition, following his death in 2012 with six of his paintings on display at the Society of Ruislip Artists (SRA) exhibition in the Cow Byre, Manor Farm, Ruislip, running each day until Saturday, March 24, 2012.

Joe Latham, 85, of Seaford Close, had been a member of the Society of Ruislip Artists (SRA) since 1985 and a member of the Guild of Aviation Artists since 1997.

He was born and raised in Worcester and joined the BBC at 17 as a transmitter assistant. He soon moved to London and helped with the 1948 Olympic Games radio coverage.

Through his job, Joe met future wife Sylvia and they married in 1950. After raising two sons, Andrew and Charlie, in Southall, the couple moved to Ruislip in 1976.

It was when Joe retired in 1983 as head of programme operations for BBC Radio that he began to concentrate on his hobby of painting.

Joe specialised in watercolours and completed more than 20 sketchbook diaries and sold more than 550 pictures. He was also a member of the Colne Group and the Ickenham Art Society and even once won the Hillingdon Watercolour Challenge.

At SRA, Joe had been secretary, programme secretary, served on the selection committee and the hanging committee.

Joe and Sylvia were married for 61 years. As well as two sons, the couple had three granddaughters and two grandsons.

Joe died on February 10 at Hillingdon Hospital after a kidney infection. He was described as 'a cheerful, kind and lovely man'.

Timothy Messack
Portrait of Andrew Murrell
1987, oil on board, 76.5 x 56.0 cm.

Messack was a South Australian oil painter active in the 1950s to 1990s and a Finalist in the 1953 Archibald Prize with a self-portrait.

Andrew Douglas Ambrose Murrell – Oil Painter Active in South Australia in the 1980s

Bill's brother, South Australian oil painter Andrew Douglas Ambrose Murrell, b. 22 July 1945 had a brief but intense career as an artist that helped him overcome alcohol addiction while in rehabilitation at a halfway house in Semaphore from 1988-89.[2] He is the youngest son of Jack and Trixie Murrell.

He held a number of exhibitions, which sold out quickly, including at the Sailmakers Gallery in Port Adelaide.

He was a prominent South Australian art and antique dealer in the 1980s, operating out of the well-known *London House* in Strathalbyn, a charming heritage listed country town located in a village-like setting 60 kilometres from Adelaide.

A deeply spiritual man, many of his works were of Icons of Saints, including Mary and Jesus. His unique signature is an iconic representation of many religious symbols, including the word DOM, short for Dominus - the Latin word for master or God and the Cross of St Andrew in honour of his Scottish ancestry.

The oil painting *Mrs Brewster Jones' Garden in Victor Harbor* was originally commissioned by the mother of John and Rick Brewster Jones – founding brothers of one of Australia's most popular rock bands 'The Angels'.

This painting of the mother of Australian rock royalty brothers, standing still and stoically in her garden in 1988 captures a historical moment at complete odds with the high-energy mayhem of the

---

[2] Personal communication, Andrew Murrell, March 2019.

band's on-stage presence of its lead singer Doc Neeson.

The artist's stunning Monet-like use of colour and the handsome gilt frame make it a worthy addition to any art collection.

Andrew Murrell's own anti-establishment, irreverent and rebellious personality is reflected in the painting and captures an intergenerational moment that is subtly at odds with the changing social values of Adelaide society in the 1980s. A cultural identity expressed and tapped into so successfully by the performances and lyrics of the rock star sons of the subject matter.

Ultimately, the painting was not to Mrs Brewster Jones' traditional taste, and it was subsequently purchased by her good friend Beatrice Alice Fairfax Murrell (nee Calvert), mother of Andrew and Bill Murrell.

Mary M Wigg,
Doyles Sydney Harbour,
1963, oil on board, 20 x 25 cm.

Mary M. Wigg (nee Lamphee) – South Australian Artist 1940s – 1970s

Six works by the talented Mary M. Wigg who was an active oil painter from the 1940s to the 1970s were held in the Bill Murrell Art Collection. This was his largest collection of any individual artist.

Mary Millicent Lamphee was born at Kensington Park, South Australia, on 8 October 1904 to parents Phillip and Clara (nee Dunstan) Lamphee. Phillip was Manager of the English, Scottish & Australian Bank in Adelaide, an iconic well-respected financial institution.

Mary died in Adelaide on April 29 2001, aged 96 years. She was a South Australian artist active in the 1940s, 1950s and 1960s where she held several exhibitions, including one at the Walkerville Gallery opened by Sir Henry Newland in September 1963 where her oil works featured two Sydney Street scenes *Kings Cross* and *Old houses, Pyrmont* which art critics described as being drawn with assurance and clarity.[3]

She is best known for her landscapes, often undertaking trips to the Grampians in Victoria, and was a member of the South Australian Society of Arts. She exhibited *The Loft – Paradise* on May 2, 1961 and *King's Cross* on 7 May 1963 held at the Society of Arts Gallery, Institute Building in North Terrace, Adelaide opened by Allan Sierp on May 7, 1963.[4]

Other exhibitions followed in the Adelaide Festival of Arts - exhibition of Australian art, March 6-21, 1964[5] and a second exhibition at the Walkerville Gallery in 1967 where reviewers described her impressions as rather tight and air-less, painstakingly accurate, and becoming almost primitive in a piece titled *South Kensington*.[6]

Her works are typically oil on board and include diverse subjects such as Churches in well-known South Australian coastal locations like Goolwa.

Mary M. Wigg,
Mt Wellington - Hobart,
1963, oil on board, 20 x 25 cm.

Mary also painted South Australian coastal scenes such as Parsons Beach also known as Pareena beach, which lies immediately west of Waitpinga Hill head, and has stunning clifftop views of the 1.2 km long beach.

She married engineer and pilot Ronald Melrose Wigg M.E. on 20th June 1931 at St. Peter's College Chapel, Hackney, South Australia when he was 35 and she was 26. He was the grandson of well-known businessman and stationer E.S. Wigg, and they had three children.[7]

---

[3] *The Advertiser*, 24th September 1963, page 18, col. e
[4] Royal South Australian Society of Arts, Associates' and Lay Members' Exhibition May 7 - May 17th 1963, Exhibition Catalogue May 7 - May 17th 1963.
[5] Restaurant Gallery (Cox-Foys, Adelaide).
[6] *The Advertiser*, 3rd November 1967, page 40, col. e.
[7] *E.S. Wigg and His Successors* – Adelaide 1992 pg. 48 and 49.

Mary painted a Tidal Mill, built c. 1100 A.D., which was at Woodbridge, Suffolk on E.S. Wigg's original farm. E.S. is said to have lost the top of his finger there! This picture is published in the book on the family history of E.S Wigg.[8]

She went to Girton Girls School Adelaide and the Elder Conservatorium of Music. At Girton she met Jessamy Bruce, the woman Mary Wigg exhibited her paintings with in 1967. Jessamy and Mary also were of the same social set and went to the same dances.

She also played the and played the viola in the Adelaide Symphony Orchestra.[9]

Mary Wigg is one of Australia's unrecognised female artists. Never collected by institutional galleries, she would have been classified by the mostly male-dominated cultural elite at the time as an amateur and hobbyist not worthy of collecting by publicly funded institutions.

Coming from an upper-class, moneyed Adelaide family, she would have been classed as a part-timer whose art was merely a past-time of the rich and idle. This view would have been reinforced by social norms at the time, and she would have struggled to have been taken seriously by the art community at the time.

Yet her work is far from this. Her landscapes are rich and well-composed. They capture the essence of what it means to be Australian.

Her nude, speculated to be a self-portrait, and one of her early works while still at art school is particularly significant and stunning.

Mary Wigg is a great example of the hidden talents of Australian women artists whose body of work has largely been invisible to the Australian art world. She was proudly supported by art collector, Bill Murrell.

About the Author – Thomas A.C. Murrell

Thomas Murrell MBA, CSP is an art collector, broadcaster and an experienced Company Director.

He is the owner of The Fairview Art collection, a nationally significant collection of women's art from South Australia and Western Australia.

The focus of the collection is South Australian and West Australian women artists from the 1850s to the present day, which are housed in a 110-year-old heritage home, Fairview, in Subiaco. Notable artists in the collection include Marie Tuck (1866-1947), Jessamine Buxton (1895-1966), Mary M. Wigg (1904-2001), Nancy Sayer (1909-2005), Mavis Lightly (1911-1988), Dr Joan Janet Bayliss (1925-2003), Priscilla Blight (1926-1990), Joy Tomcala, Genevieve Berry, Aurelie Yeo, May Courtney O'Neill, Christine Davis, Deborah Zibah and Lene Makwana.

For more information, visit www.fairviewofsubiaco.com.au

*****

---

[8] Ibid, Pg. 6.
[9] Personal communication 2020, James Neil Melrose Badger, great nephew.

Appendix 2

My Norfolk Island Connection –
Searching for Meaning and Stories About James Morrisby, Ann Brooks, the slaver Anthony Calvert and convict turned sealer Joseph Murrell

by Bill Murrell

Introduction

During my time at Norfolk Island from 7th - 14th May, 2003, I visited five museums, spoke to the Norfolk Island Historian (Les Brown) twice and have since read Gillen & Flynn's work on the 1st & 2nd Fleets, plus 1788 by Chapman, and Hell & Paradise by Clarke plus other references such as Flynn's Settlement and Seditionists. In fact, I became quite fascinated, which led to my connection to Calvert - the ex-slave trader, and Joseph Murrell - a convict, then successful sealer.

Norfolk Island

Captain Cook discovered Norfolk Island in 1774 from the ship *Resolution*. He described Norfolk Island as "paradise with straight large pine trees, and flax growing."

Norfolk Island is 5 x 3 miles, a volcanic uprising from the very deep Norfolk trough from which the height to Mt Pitt on the island is greater than Mt Everest above sea level. Recently Australia and NZ have conducted a deep-water survey of this trough, photographing and netting about 100 new deep-water species.

In 1788 after the 1st Fleet arrived in Sydney (Port Jackson), they really struggled to feed themselves, so Governor Phillip dispatched nine convicts and eight free persons plus six women 'whose characters stood fairest' i.e. 23 persons 'the best of a bad lot' to set up Norfolk Island. They were to set up Norfolk Island as a garden to feed NSW and 'supply HM ships with masts and flax for sails'. James (Alias Jos/Joseph/John) Morrisby was selected on the second ship, probably as a blacksmith so he could shackle and unshackle the convict chains.

The market garden was successful, and by January 1789 a road was built from Sydney Bay Norfolk Island (now Kingston) to Anson Bay via Mt Pitt. This was the road James Morrisby and Ann Brooks would have trudged up and down for Friday musters and church roll call on Sundays to their allocated lot 57 and their later second lot of 34 acres granted on May 1802, No.62. These lots stretch from the Ferny Lane Road, at 1st indent around Norfolk Island's fine air strip right down to Watermill Creek. Well known Australian singer and Norfolk Island resident, Helen Reddy pointed out to me the old convict track on my visit.

The market produce was very successful with "bananas, oranges, sugar cane, rice, wheat, barley, pumpkins, potatoes, turnips, artichokes, lettuce, onions, leeks, celery and parsnips", were sent to Sydney NSW in 1789. I then question why can't they be grown in Norfolk Island today? Rats and pests.

By 1790 the Norfolk Island population had grown to 150. Then a disaster - the ship *Supply* unloaded in rough weather but the *Sirius,* flagship of the 1st Fleet (11 ships), was impaled on Ross Reef. This increased the population to 650. Food became very scarce. One week's ration was eaten in one meal by some convicts!

Manna from heaven arrived as mutton-birds flew in and nested around Mt Pitt. 2 - 3000 "Birds of Providence" a night were slaughtered. Famine was averted. 172,362 birds were killed in 1795 from April to July. The birds left, never to return. They nest now on Lord Howe Island!

In 1791, two Māori were kidnapped in New Zealand and brought to Norfolk Island to teach flax weaving, but it was not successful as the flax leaves were quite different from those used for woven garments in NZ.

Settlements

There were five major settlements on Norfolk Island:

1. **c1450s Polynesian**

    These were temporary rests on their travels through the Pacific Islands. Limited digs have revealed implements but not agriculture or villages. Norfolk Island archeologists want to search further, but have been banned by the Australian government. The argument is over whose land it is! Interesting.

2. **1st Penal Settlement 1788- 1810**

    When the settlement was disbanded James Monisby and his wife Ann left with Henry aged three years and other children on the ship *Porpoise* in 1806 for Van Diemen's Land, settling on a grant of 80 acres at Clarence Plains.

    On instructions, Governor Piper razed all buildings in 1810/14 and all left Norfolk Island by 1814. Some Governors were good such as King and Piper, others harsh to bestial. Major Foveaux, for example ordered 2000 lashes to one convict over three years. During 1788 -1812, he averaged 600 lashes/day on Norfolk Island.

1805 Freemasonry was founded by Sir Henry Brown Hayes, an Irish knight and political convict. James Morrisby probably was a founding member of Norfolk Island Freemasonry. I found proof of his continued membership in Van Diemen's Land.

3. 2nd Penal Settlement 1825 -1854

This settlement was set up with 57 convicts to build stone buildings, as we see many restored today, for the doubly convicted criminals.

The severest punishment short of death, was metered out by Governor Price and others. Again there were very very cruel Governors. By 1837 letters of severe cruelty were reaching Britain and calls to close down Norfolk Island. However, this did not occur until 1854 when it was abandoned and a few caretakers left.

4. Melanesian Mission and Pitcairn Resettlements 1856 - 1942

Bishop Selwyn of NZ Church of England established a large mission in 1866 on Norfolk Island as headquarters. St Barnabas Chapel was built in 1875 as a memorial to John Patterson who was killed in the Solomon Islands in 1871.

In 1856, 193 souls from Pitcairn Is. Arrived on *Morayshire* in June 1856, i.e. eight families; Christian, Quintal, Adams, McCoy, Young, Buffett, Bums, and Nobbs. Many Norfolk Islanders today claim to be a descendant and the names carry on. Mission and whaling were the main activities.

In 1930 Francis Chichester arrived in a Gypsy Moth seaplane on his epic flight around the world.

5. Commercial Airstrip 1942 - Now

On 25/12/42, the NZ Air Force first landed on the new airstrip. Norfolk Island was a strategic supply base for the Guadalcanal campaign. This opened up the island for tourism of today. "A little piece of Paradise in the Pacific".

Britain 1750s -1780s

The invention of the mechanized weaving loom in Britain caused great disruption in the country with many people losing their craft livelihood and being forced to move to the industrial cities. Many still could not find work, so begged, stole and got on with living as best they could.

There were challenges to status quo such as Gentry and Servitude, and to the Monarchy such as Thomas Paine's *The Rights of Man* in 1791. The Gordon Riots in 1780, plus losing the American War of Independence closed in 1775 the possibility of sending more convicts and political exiles to America (30,000 had been sent before this ceased in 1772). So the British government had to think of alternative places to send convicts as Canada and the West Indies refused requests to take convicts.

So, Lord Sydney and others had the brain wave to clear the prison hulks, where James Morrisby was sent on the 6 September 1784 and Joseph Murrell in 1784 in the Thames and set up a convict colony in Botany Bay. This quickly changed to Pt Jackson after arrival in 1788.

It is in this background that watchman James Morrisby must have clearly needed a piece of iron bar for his blacksmithing that on 6/7/1784 he tried to lever it from a domestic coal cellar barred window when he was caught. Next day, the Old Bailey sent him to Newgate prison and hence to a hulk named Censor. There he stayed working during the day on river clearance and dock repairs in conditions "harsh and difficult to endure".

The dispatch to Botany Bay on the 1st Fleet was described as a reckless act on the part of a desperate Ministry of Prime Minister, William Pitt, Cabinet and King George III.

Prior to this an ex-slave trader, Anthony Calvert was contracted to transport convicts in June 1786 in his ship *Recovery* to SW Africa and up the Gambia River to Hemaine Island in 1785. This was a failure as most died during transport or vanished into the bush on arrival. More about Calvert and the 2nd Fleet later!

The successful contractor for victualling the 11 ships of the 1st fleet was William Richardson Jnr, a wealthy London merchant and shipbroker, and friend of evangelist Christian and humanitarian Sir Charles Middleton and William Wilberforce of anti-slavery fame.

The same rations were provided as on the short trips to West Indies and no anti-scurvy food was included. Fortunately Capt. Arthur Phillip overrode this and included such food at the last moment.

It is interesting that Lind discovered the reasons for scurvy in 1747 and the effectiveness of oranges and citrus, but it was not until 1795 that the findings were accepted by the Royal Navy!

1st and 2nd Fleets

The voyage of the 1st Fleet was remarkably successful, with few deaths, most arrived healthy. Capt. Phillip encouraged exercise, fraternization, and controlled the few troublemakers. He also ensured the Fleet stayed in port on the journey with sufficient time to recover health and replenish supplies. Stores planning was very poor: "no ploughs, no gunpowder for muskets" the convicts were not told and 'poor tools only for trading for the New Guinea natives'. The axes would not hold their edge on the Australian gums.

The cost of the voyage was accurately accounted at £54,518-16S-1P for 770 convicts. In 1791, five out of 25 slave traders had rations low in vitamin C and calcium. Because of the high cost of the 1st Fleet, the Ministry decided to accept the low tender of Camden, Calvert and King. "A flat payment was stipulated for each convict embarked whether they survived the voyage or not." Hill wrote "The slave trade is merciful compared with what I have seen in this fleet", "the more they can withhold from the unhappy wretches, the more provisions they have to dispose of at a foreign market, and the earlier in the voyage they die, the longer they can draw the deceased's allowance to themselves". Camden, Calvert and King were paid only £22,370 for transporting 1250 convicts. From three ships of 1007, 267 died and 31% died on one ship. On arrival, 250 (or 25%) were hospitalized in Sydney. Capt. Donald Trail sold unused food for exorbitant prices under instructions of Camden, Calvert and King in Sydney.

The 3rd Fleet also contracted to Camden, Calvert and King had a high death rate of 10%.

The 4th Fleet was contracted to the original William Richards Jnr, and only 1 died out of 700.

Ann Brooks survived these harsh conditions on the 2nd Fleet, on the *Lady Juilana*. She was healthy enough to be kept on board in Sydney while it unloaded and reloaded fit convicts, marines, and supplies and sailed for Norfolk Island arriving there 7 August 1791. The population there at Norfolk Island was then 293 female + 228 male, this included convicts, marines, settlers and officials.

It is ironic that a John Howard in 1783 demanded prison reforms in England where typhus or goal fever was very prevalent because of unsanitary conditions.

In 1987, Robert Hughes in *The Fatal Shore* wrote of the *Surprise*, one of Camden, Calvert and King's fleet. "The starving convicts lay chilled to the bone on soaked bedding, unexercised, crusted with salt, shit and vomit, festering with scurvy and boils".

A long trial of Capt. D Trail occurred over 1791-2 without result. "The only punishment Camden, Calvert and King received was the slow payment of the money owing to them 2½ years after the contract was signed".

Anthony Calvert died in 1809.

Two Murrells sailed and survived in the 2nd Fleet. Joseph Murrell embarked *Scarborough* 10/11/1789. He eventually became a Captain of a Sealer, and was probably killed by aborigines in 1816.

Robert Murrell (1758 - 1790) also embarked on the *Scarborough* on 29/11/1789 but died on 27/7/1790 less than two months after landing.

Neither of these, Murrells nor Anthony Calvert are directly related and are included as interest only. Henry Morrisby, born 11 May 1803 on Norfolk Island, was baptized by Bishop Henry Fulton 26 June 1803 - is related.

JAMES MORRISBY (1757 – 1839)

Allan Lancelot, *James Morrisby (1757 – 1839). c. 1940s*
A convict who arrived with the First Fleet aboard the Scarborough in 1788, c 1822,
pencil and watercolour, 24 x 49 cm, oval. Presented by The Morrisby family, 1988.
AG5106. Collection: Tasmanian Museum and Art Gallery.

James Morrisby is a very interesting gateway ancestor. For it is through him that his many descendants in Australia and elsewhere pass into a wider and well-documented historical process. Not that anyone ever imagined James Morrisby appeared from nowhere. It was locating him on another web of family connections in another country that was to prove difficult.

The first attempt to do this was made by a Miss Morrisby in 1867. She had written from Tasmania to Katherine Fairfax Moresby, who was then either visiting or living in Melbourne. No doubt the similarity of the surnames prompted her letter. She was right in that fact. They are both versions of the same name and the Cumbrain village of Moresby is pronounced locally Morizbi. She told Katherine in the letter that her father's name was Henry and that he had been dead for ten years (he died in 1856). Her grandfather's name was James. We do not know which of Henry's three unmarried daughters took this step nor do we know what Katherine's reply was, though we do know she mentioned the matter to her uncle Admiral Sir Fairfax Moresby. But almost 30 years were to elapse before the next attempt was made.

This time the initiative came from England. In 1894 John Robert Morrisby (1832-1923), a cousin of the Miss Morrisby, who wrote to Katherine, received a letter from Matthew Fortescue Moresby, a son of Admiral Sir Fairfax Moresby and, formerly, Paymaster-in-Chief to the Royal Navy. Matthew explained he was a keen genealogist and recognised the identity of the surnames. He went on to say he had read about a Tasmanian Morrisby who commanded a colonial steamer. This was Henry Augustus Morrisby (1862-1931), a son of another Henry, a cousin of John's. An old mess-mate had given him John Robert's name and that of four of his relatives. He added: "I would be very much obliged if you would send me all you know of your descent and family. I am anxious to know about any living kinsmen I may have, particularly so as I believe your descendant is from the elder branch." He signed himself: "Your kinsman."

The Morrisby's in Tasmania were flattered by this letter and set out constructing a family tree. None of the first generation was alive but quite a lot of the second were. In a petition addressed to the Lieutenant-Governor of Tasmania, James Morrisby stated that he had 50 descendants of the second and third generation at the time of writing and asked for a further grant of land. The petition is undated but it was minuted by Lt. Governor Arthur and surrounded by documents dated 1828, so this is the likely date. The 50 descendants pose a problem. Four of his children were still alive and we know he had one grand-child by his sons at the time. Both his daughters were married, one for thirteen, the other for fifteen years. The first had six children and the second seven.

In addition, Ann Brooks, the mother of James' children had two sons before she lived with James, so he may have counted them amongst his descendants as he brought them up. James also married for the second time in 1816 to a forty-year-old woman, who also could have had children. Despite this, there were people around, who could fill in most of the details. They were a bit thin on James though. No one knew where he was born, what his father's name was or, for certain, that of his first wife. If they knew he had been a convict and come to Australia on the First Fleet they kept quiet about it. The family tree was duly sent off to Matthew Fortescue.

They received a family tree from him which, in his words, "showed the Moresby's, as Lords of Moresby in Cumberland for five hundred years till 1499, seventeen knights in direct succession." After that history gets a little vague. "I have as yet some fifteen individuals who cannot connect from that date. One, Clement Moresby, had three sons, Christopher, Clement and John. From Christopher, I think you must descend. I come direct from John."

Well this was not so. But what does appear true is that all those bearing the name Morrisby or a version of it constitute a single family which is a rare occurrence in English genealogy and descend from the ancient family. There are, of course, some gaps. One day, no doubt, they will be unraveled, but all the evidence points to a connection.

The tree that Matthew sent was duly tacked onto the beginning of the Tasmanian one. Matthew also obliged them with a coat of arms, which belonged to the ancient family, a crest, which was actually a Fairfax crest, a family seat in Cumberland – Moresby Hall complete with a resident ghost and a living knight, Admiral Sir John Moresby, son of Admiral Sir Fairfax. It was all heady stuff. This combined family tree was passed from hand to hand among the Tasmanian Morrisby's and laboriously copied out. Errors naturally crept in. A version had showed James Morrisby as having been born in 1750 when in fact he was really born in 1757 and the name of his first wife as Mary Donaldson. His second wife was given as "the daughter of a French businessman called Lavender". Her name was Ann Brooks, she was a convict and they never married as James was already married in England. Lavender was probably her mother's maiden name as she occasionally used it and it crops up as a second name in the next generation. Lavender is a French surname and Ann almost certainly came of Huguenot stock through her mother. Another version of the same tree showed James as having come from Hull. This is not far off the mark. He came from a small town some miles from Hull. On this tree his first wife's name is given as Mary.

On a visit to Tasmania in the late 1940's, Allan Lancelot (1878-1962) produced a water colour of James Morrisby. It is now in the Tasmanian Museum and Art Gallery.

The portrait is in profile. James has a determined jaw and a good head of hair, though it is receding. He is wearing a high-collar coat and some sort of ruff around his neck. He is between 65 and 70 years old. Alfred Rowland (1893-1957) tells the story that, when he was a boy, he had met an old man of 96 who remembered James Morrisby. James, according to the old man, "always wore fawn knee breeches, white hose and buckle shoes. He carried a gold cane and took snuff from a gold snuff-box." The old man also recalled that James "was very autocratic and often in a bad temper, especially when discussing the shortage of grain in the colony or the shortcomings of the administration."

So we have two pictures of James, one painted, one verbal. Nothing else survives of him, apart from his various appearances in the records. Still it is possible to get a general impression of him, at least in his later years. But his origins were sill obscure. All we knew for certain was that he came on the First Fleet.

The place to begin searching was the Old Bailey. He appeared there before Mr Justice Heath and a jury on July 7th, 1784 (Old Bailey Sessions Papers 1783-4. Trial number 694). The indictment read: "For that he, on the 6th of July, with force and arms one iron bar, weight 10lbs, value 10d, belonging to Thomas and William Morris, affixed to their dwelling house, feloniously did steal." There was another count: "For that he, a certain other iron bar, value 10d, belonging to them, affixed to their dwelling house, feloniously did break with intent to steal".

A servant gave evidence that she had risen at 3.30am and gone to the cellar to fetch some coal. While there, she noticed dirt coming in through one of the windows and then a stick being used to wedge one of the iron bars off the window. There was already enough daylight outside for her to see a hand pulling the bar free. Quietly the servant went up to the dining-room and opened a window, which was directly above the cellar window. There was a man there. She gave the alarm and an apprentice went out into the street, but the man had gone. Then he was seen returning but without the iron bar. The apprentice seized him and the master came out of the house to ask him what he was doing. He gave no reply. They saw he was wearing a watchman's coat and had a number 11 on it. Also, his staff was split and burst. James admitted being the watchman, so they conducted him to the watch-house.

Before he went in James is alleged to have said: "I have a wife and five children. If you will excuse me now I will never do the like again." The master said he could not and, later, the constable found the iron bar he had taken away.

James was a night watchman, paid by the parish to guard the very premises he had tried to break into. This no doubt, was heavily against him, for he was found guilty, despite the fact he claimed he was only an innocent bystander and produced three witnesses who gave him good character references. He also said he had been "between nine and ten years in the guards."

The sentence was to be transported to America for seven years. He was 27 years old.

What are we to make of this?

It seems a very amateurish sort of crime. The locality was given as the parish of St. Gregory by St. Paul in the Ward of Castle Baynard. This is St. Paul's churchyard, in those days a broad street of fashionable shops on the Thames side of St. Paul's cathedral. Unfortunately, it was almost totally destroyed during the Blitz in World War II. A London directory of 1784 puts Morris & Co, cabinetmakers, at Number 15 and a contemporary engraving shows this as a tall narrow building four stories high. It is difficult to see where the iron-bars were but the master, William Morris, said in his evidence that they were attached to the kerb.

So what was James up to?

It was the height of summer, when people were up and around early. And it was virtually daybreak. Perhaps he intended to sell the information about the unprotected window to someone. Perhaps he was only interested in stealing the iron bars. He didn't try to run away. Nor did he try to resist. Instead he said nothing. It was only when he was outside the watch-house that he realized the danger he was in. Prosecutions in those days were not launched by the State but by the victim. So he attempted to play on William Morris' sympathy. Hence the story, about the wife and five children. He was married but he only had one child, a daughter, Catherine Dorcas, born on March 11, 1784, some four months previously.

The one lead given in the transcript of the trial is James' statement that he had served in the guards. There were three regiment of guards in the British army then and the Third Regiment of Guards, later known as the Scots Guards, was stationed at the Tower of London three kilometers from St Paul's.

Accordingly, to the War Office Records, James Morrisby was entertained or enlisted in the Third Regiment of Guards at London on April 3rd, 1776, so he had been a soldier for eight years. His age was given as 20 (he was actually 19), his height as 5ft 7ins (1 metre 70 cms), his "complexion" and eyes brown, his trade as labourer (probably farm labourer), his character as "indifferent" and his place of birth as Cower, Yorkshire.

At first he was in No. 1 Company but he was later transferred, first to Colonel Wynyard's Company on March 24th, 1777 and shortly afterwards on April 4th, 1777 to No. 5 Company where he remained. During 1778 and 1779 Colonel Ogilvie was his commanding officer but, in December 1781, Major General Osborn took over. Nine days after his conviction at the Old Bailey James was discharged from the army.

Presumably he had lived in barracks at the Tower of London and, after his marriage, in married quarters. By combining the two family trees we can guess the name of his wife. It was probably Mary Donaldson. Their marriage took place, presumably in London, on November 20th, 1782. There was only one child of this union, Catherine, who was married on October 25th, 1807 at St. James, Duke's Place to William Alexander Davison. Duke's Place is not far from The Tower, so it would appear his wife and daughter remained in the area. Probably James' wife came from there in any case. This wedding, incidentally, might explain how James knew of it and, later of his wife's death (which allowed him to marry for the second time, not to Ann Brooks, who died in 1813 but to Eleanor Murphy.) William Alexander Davison shipped slop clothes to the convict settlements.

The other question is why did James become a night watchman?

This was before the days of an organized police force. Security, such as it was, resided in the hands of watchmen employed by the parish. Soldiers were used but not often. No doubt the extra money came in handy with another mouth to feed. Perhaps this was also the reason he attempted to steal the iron bar. It was worth, after all, 10 pence – a small but tidy sum.

After his conviction, on September 6th, 1784 he was delivered on board a hulk at Woolwich in the Thames.

Prison hulk at Woolwich in the Thames

The hulks were disused naval vessels, moored at various places and used as floating goals because the prisons were overcrowded. In the eyes of the law those on board "were on their way to America". Unfortunately the American War of Independence had effectively stopped transportation there which was mainly to Virginia and Maryland. So, while the Government canvassed possible alternatives, the hulks were pressed into service. Convicts slept on board and were farmed out to contractors during the day. Most of those at Woolwich were engaged in repairing the Royal Dockyard.

James Morrisby must have been a hardy specimen as the Lower Thames was notorious for its "fogs and miasmas" and the hulks were breeding grounds of fevers and epidemics. He managed to survive two and a half years under these difficult conditions until, finally, the authorities made up their minds to do something about what was rapidly becoming a scandal. On August 18th 1786, Lord Sydney sent a letter to the Lords Treasury, which set forth the King's pleasure that ships should be provided for carrying 750 felons to Botany Bay.

Why James was chosen is anybody's guess but, basically they only took the fit and the strong. Sometime in the Spring of 1787 – possibly April as the ships had assembled at Spithead in March – James and a number of other convicts were put into wagons and driven to Portsmouth 120 kilometers away. It could have taken three or four days. There they were rowed out to the ship that was to transport them beyond the seas.

HMS Scarborough

In James' case this was the *Scarborough*, a not inappropriate name as Scarborough is a seaside resort in Yorkshire not too far from where he was born. She was a chartered vessel of 430 tons – smaller than a Sydney Harbor ferry. Below decks the ship had been fitted out as for troops with hammocks, mess tables and wooden stools. Thick bulkheads about three feet high and studded with nails ran across between desks behind the main mast. They were provided with loopholes through which the guards could fire. The hatches were held down with crossbars, bolts and locks and the hatchways railed around from deck to deck with heavy oak. On the upper deck a barricade studded with iron prongs had been erected to prevent the crew having any dealings with the convicts. Sentinels were placed at the hatchways and there was an armed guard on the quarter deck.

James' last view of England was the chalk hills of the Isle of Wright, which he would have seen as he paced the deck for exercise. Then at 5am on May 13, 1787 the First Fleet slipped out of the Solent. Eight months later on January 26th, 1788 it dropped anchor in Sydney Cove, Port Jackson. The Scarborough entered the heads about six pm. The voyage had been slow but unusually healthy.

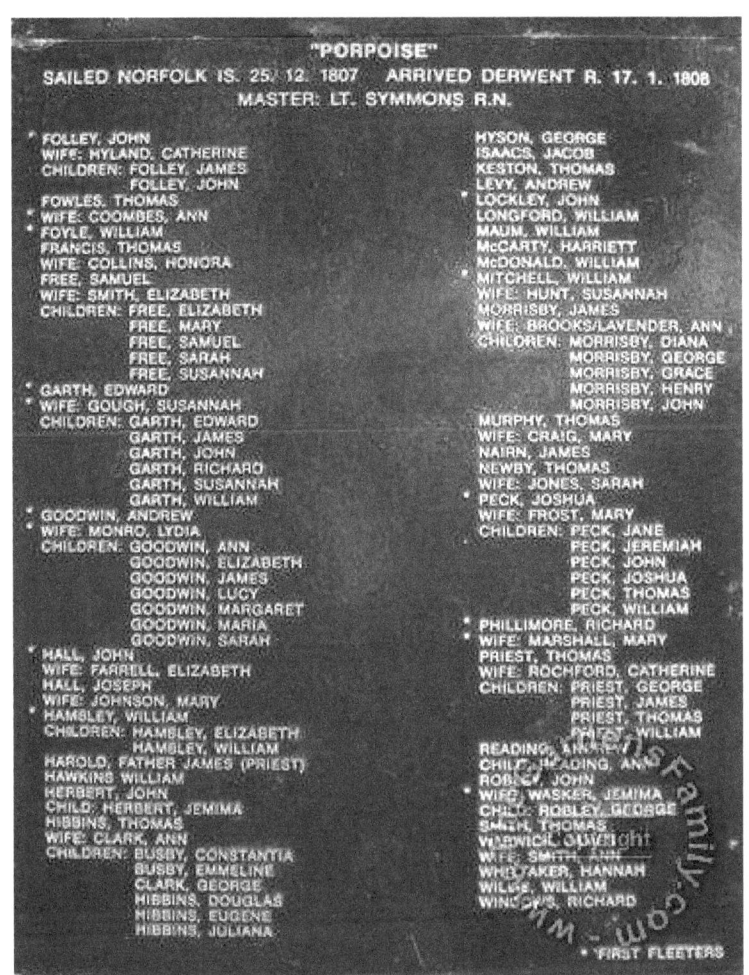

Morrisbys on *HMS Porpoise*.
Sailed Norfolk Island Christmas Day 1807
and arrived Derwent River 17th January 1808

Family Chart – Morrisby to Murrell

James MORRISBY b 23 Jan 1756 Cawood Yorkshire, England m 20 Nov 1752 London Mary Donaldson 1755 Transported 1st Fleet *Scarborough* m No record – Norfolk Island
Ann BROOKS nee LAVENDER 1790 Transported 2nd Fleet *Lady Juliana*
6th child **Henry MORRISBY** b 11 May 1803 Norfolk Island 1807 transported to Van Diemen's Land *Porpoise* with James and Ann Morrisby and other children
m **Elizabeth Mary MACK** 20 October 1824 d 20 October 1830
m **Christina SMITH** 15 June 1831 Henry d 25 March 1856, age 53 Christina d 4 April 1855, age 75 Buried St Matthews Rokeby, TAS
Catherine (Kate) MORRISBY b 1838 (Muddy Plains) d 1911

William Thomas CALVERT b 1840 (Geelong) d 1935
William Henry Fairfax CALVERT b 1872 d 1942 Married **Winifred WRIGHT**
Beatrice Alice CALVERT b 1901 (Huonville, Tasmania) d 1990 (Adelaide) Married 1926 **John William MURRELL** b 1900 (Geelong) d 1980 (Adelaide)
William John Calvert MURRELL b 8 November 1930 (Adelaide) m 4 May 1957 **Phillippa Wollaston** b 6 July 1936
Marc Wollaston MURRELL Wendell James MURRELL Lucinda Gay MURRELL William Ashley Randal MURRELL

Wendell James MURRELL	**Lucinda Gay MURRELL**	**William Ashley Randal MURRELL**
m Jill COLTON b Tullie Colton MURRELL b Hannah Kate MURRELL	b Hugo Nicolas Lindsay MURRELL	m Jane DOBBIE b Lily Grace MURRELL

Morrisby's Gum
A Threatened Legacy to James Morrisby and His Family
Now Under Threat

by Thomas Murrell

Morrisby's gum (*Eucalyptus morrisbyiis*) was first found on the Tasmanian farm of James Morrisby and his descendants. Although described by its colloquial name since European settlement it was officially described by scientists in 1939. Hence its name. It is a highly threatened tree from south-eastern Tasmania. Restricted to just two locations in the wild, near Cremorne and Risdon, south east of Hobart, this species is at imminent risk of extinction due to land clearing for agriculture and changes in the frequency of fires due to climate change.

Within the Cremorne area, the main stand is at Calverts Hill and several small nearby remnant stands, as well as from a small subpopulation 21 kilometres away in the Government Hills near Risdon.

According to the State Government of Tasmania, the Calverts Hill stand is close to being functionally extinct.

"There were 1915 mature trees in the Calverts Hill stand in 1991 and only seven mature trees were still alive in early 2018 (one dying) following a dramatic decline that started after 2005 and was first reported in 2014 at which time 70 to 80 per cent of mature trees had already died," said a report from the Threatened Species Section – Department of Primary Industries, Parks, Water and Environment, Tasmania.

The report found there were fewer than 30 mature trees in the wild that produce seed.

"The species appears to have been contracting to wetter gullies over time, exacerbated by the recent warmer and drier conditions associated with climate change. The species is highly palatable and once stressed, recovery is hampered by vertebrate and insect browsing that if left unchecked leads to the death of trees within years."

"While at imminent risk of extinction in the wild, the species is not likely to face extinction in the short to medium term due to ornamental and ex-situ plantings. The most immediate needs are to protect wild and planted seedlings at Calverts Hill to allow them to reach maturity and to ensure that the genetic variability of the species is maintained by supplementing and managing seed collections that can be used for future conservation actions," the report concluded.

A beautiful botanical watercolour of Morrisby's gum was commissioned in 2021 to celebrate its rarity. Margaret River artist, Christine Cresswell, who has links back to Tasmania, captured the beauty of this rare tree species. It is now part of The Fairview Art Collection and hangs proudly at historic 'Fairview' of Subiaco as a lasting legacy to both the tree and James Morrisby.

Christine Cresswell, *Morrisby's Gum*, 2021,
watercolour on paper, 21 x 15.5 cm.
From The Fairview Private Art Collection.

Cresswell is a botanical artist and keen gardener from Margaret River in Western Australia with family links back to Tasmania.

Appendix 3

Mother's Memoirs

Written by Beatrice Alice Fairfax ('Trixie') Murrell (nee Calvert) – (2/3/1901 – 4/6/1990)

A Vision to Visit Birmingham

In my early days living in Tasmania, I often dreamed of visiting England where my own mother, Winifred Calvert, nee Wright, had lived with her parents in Birmingham. She migrated to Australia in the 1880s at the age of 12, the only daughter with nine brothers.

Emma and Alfred Wright circa 1910 at "The Homestead", Niagra Park,
a suburb of the Central Coast region of New South Wales,
six kilometres north of Gosford's central business district and
on the northern branch of the Hawkesbury River.

**Standing in front of a plaque of my ancestor,
John Skirrow Wright,
in the vestibule of the Birmington, UK Town Hall.
Wright was a notable person and Mayor.**

How she was adored. They were very English and I remember so vividly my Grandfather Alfred Wright, who wrote entrancing letters and spoke such beautiful English and was a wonderful gardener. Wherever he went he made a garden, and yet he suffered very much from asthma. His curly beard, the flower in his buttonhole, and his frock coat and striped trousers were all such vivid memories.

I also remember seeing on the wall of their house the picture of a statue of another Englishman, who was tall and erect. This was my Great Grandfather, John Skirrow Wright (2 February 1822 – 15 April 1880). He was elected as a Member of Parliament for Nottingham/Birmingham to the House of Commons and also a member of the City Council of Birmingham and was a co-member with the famous Joseph Chamberlain of England.

He died tragically of a heart attack at a large Council meeting. The statue in the picture was erected by the workers of Birmingham and used to stand outside the Great Town Hall of Birmingham beside that of Queen Victoria for many years.

One of my great joys of visiting England was the realisation of one of my many dreams. It was to stand beside his bronze bust, which was erected of him in the foyer of the Birmingham Town Hall. He was a great leader, a great preacher and debater, a humble hospital visitor, often carrying books and posies of flowers to the Local Hospital on a Sunday afternoon after preaching in the Tabernacle in the morning. This great man owned a· Button Factory and he helped bring Bibles into Schools. He was a man of Great Faith in the Lord and Savior. When he died, thousands of people lined the route of his funeral. He was the friend of many. His death was a stunning blow to many of his committees and activities.

After his death, his son, Alfred, my grandfather decided to leave the partnership of his brother Frank and migrate to Australia. I still have in my possession a gold and black Mourning Bracelet, which my Grandmother and then my Mother possessed. They wore these when dear ones passed away.

My grandfather, Alfred Wright of Neutral Bay, Sydney, wrote me this letter in 1919 when I was 16.

```
My dear Trixie,

    Here's to -- what shall I say?  not the head
and the arms and the legs and the body, that goes
by the name of Trixie, to distinguish it from
other forms -- but here's to the Trixie that lives
in that body, and who makes it beautiful -- the
eyes to sparkle and the lips to smile, that which
speeds the feet to serve and the arms stretched out
to comfort and to shield.  She brings the care of
pity and sympathy and the laugh to make glad.  She
has that which plays the grace notes in life's
scales -- what shall we call it - the spirit - the
ego or what?  No, its just Trixie, the Trixie I
think of, and the Trixie I love.

    In all the years to come, I am not careful
that you remember me, all I want you to remember
and cherish is that this is what your grandfather
always thought and felt of you, to my daughter's
daughter, Trixie.

                                Alfred Wright.
```

Read by Rev. Reg. Piper at Trixie's funeral service in 1990

So many of these facets of my early childhood are being revealed now in this part of my life, even at this stage, in the year 1973. What memories, fragrant memories of beautiful letters of a loving mother, who loved and was beloved of her parents. An only daughter, she was loved and often later in my girlhood we visited Sydney.

My Grandfather and Grandmother thoroughly spoilt my sister and I with their care and affection in taking us to places of interest, saving the lovely navel oranges on a special tree for our visit. No one else must touch that fruit until my mother, sister and I arrived. She, in her devotion made, or had made sweet bonnets for Grandmother. I can remember the violets and the velvet pansies and the veiling tucked into theses bonnets that grandma wore. She was upright and slim and loved taking us shopping in the neighborhood. Everyone loved her. She was so proper and English. She made the most wonderful Boiled Custard I ever tasted. Now, most of my grandchildren hate boiled custard. I just love it!

This dream of my childhood really became real, when, after my marriage on the 30th December 1926 at St. John's Church, Hobart in Tasmania to a Civil Engineer, John William Murrell of Geelong, Victoria took us to the mainland and Adelaide. There we brought up our family of five children, of which two were doctors, one a nurse who married a doctor and one an engineer and one (the youngest) is in an Airways officer and later became a talented oil painter. Two daughters and three sons.

Beatrice "Trixie" Alice Calvert outside St John's Church, New Town, Hobart on the 30th of December in 1926 on her wedding day with two bridesmaids, Miss Mollie Calvert, sister of the bride, and Miss Iris Cuthbertson (Melbourne) cousin of the bridegroom, who were frocked alike in delphinium blue georgette frocks over silver lace, finished with diamante trimming and buckle, and wore silver turbans. They carried sheafs of delphiniums and wore long crystal bead necklets, gifts of the bridegroom.

Beatrice "Trixie" Alice Murrell with three of her five children and her sister, 1989. From left to right: Bill Murrell, Ruth Barbour, Trixie Murrell, Tim Murrell, Miss Mollie Calvert. Note artwork in background LHS, Andrew Douglas Ambrose Murrell, *Mrs Brewster Jones' Garden in Victor Harbor*, 1988, oil on board, 34 x 44 cm.

These 40 years were very happy ones with many up hills and down dales, which everyone in life goes through but always we had great Faith in God and I know He helped us over many hurdles which we ourselves could not have faced alone. We are still privileged to have our family around with their children, which number 11 grandchildren, and what joy these little ones bring into our lives.

Trixie Murrell and grandchildren.
Left to right: George Murrell, James Murrell, Simon Barbour, Marc Murrell, Tom Murrell, Trixie Murrell, Angela Barbour 1967

An Unexpected Family Tragedy

My sister Mollie and brother Douglas were living in The Huon Valley, Tasmania, when we suffered a bad loss. We were 19 and 20, and my brother 24 years old. My Mother and Father had gone to Sydney, really expecting to move there and buy a sheep property. My brother was engaged and would take over our apple orchard property, 'Forest Home' at Judbury in Southern Tasmania. My Mother (Winifred Calvert nee Wright) had a sudden illness and died very suddenly. I remember so vividly that day. She and my father were preparing to come home in a week. And instead, a car coming into the drive at 8 o'clock in the evening, bringing friends from Hobart, their faces so sad. It was to tell us Mother had passed away that afternoon in Sydney.

The awful news and heartache it was. I remember so well a sleepless night, (no sleeping pills in those days, or I don't remember them). I got up very early in the morning, and in my anguish, I remember going to the piano, playing some of the music Mother used to love. I was also learning singing from Mrs. Lucy Purches. Her husband was a cousin or nephew of Dame Nellie Melba. She and he were well known singers in Hobart. I played Mendelssohn's *Remembrance* and several other pieces and songs; one was *You in a Gondola When Loving is Sweet*. I believe those who were in the house were really brought to tears, but the music seemed to soothe my soul at this dreadful time of losing a most wonderful Mother. She incidentally was a very good trained nurse. I still have her credentials in that walnut letter box which her father's Bible Class in England had given her at aged 12 years, when she left England to live in Tasmania.

Many times I remember neighbours of our district coming to ask her to come and help when people were sick; she would go to them at any hour in the night. Our life seemed empty from then on-but we did have memories, memories of wonderful friends and relations coming to see us, bringing beautiful apple pies and cakes, even casseroles of meat to help us. She was buried in Rookwood Cemetery, SE Sydney. After my marriage, Jack and I went to Sydney. I took my lovely sheath of gladioli, which I carried at my wedding and managed to keep fresh enough to place on her grave.

In challenging times, this is the prayer I refer to most:

```
My Prayer and Thoughts of God:

The Light of God surrounds me,

The Love of God enfolds me,

The Presence of God watches over me,

The Power of God protects me,

Wherever I am God is, and I am safe,
    and I manifest my good now.

"EXPECT A MIRACLE"
```

Left: Read by Helen Murrell at Trixie's 'wake' at Tim and Pat Murrell's home after the funeral in 1990.

Beatrice "Trixie" Alice Calvert outside St John's Church, New Town, Hobart on the 30th of December in 1926 on her wedding day with her father, the Hon William Henry Fairfax Calvert MLC (14 February 1871 – 8 June 1942) and her sheath of gladioli, which she managed to keep fresh enough to place on her mother's grave in Sydney.

After my mother's passing, I remember going to a small Methodist Church two miles away one Sunday morning and feeling very close to God there, still full of sorrow. I asked Him to take my hand and lead me through my life. I felt so helpless and alone – and this I think He has done. I have failed Him often, left undone things I should have done and done things I should not have done, but always He has been there to help, my constant Friend and Savior.

My Mother, the Respected Nurse

There were many important letters, such as a letter from my Mother in Sydney, nursing her own Mother, and a few days later my Mother had died.

My Grandfather was a wonderful letter-writer. I was his only daughter's daughter, whom he adored, whom everyone adored in the district where she lived and nursed. When a very bad epidemic of Infantile Paralysis, now called Polio swept through the Huon District, my sister and I went down with the illness. I was left slightly paralysed, but my sister escaped with just the illness. For two years I was lame but my Mother nursed me and massaged me through those two years from when I was aged from five to seven years old. And there is not any trace of it now. It completely healed.

Life On the Orchard

My vivid memories of my life have been visiting the various apple shows. My Father was a great exhibitor of fruit.

In my childhood there were lovely all-day cricket matches, travelling often long distances as My Father and brother, Douglas, were keen cricketers. There was even a cricket team composed only of Calvert men at South Arm in Tasmania.

Travelling to Sydney on a ship with Mother, to visit my Grandmother and Grandfather Wright in their different homes, as they moved often was another fond memory.

Celebrating Christmas at South Arm, Tasmania to visit my Father's Father and his Wife in a lovely old house with cherry trees in the garden and gooseberries, with the lovely smell of their gorgeous pantry containing, ham, Christmas Cakes, and cinnamon biscuits. We had very few presents, but memorable days of happiness.

My Wedding Day on the 30th December 1926 at St. John's Church, Hobart was a dream come true. The help given me by my sister Mollie, my sister-in law Rowena, brother Douglas and so many other friends, because I had no Mother.

I wore a beautiful silver brocaded gown made in old-fashioned style, with a tight bodice, and full skirt which was wired at the hips forming an uneven hem, long tight sleeves finished with a pointed cuff. My long veil was of plain cut tulle, with a tiny wreath of orange buds finished with clusters at either side. My only ornament was a diamond and platinum wristlet watch, which was a gift of the bridegroom. I carried a bunch of white roses.

Going to Boarding School at Collegiate Girls School, Hobart and spending super holidays in the Midlands in Tasmania. Such lovely parties in a lovely old 'English' home and afternoon teas in lovely sitting rooms on sheep properties and watching polo matches with friends such as Gertie and Tom Green's families.

Travels Abroad in 1967

**Jack and Beatrice "Trixie" Murrell with Helen Murrell in London
on one of their many overseas trips.**

Our first trip was via a Greek ship *M.V. Patris*, via the Panama Canal, after my husband's retirement in 1966. Again, we had the thrill of meeting our son (Timothy) and his wife (Patricia) my daughter -in-law and two Grandsons (George and Tom) in England. Also, my brother and sister-in-law, who were visiting England from Tasmania. We also intended to visit our daughter Helen in India on the way home. Our shipboard voyage was most interesting, there were 40 Masonic people on board and many meetings were organised amongst the men folk, the wives joining in. We went via Sydney, Wellington New Zealand, then Tahiti. This enchanting island of tropical flora and fauna has changed somewhat with the French Air Force Base having based there. Prices seemed very high for food and goods. Our next Port of call was Panama and Balboa; this city was most interesting, visiting it late at night, as we were late arriving. There were many Indian shops, I bought a lovely Spanish doll and my husband bought a Panama hat.

I remember many Indian-owned shops and we were glad to return to the ship in the early hours of the morning. We received quite a bundle of mail. How we looked for news from home. Then leaving Panama, we passed through the Canal after a few days. What an experience! Especially to the men folk with engineering experience. Lunch was served on the Deck as a smorgasbord so as not to miss the grandeur of the Canal. Passing many ships so close by, and the glorious tropical trees and foliage right at the water's edge. It was all very unbelievable seeing our great ship come down the locks and to watch the mechanical mules clunking, drawing the great ship into the large locks. What an engineering feat! Then to Christobal, so brilliantly lit with light as it had taken us all day to go through the Canal itself. Then in the early hours of the morning, we saw in the distance, Caracas, the wonderful houses of all different hues of colour of Dutch style and most attractive. Here we hired a taxi to take us around the city, spending $1 for a small bottle of Coke, it was quite hot. Here they turned sea water into the water they use and drink. Lovely hotels with swimming pools and also we viewed the floating market of ships bringing all sorts of goods from South America. This was a most interesting place to visit and our last port of call until we berthed at Southampton.

There were many concerts on board ship and a very good entertaining officers, with a special Greek night of dancing and Fancy Dress Party, also a Hawaiian night, Children's Fancy Dress when a little boy was dressed as Adam with an apple on his head and fig leaf- very good. There were many swimming sports and plenty of activities. It was a very smooth trip, with glorious sunsets, wonderful united services on board, including many denominations taking part.

Then Southampton and our first glimpse of England and the countryside, going up by train to Waterloo, where our son and grandson met us. He took us to our flat at Hans Place, Kensington, which was to be our home for four months; with a large bed- sitting room, two very comfortable divan beds, a writing table, easy chairs, a small bathroom off the hallway and little kitchenette with fridge and small stove; all serviced with linen and crockery and a Spanish maid and very nice landlady, who looked after us so well. This flat was off Sloane Street, very near Harrods. How good it was to unpack and leave everything in our wardrobe as we did our trips around England and the Continent.

We went to Pont Street Church of Scotland quite often, a lovely church and very friendly; also to All Souls', Langham Place. We had so much to be thankful for in praising the Lord for all His Goodness to us in such a good trip, such interesting people and places to visit and to see one's family. They had a flat at Regents Park and we could visit regularly and they visited us too.

After a fortnight in London, we did an eight-day tour of Devon and Cornwall, that delightful part of England so well known by so many people. Never will I forget the cottages of thatched roofs, the little roads with close hedges, bluebells growing under trees and slopes. There was a lovely house with rhododendrons growing in the garden and climbing roses on the grey stone walls, all with their small glasshouses of geraniums and hanging baskets. So picturesque! We stopped and bought boxes of luscious strawberries and looked down at the cliffs of Tintagel Castle where King Arthur and his knights used to meet. The wonderful history of England one could never tire of this fascinating country. Even standing on Land's End, looking over on the Scilly Isles in the North Atlantic, a really rugged coastline where much of the smuggling used to trade things such as food and brandy from France into England. The lovely cities of Exeter, Bath and Well and their glorious Cathedrals. One could write chapters on these glorious places and history. The architecture and workmanship was a revelation to us. Oh! If only these cathedrals were being used by the people of today as they were used in the old days and God worshipped in the world as he should be; but so much of the material world is more important than worship these days. The places are kept going by the tourists giving their money for entrance fees and literature on stalls or perhaps they are helped by this method, as the maintenance of these glorious places must be considerable. May they be kept for many more years to come for people to enjoy and wander through their portals of wonder and worship.

Visiting such places as Penzance, St. Michael's Mount, an island of the mainland of Cornwall, Helston noted for the Flora Dance, that wonderful rollicking song and on to Plymouth, associated with Sir Francis Drake and his game of Bowls at the Hoe as the Spanish Armada was sighted, as well as later the departure of the Pilgrim Fathers in the Mayflower for America. How strange that we stayed in our recent visit to USA at the Mayflower Hotel in Los Angeles, which was adorned with pictures of the ship and relics of this epic journey of Christians from England to USA. We went on through country where Sir Walter Ralcigh spent his childhood, then visiting Bournemouth, that lovely seaside resort of parks, gardens and lovely houses, and avenues and avenues of rhododendrons. Then onwards, through the New Forrest where we enjoyed seeing the fascinating Ponies, some so tame and others quite wild, all colours and sizes. We adored Beaulieux Abbey and Lord Montague's collection of old cars; so, on to Lyndhurst where we stayed at a lovely hotel on the edge of the Forrest. Our last day on to London and we visited Winchester Cathedral. What a fascinating town with the lovely stream and quaint Bridge behind the Cathedral, in which Jane Austen is buried. There was also a large school, a chapel as a memorial of the Crimean War and also Mary Sumner House, the lady who started in her sitting room a meeting of young mothers and children which later became known as the Mothers' Union of the Church of England. Now there are different groups all over the world. I count it a privilege to belong to this wonderful organisation where mothers and children of the Church can meet for Prayer and Fellowship with each other. Next, we went on to the great new Cathedral of Guildford on top of the hill, where again loving bands of worshippers the world over, had done tapestry kneelers for this great place - so many patterns of beautiful tapestry work.

Then we came home to our haven of rest, our delightful flat and spent the next two weeks in and around London. We had a boat trip on the Thames, visited Kew gardens, saw our son and his family again and also my brother, Douglas and his wife, Rowena at the Royal Overseas Club. What a wonderful place this is for meeting folk from all over the world also the English-Speaking Union and the Victoria League. They were also helpful in making overseas visitors feel welcome in this large city of London and in England.

Whilst looking at Buckingham Palace at the Changing of the Guard, we caught a glimpse of Her Majesty the Queen going out to unveil a tablet memorial to the late Queen Mary. The Queen looked really lovely as she always does. We visited Chelsea Hospital for the Founders' Day ceremony when Lord Montgomery was the speaker. Later, watching the Trooping of the Colour parade we marveled at the wonderful patience of the London Policemen in coping with crowds. It was such a sight of pageantry. We were also fortunate to have an invitation to a Commonwealth reception at Marlborough House where the Duke and Duchess of Kent were present and many other interesting people - a consulting engineer and his wife, Jean, diplomatic service personnel, people from India, who lived in Bombay. We worshipped in the Guards Chapel, which had been completely bombed in 1944 on a Sunday morning during the reading of the lesson so many lives lost, such a hallowed place and now beautifully rebuilt. We also visited the Tower of London, seeing the glorious Crown jewels, then to the British and Foreign Bible Society and their 2000 copies of Bibles in different languages and translations including Papua and New Guinea and hearing the stories of many of the early translators of the English Bible. We also met D.G. Watson and Mr Ashley who had been out to Australia and many people who had been connected with this great Society.

The art treasures that are in England, with pictures, books and works of art, one cannot describe adequately. One has to see them to behold their beauty. We visited Windsor Castle, near the Thames, the sweet town of Windsor, Eton and Eton College and the Ascot Mile and avenue of trees, the Long Walk of Windsor Great Park. We wound around the lovely countryside to the American Air Force Memorial overlooking Runnymede. This really moved me, a simple building the many windows looking onto the Valley where the planes come into Heathrow. I liked the little Chapel of Peace, with prayer desks and such quietness, then reading in the Visitors Books were such harrowing phrases as 'Where so much was given by so few'; and another writing, 'I felt nearer my loved one here than anywhere else' were written by loved ones of those who had sacrificed their lives for us and all men. Inscribed in columns around the semicircular walls were the names of 20,000 airmen who died or were missing, remembered here overlooking the fields and hills where the Magna Charta, the Great Charter of English Freedom had been signed many years before.

At a delightful reception at Australia House, Sir Alex and Lady Downer being the hosts, we met many friends and fellow travellers also present from South Australia; one felt like being at home in Adelaide.

Tours of Scotland

We passed through Baldock and Uppingham, a great public school where Jeremy Taylor preached to Charles 1st. It was a different country to Devon and Cornwall, but lovely with Brier

Rose hedges, Ragged Robin and Cow Parsley lining the roads. There was a Floral Festival at Leicester Cathedral and many nurseries outside the town. Melton Mowbray reminded me of my school days, holidaying on a sheep property in Tasmania at Melton Mowbray, where they had numerous Hunts of Foxes with the Hounds and Horses. Then an overnight stop at Darlington, where Robert Stephenson's steam train was viewed. We went over the slopes and glades and being Sunday morning, we had arisen early to partake of Holy Communion at Holy Trinity Church in Darlington. Then on to Dryburgh Abbey where there was a glorious service in progress in memory of Sir Carl Hewes, with massed bands playing. Sir Walter Scott is buried here between the ruins and on the green lawns, the birds were chirping. The glorious hymns as 'Abide with Me', echoing over the hills were a real joy. It was a short service but very uplifting. To our souls and bodies.

So on to Melrose, then Edinburgh, so gaunt that great city but so grand and good and true. It was lovely to be amongst the Scottish people and 'My Ain Folk'. We had a wonderful Scotch guide on our tours of this great city and so to Holyrood Palace, where the Queen regularly entertains. There were lovely bright flowers in all the rooms matching each colour scheme. We climbed the tower where Mary, Queen of Scots slept and where David Rizzio was murdered. She took herself over to the Castle where James 6th of Scotland, to be James 1st of England was born and baptized as a Roman Catholic. Then we went on to the Cathedral where the great long windows depict the Life of Christ and the Chapel, where the Knights of the order of the Thistle sit, were glorious carvings. We then visited the Castle on the hill, the War Memorial St. Margaret's Chapel and the wonderful jewels and armour, all connected with so much history.

On leaving Edinburgh, we went to Allen Water Hotel situated in a lovely position on a hill. We wandered down to the Bridge and Banks of Allen Water. Sixty years ago in our sitting/dining room at Forest Home in the Huon district of Tasmania, we used to gather around the piano singing 'on the banks of Allen Water'. What memories we had as we leaned over the bridge and saw the lovely running stream, with the great Stirling Castle, standing out like a sentinel on the distant sky line. Passing Port Augustus, we saw the house near Stirling of the TV series of 'Dr. Finlay's Casebook'.

We visited the Island of Skye. What scenery as we skirted the lakes before arriving at Kyle of Lochalshel. Then we went across on the Ferry to the Isle of Skye, and after a trip via Arundale to Portree, an all day trip around the island. Flora McLeod's Castle of Dunvegan, 700 years old, is fortified be the sea and Loch against invaders. She has many associations in Australia, it was very interesting. Then wending our way back again, through the Cuillin Mountains, never will I forget the heather on the hills in the distance. We went on to stay with friends, as we were leaving for home and had so much packing to do. We were so disappointed to be leaving the Highlands.

We viewed the Great hydro-Electric Scheme, Lock Rannoch and Lock Kinnock, the salmon breeding grounds and on to the Pass of Killecrankie, where the great battles were fought between James 1st and Graham of Cloverhouse. Blair Athol Castle was an experience- over 100 rooms and much armour, with deer roaming on the moors surrounding this glorious castle. We saw letters written by James, Earl of Derby before his execution for his faith in God. They were written in Gaelic. It was very moving to read the translation. He showed no bitterness, but was willing to die for what he believed-his faith in his God. The hillsides and roadsides were lined with yellow-brown bracken and gorse, behind were the great fir forest used for timber and Scots pines. We passed Kincraig and this brought back memories of lovely home, also called Kincraig, belonging to our friends, Mr and Mrs K. Ford near Mt Lofty station, South Australia. This lovely residence had a lift in it, which made it unique. We stayed for two nights at Nairne on the water, a lovely town. From here we did our trip to John of Groat's, through Caithness and Golspic. We saw the Orkneys quite clearly and Scapa Flow, where the German Fleet surrendered to the Allies in the First World War. We also saw the Castle of Mey, the home of Elizabeth, the Queen Mother. On over the Peat fields to Thurso, then we went through some isolated country to Inverness. We saw again Dunrobin Castle, belonging to the Duke of Sutherland. Then on to Culloden, where the great battle between the English and the Scots was fought, which involved many clans under Bonnie Prince Charles against Montrose, Duke of Cumberland, - 'Sweet William as he was called the 'Stinking Billie'; hence the name of 'Sweet William' for the very attractive flowers. Along the shores of Loch Ness we saw the highland cattle too, then on to the Caledonian Canal and the Great Monument for Commandos, who trained in this area and did so much during the Second World War.

We went on south to Fort Augustus, saw the Abbey School and that lovely place Fort William. Here we had the loveliest roast beef I've ever tasted- Scottish of course, and saw the Great Glen Cattle Ranch and beyond was Ben Nevis, 4,400 ft high, and other snowcapped mountains. Then we stayed at the lovely Loch Awe Hotel on the side of the Loch. The very picturesque drive through the mist and past lochs to Loch Lomond brought back memories of the song 'By the Bonnie banks of Loch Lomond', which we used to sing on Sunday evenings at home as a family. We would gather around the piano at Port Road, Thebarton singing these songs as I played them from one of my several books of songs and music. The one with the songs had a brownish hard cover and the hard-backed dark blue covered book contained my favourite music of a more classical style: Brahms, Mendelssohn, and Chopin. Later Ruth and Helen would play from these books. Ruth was a much better pianist than Helen. Who knows where these books are now after all the family moves? Ben Lomond and Inverary Castle belong to the Duke of Argyll. From the tiny village of Luss on the edge of the Loch, we enjoyed a cruise on Loch Lomond. We then passed Glasgow and the Forth Bridge, staying at a small place called Symington. We took photos of the lovely gardens of the hotel, full of antiques and coloured glass, all attractively displayed.

Back to England

Then, we went on to the Lake District, passing Carlisle, to Keswick and memories of Thomas Carlyle, the essayist and writer, whose home is by Coniston Water. We had a delightful hotel at Keswick and bought some delicious shortbread. Then we went on to visit Grassmere and that sweet place where Wordsworth spent much time and the church and cemetery where he was buried. Dove Cottage was the name of Wordsworth's cottage. Then we went along Lake Windermere, associated with Sir Donald Campbell's attempts at speed boat records, the last being fatal; and on into Kendal, where the Bronte sisters went to school. Further south we passed Bradford and Huddersfield, before coming to Buxton in Derbyshire. It was a lovely Spa town, great culture, lovely shops, hotels and theatres. Soon we were on our way back to London, and into our own homey flat enjoying the mail from home in Australia.

Next day, we saw the Rose Show at Alexandra Palace. What an aroma of scents! The array of colours had to be seen to be believed! We also heard that Great Evangelist, Billy Graham at Earl's Court that evening. He gave a wonderful address, the text from Mark 8 v.24-25. The man looked up and said: 'Yes, I can see people, but they look like trees walking about.' Jesus again placed his hands on the man's eyes. This time the man looked intently, his eyesight returned, and he saw everything clearly. Good News Bible. This address was relayed to many cities in Britain. How privileged we were to hear him. This great man has done so much for His Lord in this world and age. We thank God for his life and witness and pray that he may be kept in health and strength for many years to come.

We visited Cirencester and were guests of Mr and Mrs Benson, members of the Victoria League. He was a Commander in the Navy, and an old Etonian. They had four children, two at Eton, they were such gracious people; Mrs. Benson taking us to the Floral Festival at the Duke of Beaufort's home at Badminton where the famous Horse Trials are held. We also visited 'Starway'. The lovely home of Mr. and Lady Violet Benson, Mrs Benson, our host's Mother in their 14th and 15th century home. He is brother to the Earl of Wymyss, who lives in Scotland. There were priceless antiques and furniture and china in the house with a lovely sweeping lawn and a church on the property. We enjoyed a Masque Concert in the old 13th century Tithe Barn and also enjoyed seeing a game of Polo, that popular English sport. It was a really lovely weekend in that glorious part of England, the Cotswolds. We will never forget the hospitality and kindness showered on us, complete strangers, in the beautiful countryside.

We were honoured to be invited to the House of Lords reception, being received by the Lady Dunrossil and her son, also a Lord. It was also wonderful to see the Centre Court at Wimbledon. What an experience to enjoy strawberries and cream there! That day we saw John Newcombe defeat Fletcher, and two Australian girls defeated two American girls; we also saw the Duchess of Kent in the Royal Box. On another great occasion we visited Cambridge with the English Speaking Union and had a lovely lunch, soup, salmon with tartare sauce and dessert, at St. John's College Dining Hall. We also saw King's College Chapel. I just wished we could have attended a service there to hear the choir.

Another memorable occasion was to attend the Garden Party at Buckingham Palace; to walk through the entrance and come out the other side on to the sweeping lawns with over 6,000 people there. The Queen looked lovely in green chiffon and green chiffon beret type hat. It was a lovely afternoon, but we were very foot weary on arrival back at our own flat. We often said 'Thank you' for that flat and bath of hot water to refresh us, just a plain cup of tea and something simple for a meal which we prepared ourselves

We visited Earl's Court again for the Royal Tournament: a wonderful spectacle of Horsemanship and entertainment. We had dinner with friends at Regent Palace, carving our own dinner, a lovely meal.

Now! Our Tour of the Continent to that great city of Prague.

Tour of the Continent

How fortunate we are with lovely weather, interesting travelling companions.

Our tour started from Liverpool Street Station, by train to Harwich, where we joined Avalon Ship across the Channel to Hook of Holland. The Coach included many folk from U.S.A., Canada, and Hong Kong with two New Zealand couples and ourselves. We had a lovely run to Amsterdam, a trip on the canals, lunching at The Hague. Holland is so clean and fresh looking. We were amazed at the number of bicycles everywhere, also the fresh curtained windows and window boxes of flowers. I really wanted to put window boxes on every house when I returned to Adelaide and Australia. After lunch at The Hague we arrived at Arnhem, where the great Battle of 1944 was fought in the Second World War. Was it a war in vain; so many lives were lost: 'At the going down of the sun, and in the morning, we will remember them.' These lines come to me when visiting these places of history. Then to Washaf, which was 90 per cent bombed during the war, but now we enjoyed the lovely shops as we walked along the streets in the evening.

At Cologne, we bought the cuckoo clocks for the family and ourselves. I have always wanted a cuckoo clock and ours has dancing girls as well. The country we passed through was farmland growing potatoes, spinach, barley, oats between little German towns. As we passed along, I must mention the statues of Christ and His Mother and the Christ-Child, standing on the roadsides or overlooking the fields. We visited numerous very interesting cities with quaint arched bridges, and water-pumps in the Market Square. Renowned for the trials of the War Criminals after World War Two, was Nuremburg. Then, over the border at 4pm where we were held up for an hour or so by very important looking guards, so arriving at Hotel Flora at 8pm in time for dinner we were very tired. We were very tired of veal, veal, veal for our meals too!

Prague is a wonderful city; we were fortunate to visit it just before the big military coup a year later. We stayed here two nights, visiting the Great Castle, which was an old monastery, where there were great archives of literature and Bibles in all languages from all over the world. The monks were forbidden to read some of the Protestant books. The ceilings consisted of paintings of the life of Christ, of the disciples and from the Bible. It was a really glorious building overlooking the city. We saw the Presidential Palace with official looking guards, the Chapel in the palace and the Cathedral, which was named St. Vitus Cathedral. As a young monk, St. Vitus was burned with oil which caused a shaking disease, called St. Vitus' Dance. It is also the place on which the story and carol of 'Good King Wenceslaus' is based. The people of Prague are 80 per cent Roman Catholic and 20 per cent Protestant. John Huss, an early Reformer, preached here in the Bethlehem Church. We visited the Town Square, where the clock struck midday, the figures of Christ and His disciples moved in a row across the clock-face. It was glorious to hear the church bells ringing. We also went to the Jewish Quarter of the town, the synagogue and cemetery, where there was a memorial of all Jewish people murdered by Hitler's orders up to the year 1942. Over 77,000 names are printed on the walls in a perfect mosaic pattern of print. It was a really emotional place to visit, memories we would like to forget, but what dreadful memories for so many people.

Our Guide could speak French and had resided in Paris for two years. She was very interesting and helped us quite a lot. So many of the guides are university trained folk and very intellectual. One

Courier was Belgian-born. We had given up our passports on arrival and when leaving Prague, quite a way out of town we picked up our Courier, who had our passports all intact. Soon again, at the border of Austria, we were to lose them again but they were soon returned. The drive through Moravia and Bohemia through Bennus and then to Vienna was full of interest. The avenues of cherry trees bordering the roads, still no fences, all community owned, large farms, fields of sunflowers, were so picturesque. Memories of our trip were brought back when we viewed the lovely picture of Sophia Loren and the fields and fields of sunflowers. Then we went through the stark country of the Second World War again. We were amused at the storks nesting on the tops of the chimneys and the women wearing black working in the fields and sweeping the streets of the villages.

Vienna, in this glorious city we had a lovely night in a very nice hotel, all chandeliers and formal in every way with a lovely dinner and such courtesy. After dinner we viewed the city at night, all the churches, palaces and the Opera House were beautifully illuminated. The river Danube was quite near. We went to a delightful Honheiger, a restaurant in a garden under the trees, and of course, we were serenaded with music, those glorious songs of Strauss, including Vienna Woods and the Barcarolle. We arrived back at our hotel at 12.30a.m. at the end of a Perfect Day!

The next day we visited the Great Palace of Emperor Franz Josef and all his ancestors. What a glorious place of quiet dignity. All the rooms were full of mirrors and gold furniture and chandeliers, so beautiful. The Palace contained a thousand rooms but he only lived in 300 of them! We also saw the wonderful Opera House of scarlet and gold which was bombed during World War Two, but restored in a very dignified way including a beautiful marble staircase.

Then we went on to Budapest and Hungary where we experienced quite hot weather. It was flat country again with many walnut and cherry trees lining the road, crops of maize, which is made into cornflour for export, and sweetcorn. Here at Budapest Hotel another large tour had arrived from the U.S.A.. It was July 22nd, my youngest son's birthday. How our memories go back to those we love; we have been remembering them all and our friends in prayer. It has been such a privilege to visit these interesting places amongst such good folk from U.S.A., Australia, New Zealand and Hong Kong. Looking over the Danube again, we saw that lovely city which is Buda on one side of the river and Pest on the other. We also crossed to Margaret Island and saw the Roman Amphitheatre, 2,000 years old.

Ships trade up and down the Danube into the Black Sea. Hungarians are very happy folk. We met a local man who helped us with our shopping and language. He was a lawyer, but was teaching and seemed very depressed with conditions. How different they are in our Country! As we crossed the border our coach was searched and we were all glad to be clear of restrictions. So, on we went to Lake Ballaton. Literally thousands of people were lining the shores of the Lake and in the very shallow water. We were glad to sit in the shade and cool of the Hotel foyer and have cool drinks. The road follows the Lake for 45 miles, with camps with coloured awnings and houses lining the road, it all looked so clean and cheerful. We had lunch at a restaurant at the Lakeside under a huge walnut tree: more goose soup and veal, which I could not like. Travelling on, again the country was very flat with maize, corn and collective farming. The women, dressed in black, were sitting outside their cottages, which all needed a fresh coat of paint, looked so poor. We passed some young Army folk and a few hillsides of grapes and the various flocks of geese and herds of cattle. Then, we went on to that new city of Zagreb with 750,000 people, full of flats, gaunt not very attractive. We were really only there to sleep, so cannot judge the place. We had a very modem Hotel, which was a complete change.

Now the country is changing, as the road climbs and winds through hills, passing big fir trees and oaks and the Gava Caves. There are still more crucifixes and statues guarding the fields and roadsides all through the Continent. It was great to stop at Timprana for cool drinks. We met two charming young people from Yugoslavia, who could just understand our English. How they would love to come out to Australia!

Our next stop was Venice. Passing through the borders of Yugoslavia and Italy was much easier than the other borders we had encountered. We stayed at Lido Island, so crossed by ferry. It was very hot but had wonderful service at the Hotel Astorias. We even breakfasted, Continental style, under the grape vine pergola. Our housemaid also served iced tea and lemon, which was so much appreciated. The gondolas, St. Mark's Square and all the usual sites of Venice were a wonderful experience. I still have my lovely Venetian Glass Candlesticks and Bowl of gold-leafed grapes on stems on my mahogany sideboard to remind me of Venice. We spent some of my husband's retirement cheque on this, which I never regret and also some linen, all of which were passed on to Ruth Barbour.

Then on we went to Milan where we saw the mural painting of the Last Supper by Leonardo Da Vinci and to Verona where there was the balcony of Romeo and Juliet. It was a lovely little town to shop in, but never enough time. We had wonderful service in Italy, people were very courteous and attentive everywhere. We saw Lake Como, then we were driven on into Switzerland and Berne, that a lovely city with performing bears, unusual buildings and clocks. It was all so quaint along the winding river an arc, like a horseshoe around the town. At Interlarken we bought watches, a fob watch and two men's watches. We then drove through the great Gotthard Pass, but it was not cold, just glorious mountains scenery in the sunshine. We passed waterfalls, Swiss cattle mountain goats and the glorious Swiss houses with their gay window boxes as well as skiers and beautiful wildflowers.

On we went through Alsace Lorraine to Strassburg, a very quaint town, where we walked around the canal and quaint houses. Our bedroom was a real attic, with china plaques and interesting check curtains. We had a lovely egg and bacon pie, which was so nice after so much veal, chicken, salads and cheeses. Then we were on the way to Paris, a lovely city but everything very expensive. We did the Paris by night trip and sat on the Boulevards eating our rolls and coffee. We went to the Art Centre on the hill, Monmarte, and visited the Sacre Coeur Roman Catholic Church as it was Sunday. It was nice to ponder and worship in the Lord's church although we did not understand the French Preacher. We have kept so well and so thankful to the Lord for His help and strength and the wonderful travelling companions from U.S.A., N.Z. and Hong Kong. The Wardoque Art galleries were so well explained by guides, especially the wonderful painting by Rubens. We also visited Versailles. Leaving Paris in the early morning we passed through Flanders and Calais, never dreaming that in six years' time we would be revisiting Calais during another trip to England. How good the Lord has been! Can I ever thank Him enough for His Goodness and Mercy which endureth for ever and ever? After crossing the Channel we were excited to see the White Cliffs of Dover again. Then we caught the train to Victoria Station, and got a taxi, one of those wonderful blessings of London, taxis and their drivers, to our flat. So, a wonderful three-week tour of the Continent had ended, with many memories of friendships made.

We did many visits to shops, including Harrods, that wonderful store quite near our flat. We took our grandsons George and Tom to Chessington Zoo, saw a cricket match at Lord's, visited Kings Road, Chelsea with it's exclusive shops of clothes, china, antiques. We also visited friends in Beckenham, Kent and an old 11th century church; Mr & Mrs. Bowker, who had lived in Sudan at one time. We had a lovely trip by train to Canterbury, viewing the Cathedral and town, then we caught the bus to Heme Bay and back to Surrey and Fordwick. We were shown this quaint place by a Mr and Mrs Williams, whom we met on route. This is the charm of England: so many places and so interesting for example Brighton, the Pier and the Great Pavillion with all its treasures and the antique shops in the Lanes. I could spend hour and hours there.

Again, we visited our favourite church, All Souls, Langham Place, so like our own Holy Trinity in Adelaide. We also visited the Church Missionary Society office at Waterloo and the B.M.M.F. office in Kennington. We did a Frame's tour of Oxford, Warwick Castle, and Stratford -on-Avon, visiting Shakespeare's birthplace, and Ann Hathaway's Cottage, which brought back so many memories of Home and our little Hathaway cottage at Stirling in South Australia. When we returned home we sold it on account of the large English garden, which got too much for us.

Another day trip was to Birmingham and Coventry Cathedral. That new Cathedral so hallowed with the ruins around and the stark burnt Cross, with the words 'Forgive them' inscribed across the bar. Every stone seems to be a witness too God and the welding together of people and nations. The Germans gave much to the building of the new Cathedral; nails from the fallen, burnt roof form a small cross; the baptismal font from Billileban. We had evensong here in the twilight, the service taken by an African minister. It was a day of remembrance: 'From the rising of the sun even to the going down of the same, My Name shall be great amongst you.' Malachi ch.I:1

Our second trip to the Continent was a very short one, but very beautiful doing Austria and Switzerland and a wonderful day tour around Lake Geneva. We stayed at Villinervre, on the lake-side with mountains at the back and those glorious Swiss valleys. The houses on the slopes of Vivey were those of many famous people- Charlie Chaplin, Sophia Loren, Noel Coward. The esplanade at Montreux was fascinating amongst the gorgeous homes, as well as the cruise boats lit up at night touring the lakes. In Geneva itself, we saw the house where Churchill used to stay and where he did many of his paintings. The terraces of vineyards and the lovely white house with Florentine coloured blinds were so picturesque. The glorious Swiss scenery seen from the little cable cars climbing up and climbing up, going from one mountain top to another was amazing. Some of the chalets were carved wood and of course a picture with window boxes. We passed up the Gotthard Pass on to Interlaken and then to Lake Lucerne, making our next stop on the side of a lake. From here we went to the water's edge to Telleschapel. The boats come by and they have a service in this little chapel, in memory of William Tell. Next day we went through the glorious mountains and roads of forest to Lake Zurich and on to the Rhine Falls. What a treat that was! We wandered around meeting some local folk in national dress, it was such a charming place. We then passed many ski lodges on the slopes, one had 40 ski lifts. We went on into Baveria seeing the amazing castles along the way and the town of Oberammegau, where the wonderful play on the Life of Christ is held every 10 years. The little town of Merona was gorgeous, with the river running through it and a lovely formal garden. From a cafe on the hill, we saw the city lights of the quaint town of Innsbruch on the River Inn. We enjoyed a lovely concert in the part where the trees were all floodlit. Another wonderful experience here was to see of a little tiny church on the hillside, it looked all alone and miles away, but several times a year pilgrimages are made up there when the people who believe and worship meet for fellowship together.

Our trip back to London was uneventful. Then it was only a few weeks before starting our package tour back to Australia, taking in most capital cities and spending three days in each on our way home. We flew to Amsterdam and then to Paris both cities which we had visited before. We enjoyed watching a lovely opera 'Faust' at the famously beautiful Opera House in Paris. We flew from Orly Airport to Rome, this glorious city of statues, fountains and alleyways. We stayed at a quaint hotel, Hotel Lumera', but it was hard to make ourselves understood. We went to a lovely church service at St. Andrew's Presbytery-on-the-Hill. Everyone there was very friendly; it was lovely to worship Christ in this way in Rome, even though we were just passing through. How good He has been in caring for us during this wonderful trip to England. Now we are on our way home. We visited the seaside by train to Lido, but the sand was very grey and not golden or white like our Australian beaches. I believe that in Northern Italy the beaches are much better. Leaving Rome airport for Athens we had another wonderful lunch on board - roast duck, salads, icecream, blancmange and coffee rolls. We were wonderfully well looked after all the way. Our hotel in Athens was facing the main Park and Gardens. How strange that our morning reading was from 1 Corinthians chapters 1,2,3, so appropriate for Athens and its surroundings. We visited Areopagus where St. Paul preached with only one convert, and thoroughly enjoyed the beautiful sound and light concert sitting on the hillside.

India to See Helen

From Athens we flew to Beirut, Lebanon where we bought an old Persian carpet, probably its origin was Tabriz. Helen had the carpet repaired by an expert in Kensington, London, and this lovely rug is in her living room at 8 Lawkland.

From Beirut we flew to Delhi, India, where Helen met us at the airport. After some sightseeing including, the Red Fort, including the 'Son et Luminere', Chandi Chowk, the Jamma Masjid Mosque and a modern Hindu Temple, where Jack accepted a garland of orange marigolds put around his neck. One day we went by train to Agra and Jack chatted up a Hindh sadhu, holy man, whilst on the train. We were thrilled to see the beauty of the Taj Mahal. Helen and I both reminisced about the floral 'Taj' float produced by a group of ladies from Prospect or Enfield, I think, for the Floral procession during the Centenary celebrations of South Australia in 1936. The three of us flew to

Lucknow where we stayed at a typical old Raj type hotel, with a stuffed tiger in the entrance hall. Jack thought it was great, but I got a shock every time we re-entered the hotel.

We did some sightseeing whilst Helen attended the BMMF/Interserve North India Field Conference. We joined in some of the Bible Studies led by Rev. Subodh Sahu and other 'open' sessions. It was a great opportunity to meet some of Helen's friends and colleagues. Usually, this conference in late August or September was held at Edgehill, Landour, Mussorie in the Himalayan foothills. Helen was disappointed of the change in venue as she had hoped to show us something of the magnificent Mountains. After the conference we travelled by FIRST class train to Ludhiana. We had a 4-berth compartment I thought, to ourselves, until a Sikh gentleman was directed in with us. However, we coped very well although it was a hot dusty trip. We were amazed by the crowds on the station and the coolies carrying our luggage. Fortunately, Helen had arranged for transport from CMC to meet us. We stayed with Dr. Kenneth and Mrs Betty Scott in their home, The Director's Bungalow. Again, we had the opportunity to meet other medical colleagues of Helen and we were quite amazed at the extent of the hospital and college buildings. Helen arranged through local doctors for a taxi to take the three of us a hundred or so miles north to the Bahkra Nangal Dam, the largest earth work walled dam in the world at the time. Jack was quite impressed with the dam but not with the trip or driver as we had two punctures. During the repair of one of the tyres on the way back in Chandigah we had a pleasant snack meal and icecream in the coolness of Kwality's, and eventually arrived safely back to CMC Ludhiana. We also visited Amritsar by train to see the Golden Temple, the Holy shine of the Sikh religion. Helen went with them back to Delhi and waved goodbye as we caught the plane on the last lap of our journey back to Adelaide.

Jack and Trixie Murrell

About Beatrice ('Trixie') Alice Fairfax Calvert (2/3/1903 - 4/6/1990)

Trixie was born in Tasmania, the second child of William Henry Fairfax Calvert and Winifred Wright who had married in 1898. The family lived at 'Forest Home', a large apple growing property, in the Huon Valley. There were many Calvert farmers in south east Tasmania, including others in the Huon, at South Arm and Bruny Island. Many were prize winning orchardists and representatives on fruit boards. They were also very keen cricketers and there was an entire cricket team at South Arm made up of Calverts. The Calvert families were heavily involved with the church (Anglican) and Calvert women were kind and warm hearted, hospitable and hard workers. The Wrights were strong baptists.

Trixie and her siblings, Douglas and Mollie, helped on the orchard. Trixie had polio as a child and was lame from age five years to seven but recovered completely. Trixie and Mollie went to the local primary school at Ranelagh and a local Methodist Sunday School. They later boarded at The Collegiate School, Hobart. Trixie played piano and sat a number of Trinity College of Music, London (Hobart Centre) examinations. Trixie had an idyllic childhood on the orchard, attending cricket matches, visiting her Calvert relatives at the different farms, including Christmases at the Calvert grandparents at Clifton, and visiting her Wright grandparents in Sydney.

The Wrights had been living in Tasmania at Wyre Forest, New Norfolk at the time of Trixie's parents' marriage. At some stage Winifred's parents, Alfred and Emma, moved to Sydney. The family often visited them. Trixie's parents had been considering moving to NSW.

During a trip to Sydney in 1922 to look at sheep properties, Winifred developed 'quinsy' and after a short illness died on 24 November. Trixie was 19-years-old. The family was devastated. Trixie's father, William married again in 1925 and Trixie never really got on well with her new step-mother.

Mollie and Trixie lived in Mercer Street, Hobart. Trixie met Jack Murrell on board ship travelling between Tasmania and Melbourne. They were engaged for two years before marrying.

After their honeymoon they went to live in Adelaide.

They initially lived in apartments in Norwood, then at Port Road, Thebarton. Then "Hathaway", 43 Ayers Hill Rd, Stirling, 90 Devereux Rd, Beaumont purchased 14 July 1970 and sold 9 August 1974, then Tusmore Avenue. In 1980 they moved to 8/10 Newland St, Victor Harbor.

There were many pets at Port Road, including chickens, cats, dogs, cows and horses, and there was a large garden with flowers, vegetables and fruit trees. Trixie loved flowers and flower arranging. Trixie and Jack were very hospitable, having many parties and dinners. The family had interstate holidays including to Geelong and Tasmania to see relatives.

Trixie and Jack were strong Christians and were invited by Reverend Fulford to worship at Holy Trinity Church, Adelaide, not far from their house at Port Road. They subsequently became parishioners and the children attended Sunday School there. Their association with Trinity spanned many years. Jack was on the parish council for 31 years (1947 - 1978) and chairman for at least half this period. He was instrumental in hiring ministers Graham Delbridge, Lance Shilton and Paul Barnett. Trixie was on the flower roster and they were involved in supporting missionary work especially that of the Bible and Medical Missionary Fellowship (BMMF) and Church Missionary Society (CMS). Trixie was a long-term member of the Mothers' Union. She was involved in recommencing the Mothers' Union at Trinity in 1950. During her membership she served as treasurer and vice president and was a member of the Diocesan Mothers' Union executive. From 1960 - 1969 she was Mothers' Union Diocesan Convenor of hospital visiting at the Royal Adelaide Hospital. She was also a visitor to patients at Glenside Hospital. As a thanksgiving for the life and work of Trixie and Jack, Ruth and Bob Barbour donated pew cushions to Holy Trinity Church in 1996. They were well loved parishioners.

Jack worked in the Engineering and Water Supply Department in South Australia for many years, retiring in 1966. He held various positions including Engineer for Sewerage and Deputy Engineer in Chief. He was president of the South Australian Division of the Australian Institute of Engineers and also of the Town Planning Institute. This position was indicative of the esteem in which he was held by his colleagues and his eminence in his profession. He was a member of many committees, including school committees of those his children attended and professional societies. After his retirement he held various temporary positions as a consulting engineer. He played bowls and was president of the Adelaide Oval Bowling Club. He was also a member of the freemasons for many years.

Trixie and Jack loved sport – especially Australian Rules Football, Jack's old team Norwood in particular and cricket. They were members of Adelaide Oval. They loved family and adored their 11 grandchildren. They had a lolly jar for the grandchildren and a doll's house for the granddaughters. Trixie didn't like the grandchildren saying 'shut up' and she'd tell her grandchildren she would wash their mouths out with soap. They hosted big family Christmas gatherings at Trixie and Jack's or at one or other of their children's homes. "Hathaway" at Stirling had a big cold climate garden which the grandchildren loved to explore.

They had many trips back to Tasmania, including in 1979. Trixie's sister, Mollie, died in April 1975 from breast cancer.

Trixie and Jack celebrated their golden wedding anniversary on December 30, 1976 with family at the Alpine Restaurant, South Parklands, Adelaide.

Jack died not long after they moved to Victor Harbor in 1980 of complications related to aplastic anaemia. 'Lead us heavenly father lead us' was a favourite hymn sung at Trixie and Jack's wedding and at Jack's funeral.

Trixie stayed on at Victor Harbor. She became an active member of the community and drove regularly up to Adelaide to see friends and family. She attended St Augustine's Church and became an active member of their Mothers' Union. They made a new Mothers' Union banner in memory of Trixie's life and dedication to Christian work. She became interested in spinning and weaving, was a member of the local spinners and weavers club and spun and knitted woollen clothing for family.

She continued to travel with trips to Tasmania in February 1983 and in 1985 for a Calvert reunion where she gave a speech at the launch of Beth Robb's book. On March 2, 1983 there was a family party for her 80th birthday.

On one of her visits to see daughter Helen in the UK in 1983/1984 she met Yvonne Farrow (1913 – 1997) at a bus stop near Helen's house. Yvonne lived at 'Ashleigh', Stoke Park Ave, Farnham Royal, a lovely house with large garden near Helen. Trixie and Yvonne became great pals and the family got to know Yvonne also. Yvonne used to make cards and bookmarks with flowers she had pressed. Trixie also got to know some of Yvonne's friends such as Freda Armstrong who lived at 'Christmas Tee Cottage'. Yvonne at least once came out to Australia to see Trixie. In one conversation, they worked out that during World War I Trixie wrapped apples for export in tissue paper with the Calvert logo, and that Yvonne, as there was a shortage at that time, had used the same wrappers as toilet paper!

Calvert Apple Labels recycled as toilet paper during the war in the UK.

Trixie and Jack's many friends included Maisie Newland, who was Jan Muecke's mother and was from Tasmania. Bessie Hopkins and many others from Trinity were part of a close-knit community.

Bessie Reiger, Doris Schafer, Doris Ford and Betty Forwood were other close and adored friends.

Trixie died in 1990 of severe acute pulmonary oedema occurring as a result of ischaemic heart disease, though she had still been very mentally and physically active and independent.

Mollie Maughan Calvert, Trixie and Jack Murrell are buried at Centennial Park Cemetery, Adelaide.

About John Skirrow Wright (1822-1880), Alfred Wright (1846) and Eric Wright (1879 -)

John Wright (of Preston, England) married Jane Fawcett (1772 - 1811 died Liverpool). Jane Fawcett's parents were John Fawcett and Susannah Skirrow. This may have been the John Fawcett (1740 - 1817), originally from Yorkshire, who wrote hymns.

John Wright and Jane Fawcett had children including Edward Fawcett Wright.

Edward Fawcett Wright (1799 born Yorkshire - 1856) married Ann Wilson (died 1857). They had children including John Skirrow Wright (1822 - 1880). Edward and Ann are buried in Key Hill Cemetery, Birmingham.

John Skirrow Wright (1822 born London - 1880 died Birmingham) married Sarah Tyrer (1818 - 1893). John Skirrow Wright was a prominent social reformer in Birmingham. A statue of him was erected in Birmingham. This was later replaced by a bust in the Council House. John and Sarah are buried in Key Hill Cemetery Birmingham. Children of John Skirrow Wright and Sarah Tyrer (born in UK): Egbert, Alfred (1846 - 20/12/1920), Amy, Kate, Frank, Harold.

Alfred Wright (1846 born Birmingham - 20/12/1920 died Sydney), married in 1867 in Birmingham UK, Emma Maughan Smith (1842 born Birmingham – 20/7/1926 died Sydney).

In the 1871 and 1881 censuses of England and Wales Alfred is listed as being a button manufacturer. They migrated from Birmingham on the *Pekin* arriving in Victoria in July 1883 with their nine children. They lived in Tasmania for 16 years. Wyre Forest, New Norfolk 1898 at time of marriage of their only daughter Winifred to W.H.F. Calvert. then in Sydney. Alfred loved gardening. Children:

- Winifred (Winnie) (17/2/1870 - 24/11/1922). Winifred received training as a probationary nurse March 1891 – February 1893 and passed relevant examinations at Hobart General Hospital. On 9/11/1898 Winifred married William Henry Fairfax (WHF) Calvert in Hobart. They lived in Tasmania and had three children Douglas, Beatrice, Mollie.
- Walter born about 1870. Married Gertie Pillgrem. Auntie Elsie Pillgrem from Fingal Tasmania was friends with Trixie and Jack Murrell. She often visited Adelaide in the winter. Andrew was very fond of her. She was Gertie Pillgrem's sister and sister-in-law of Walter Wright. Elsie's siblings drowned in a boat accident in Tasmania. She died around 1962, 63 or 64 age 90.
- Percy born about 1872. Age 22 when married in 1895
- Norman born about 1875
- Oscar born 1876
- Eric born 1879. Eric Wright was an artist and two-time Archibald Prize finalist
- Kenneth born 1879
- Archibald 1880
- Reginald 1881-1947
- 2 more males

Winifred Calvert and Alfred Wright are buried in the Baptist section of Rockwood Cemetery, Sydney.

Appendix 4

Letters of Bill Murrell from USA to Adelaide
17th September 1952 to 10th of June 1953

Hotel Wellington,
<u>NEW YORK.</u> U.S.A.
17/9/52.

Dear Jane,

I was all smiles to-day when I walked into the morning lecture and the Chairman handed me three letters, one from Dad, Tim and yourself, (the one you sent from W.A. to home). It was grand to receive my first letters from Australia – now 12,500 miles away. Well, this is my sixth day in New York, and I guess you would like to hear a little about things so far.

Well, for details of the flight to San Francisco (S.F.), ask Tim to read you the letter. Generally, I was glad when I stopped flying, as I was getting quite giddy, and my nose bled (not badly). The other three students were affected the same way.

First impressions of Los Angeles. A very large sprawling place, composed of hundreds of small towns just like Adelaide! A smooth scrumptious (not literally) sultry voice of a slow southern drawl echoed over the speakers making all the announcements. She made us a little fidgety with her "come hither" voice. The service while having a meal at the airport was "out of this world" to us. We have even seen much better while on the train.

The trip (flying) to S.F. was the most interesting of any flying we did, most picturesque. I hope I have some good colour shots of the Sierras. Now, S.F. reminded me of Sydney – marvellous bridges, water all about, terrific apartments and grand hotels (we looked over the four main ones). I had an address which I fortunately looked up, and I guess I travelled 200 miles sight-seeing in their '50 model "Kaiser". I had a sore finger ever since, as I crushed the tip of the left forefinger in the door lock and bent back half of the nail.

After hectic 20 hours in S.F. we eventually caught the train – the Californian "Zephyr" (C.Z.), the world's best tourist train. Gee, am I sick of the world's best this, the world's best that, the world's "largest that", etc. etc.!! This railroad was really good (so was the beaut. Zephyrette that bandaged my finger for three days). Heating, ventilation, fan, radio, etc. in each compartment, in fact so many gadgets that we often used to put on wrong switches. Americans are gadget made. Next time you see a "National Geographic", have a look at the C.Z. "Vista Domes". We sat in these most of the days, and began to get to know some American people, including other students returning for winter semester. Again there was one superb woman, but she was very standoffish (unusual for the girls here). Perhaps a few lines about this topic might interest you (it has me). Generally, women here are striking. They "make up" marvellously. Everyone does – 12 years to 72 years. I have only seen one female out of that age group "undressed" as they call it. Black suits seem to be the fashion. Shoes are ankle affairs that remind me of about 1920 – and they call it advancement.

Imitation jewellery here is prolific. Everyone has three or four gaudy bulky rings (one for high school graduation, and another for college etc. and they wear them all, even the men). Clothes seem expensive. I've seen several girls with the nail polish that Jill had, but here they know what to wear it with, and it didn't look out of place. Colours are terrifically bright. Men's shirts, phew!

I haven't taken any women out yet, so I can't tell you anything more about them. I have arranged a date in Chicago the week-end after next with a girl who openly told me she was interested in me.

Doesn't look as if I have room for the Zephyr trip and New York.

Generalizations:- U.S. Cars, cars, and even more cars. The difference between a poor worker and a rich American? The latter pays a fellow to wash his "Cadillac", but the poor man has to wash his own. The main aim in life is: 1. to own a car, 2. a television set and 3. never stop moving. At 3 o'clock in the morning, looking out from our hotel window in 7th Avenue, New York, is like Rundle Street at about 11.30 a.m. on Saturdays.

Guess that is all I can fit in for now.

Lots of love,

(Sgd.) BILL.

<u>NEW YORK.</u>
20/9/52.

Dear Family,

It was grand to receive your letters a few days ago, although they made my stomach a little queer. I thank you, and please continue writing about anything.

Now, San Francisco. We landed just before Senator Stevenson (running for Democrats) arrived. My, what a show! Banners, newsreel & T.V. cameras, loud speakers, photographers, press men and police cyclists with sirens, trudgeons and even loaded revolvers in a great procession of about 50 current model (all types and gaudy colours) convertibles. We didn't wait, so caught a bus to the hotel. The Airways do not supply that free here, it cost us 1.25 dollars & 25 cents tip. We knew we were in America then.

The Hotel St. Francis was most luxurious and the service excellent. I immediately rang up the South's to get rid of the wretched awkward parcel. While waiting for Mrs. South (Kip.) I had a much needed bath, then heard a terrific din of loud speakers. On looking out of the windows I heard "one minute from now you will have the honour of seeing Senator Stevenson pass before you" (on his way from the Airport to give his first campaign tour address at S.F. City Hall). Exactly one minute later sirens, police, traffic hooters (and jams) and the long line of pageantry, and finally, Senator Stevenson. I swallowed and resigned myself to the fact that I just have to accept the American approach in doing anything.

Vin. Came in a little later and took me for a drive around S.F. (got into several traffic jams, where everyone just leans on their horns until the mess sorts itself out. I don't think the noise really helps!) across the beautiful Golden Gate Bridge (six lanes, minimum speed 45 m.p.h.) to their home at Marin County.

In the centre of San Francisco Bay lay Alcatraz Federal Penitentiary, a very sinister looking place (no one has ever escaped).

Marin County is a copy of an English village, quite picturesque. I commented about likeness to England, and could feel that I had injured the American's pride. England cannot be compared with mighty America. Australians are accepted, Englishmen, for whom we have been mistaken often, are only tolerated. Don't get too wild, Mother.

The dinner was quickly prepared (in ½ - hour) from frozen foods and tasted well. I was sorry that I had not got my land legs and my appetite back. The South's home was neatly set out; they have two cars and a private aeroplane, yet are by no means wealthy. Vin. Drove me all about Marin County, down to the Airport, to see his plane, to a "Super Market" (tell you about these and "Automats" some other time).

During this drive I managed to slam the door on my forefinger. Since, I have had to receive medical attention (it is not broken, but badly bruised, and I will loose the nail). It has hampered me quite a lot, as it's hard not to knock it. The infection and pain has gone, and I guess that it's only a matter of time before the nail falls off and a new one grows. Don't worry, it's O.K.

Back to San Francisco. After dinner we drove in the "Kaiser" back to the Hotel and picked the others up and toured the city. We went "downtown" (i.e. around the city streets), then across to Oakland, via the famous Oakland Bay Bridge (a marvellous structure 8 ½ miles), to "Calemount Hotel" and saw this castle palace; also, my first T.V. show (horrible). It has a beautiful view across the Bay to the glittering lights of the city. This reminded me of being on the North Shore of Sydney (say Mosman) and looking across, the only difference being an arch bridge instead of graceful suspension type, as popular here.

Returning on lower deck of bridge we called in at the control tower and had the lighting, policing, tolling and traffic control systems explained to us. Next we went to "Mark Hopkins" Hotel, probably the most popular of all places. It's central, and on the highest point of the peninsular, and being itself about 25 stories high, one gets a magnificent panorama from the cocktail bar on top. I could work out the street layout quite easily.

Next, we crossed the road to the "Farmount" Hotel, and this place is most interesting because of its number of unusual rooms (dancing and cocktails) catering for all tastes. An English "Birch Room", "Venetian Room" and "Cirque Room", the Spanish "Papagayo Room" and South Seas "Tonga Room" (this has a pool within the dance floor 50' x 30' on which floats a raft on which the musicians and hula girls play and dance – most captivating! Then the last place we saw was the "Merry-Go-Round Room" which had a medium sized carousel constantly and slowly rotating.

Enough of the "Fairmount", on to Fisherman's Wharf. We picked a bad night as nothing was doing, but it is an uncanny place. We had supper at a "Drive In", again excellent service (there's a lot of these "Motels" and "Drive In Movies" over here, and will tell you in another letter about them).

Next we saw the "Cliffs" and "Seal Rocks", and on the way home the Amusement Parks (like St. Kilda, but much cleaner). After driving down Lombard Street (a steep road that twists like a serpent and drops at least 200 ft. in as many yards) we came down in between 30-40 m.p.h. and Vin. did a marvellous job to keep on the course. This is the nearest approach to a big dipper that I have been on. Some streets are so steep that cars are ridiculously parked 90° to footpaths, which have steps.

Next we went to Chinatown and then home to the "St. Francis". We were pleased to go to sleep at 3.30 a.m.

Next morning we left on the ferry to catch the Zephyr, and Don. was shown the largest dry dock in the world. On enquiring we found that the Capt. Cook Dry Dock was more than twice as large, but everything, as far as they are concerned, is the largest, smallest, costliest, highest, lowest or somethingest (it doesn't matter what) in the world. It's annoying trying to get used to continual boasting without saying anything that might hurt feelings.

I didn't count the number of carriages, but we must have had about 11 or 12 strung behind the two G.M. diesels. The Zephyr is America's foremost tourist train, expensive eh! (one piece of steak 4.50 dollars, i.e. £2 – meals cost us on an average of £5 per day). The Zephyr travels slowly in the day through scenic parts (about 45 m.p.h.) but at night averages 85 m.p.h. The country before the Sierras was like N.S.W. Eastern plains; agricultural, with the occasional large town or industry flashing by.

We passed through "White Feather Pass", but the light was bad and I could not get any photos. Nevertheless, it's an awing sight. After going north for 150 miles we passed through the pass 50 miles east, then due east all night over plains, I think, and travelled through several canyons next afternoon. These were exciting times indeed.

William John MURRELL.

"WEEK-END IN CHICAGO"

26th – 28th September, 1952.

Due to a letter of introduction that was given to me in Australia, I had a two-hour drive around Chicago while on the way from San Francisco to New York.

The "Smith's" invited me to come and stay with them any week-end that was free. Well last week-end it was then or never. Mich. Wylie's ride fell flat, and I became despondent, so to add new life I decided to hitch-hike down to Chicago (about 280 miles). I left Buick Plant (where I'm working for the first four weeks as a Safety Inspector) at about 3.30 p.m. First hitch to Battle Creek in '52 Pontiac" (average speed 60 m.p.h.), then to Benson Harbour in '51 "Oldsmobile" Rocket (not in Australia). At Benson I picked up a "couple" going for a short drive, and they were so interested and amused by my funny speech that I talked them into going as far as Michigan City. Here I travelled by truck to Gary, and intended to catch a train into Chicago, but as it was then 11.30 p.m., and the next train did not leave until 1.00 a.m., I decided to continue "thumbing".

Although I was dumped in the middle of nowhere, I managed to pick up a student from North-Western University, in a new "Cadillac", and he took me right in.

Downton I was given wrong directions and ended up arriving at Smith's home at 2.30 a.m., but it was tremendous fun.

I slept in on Saturday morning and then Jeanette took me in their "Dynaflow" '51 Buick (no gears and no clutch needed) (by the way she doesn't know how to drive a car with gears – nor without) to do some shopping at a super market. After "Brunch" we went for a drive along Sheridan Road, through Evanston, Fort Sheridan (an enormous training camp), Winnetta to Great Lakes Naval Training Depot, etc. At night we went to Chicago Vaudeville Theatre – good, but weak after Rockefeller City, N.Y.

On Sunday we went on an all day picnic into the woods. It was tremendous. A picnic is a picnic here (about 4 courses). It was most enjoyable in the autumn tinted trees (beech, oak, poplar, aspens, etc.) with squirrels running about and robins chirping above. I amazed them by saying it was usual to grill lamb chops at home. Cost is terrific here; in any case, they're mutton. I had one slice (area about 6" sq. and about 1/6" thick) of beef (no vegetables) for tea tonight – cost 80 cents, i.e. 7/6d. ! "dinkum".

William John MURRELL.
ELWOOD, U.S.A.
30/9/52

Dear Family,

Guess you will be anxiously awaiting this letter. Well, here it is at long last. I simply have not had time to settle down for an hour or so and write.

I will start at New York and interject remarks and thoughts as they occur.

We wondered what we were coming to when we stepped out at Central Station, New York. Dark, dirty and depressing, but with a sigh we took up our bags and went into the foyer. This was much bigger, brighter and better than any station I had seen. At one end was an attractive Kodakcolor display – the other, in good New York fashion, full of people.

The Wellington Hotel was a disappointment, at least the old section we were in was. The other students – 19 of them, were in the new section.

Brian and Mick think this year's intake are a much better bunch than they expected. The others comprise two Englishmen, four Germans, two Belgiums, one Frenchman, one New Zealander, two South Africans, two Brazilians and one Mexican. Most of the lads are co-operating (i.e. sponsored by and working at plants outside of Flint). About eight of us are continually in Flint. Peter Green (Aust.), Ray Springham (Eng.) and Joachim (Germany) and self are at Buick Motor Division at Flint. I'm lucky because I'm the only one at Aust. House (1633 Elwood) that is earning this month. Roy Martin, Bill Dobell, Brian Stanton (all last year's students) Peter Green, Frank Pound, Don Enderby and self have the top floor of Mr. & Mrs. Webb's home – three bedrooms, two studies and two bathrooms, so we are well set up – cost 1 dollar per day without meals.

Meals have cost me approx. £1 pe day here. A plate of Kellogs 3/-, a drink of milk 1/6d. – 2/-d. (one small glass), but the best "horse" I have had was one piece (slice) of beef about 6: square, cost 80 cents i.e. 7/6. We have found the cheapest place to eat (above prices) is the Y.W.C.A. Cafeteria, that is where I have tea.

I catch a bus at 7.15 (it's beginning to get cold now too) into the city (downtown), cram a snack at the Greyhound Bus Depot at 7.25-7.35 a.m., then catch another bus to Buick, arriving at 7.50 a.m. Work starts at 8.00 a.m. I'm working office hours, 8.00 a.m. to 5 p.m., and 1 hour for lunch (buy it at work for 8/-), but later I may have to work factory hours i.e. 7.00 a.m. – 3.30 p.m. and ½ hour for lunch (not looking forward to this). Pay day is next Friday, but I'm not worried financially due to my extra money, but the others will be really worried in six weeks time when they draw their first pay! Although I get up earlier than the others, I've got the best deal.

Flint itself is just a place. A big untidy, overgrown industrial town. I will be clearing out of it on all week-ends possible, that's when I get a car.

Cars are amazing here "cheaper by the dozen". I've seen '39 Pontiac's, like our old one (but beaten up) for 150 dollars. I think I'll try to hang off until next Spring to get a jalopy, as prices will be lower then and I may be able to afford a later model. The temptation to buy now is terrific.

I must tell you a little about last weekend. I had a marvellous time down in Chicago. Wylie's ride fell flat, due to him working overtime, and all looked dim. The Smith's (wonderful people) had previously invited me to stay (and since invited me for 10 days at Xmas, and a week at their summer lake residence next Aug. vac., good eh?. I was feeling disappointed and despondent when I decided to overthrow the bad feelings and travel, making it in excellent time to Battle Creek then to Benson Harbour and Michigan City about 9.30 p.m. but I missed out badly from Gary into and through Chicago. Still I would not have missed the adventure for anything. Tim, I travelled at 102 m.p.h. in a '52 Oldsmobile 98 Rocket", the new V-8 Firedome engine. It's terrific, also had two brake pedals (one needs them too) but no gears due to the hydromatic transmission (an automatic torque convertor – much superior to a "fluid drive"). This has an automatic passing gear that cuts in at 70 m.p.h. when you depress the accelerator sharply, swish and you are doing 80, 85, 90 and up to 110 m.p.h. as quickly as that, hence the name "Rocket" (sorry to bore some of you).

On Saturday morning I did some shopping with Jeanette in a Super Market, and in the afternoon went for a drive up the "posh" western drive of Lake Michigan, halfway up to Milwaukee, then back along Super Highway travelling 70-80 miles per hour (and being continually passed) in a '52 "Buick" 4-door. In the evening Mr. Smith took us to the Chicago Theatre – seats 3,600, and we saw a stage and the film "The Quiet Man" – a good show.

Chicago City is a very pretty place at night, rather stark in the day (the reverse applies to the suburbs which extend in 20 miles radius).

Next day, Sunday, was one of the best days I have spent in America. On what? A picnic in the wood. This was superb. Away from the hustle and bustle and noise (except jets overhead) in the peaceful autumn-tinted woods. I first discovered Americans can slow down to our pace. We cooked hamburgers, onions, fried potatoes, then salad, pickles, etc. followed by fruit pie and delicious cake by which time everyone had drank at least four glasses of iced tea, ugh! To me this American picnic resembled a banquet, or feast, as we had everything and a little bit more. Yet, when I described cooking lamb chops and boiling billy, etc., I made them envious of Australian picnics (Lamb is very expensive and a real treat here).

Well I guess there are many different types of picnics one could have, but this was one I'll never forget.

I travelled back to Flint by railroad – a dreadful trip, and it cost me £6/10/- and I got to sleep at 3.15 a.m. on Monday morning. Now you know why I "braved" hitching.

New York is still in my mind, but I don't know quite where to start. First I didn't buy anything there, because (a) I have not acquired my money values, (b) the place is full of rogues and (c) I hope to be back there again before I come back. We arrived there on a Saturday and Hans showed us around Broadway at night. This famous diagonal street running right across Manhattan. Neon lights all over the place, terrific advertising stunts.

I spent the week-end with Hans at Maplewood. Monday G.M. welcomed us and explained arrangements. In the afternoon we walked around Central Park, a glorious place in a humming metropolis.

Tuesday – mostly G.M. propaganda, and wandered the streets in the afternoon. At night saw "Les Misérables" – a good film.

Wednesday – a G.M. discussion, and saw N.Y. "Giants" beat the Chicago "Cubs" in a big baseball game. I was bored!

Thursday – Toured Rockefeller Centre. Given a reception and swanky dinner at "Mampshire House" in the evening, followed by a Vaudeville Comedy "Top Banana". This show is really hilarious.

Friday – More films and discussions. Saw Hayden Planetarium, a wizard place in the afternoon.

At the week-end I again went out to Maplewood to stay with Hans. Mrs. Mantner, Hans' mother, was very good to the boys as we had two wonderful dinners at her place. Mum would you please send her recipes of your scones as she has never been able to cook them since she left Australia and would love to taste them again. You've guessed right, you cannot buy scones here, as there is no such thing. Also, she would appreciate a letter covering any social events, especially those connected with "Saints". Many thanks Mum.

Monday was a mad rush of packing, and we caught the "Detroiter" to where? Detroit, of course.

I've left out another dinner we had at Mantner's during the week, and a dinner and evening we had a "Droogams", and also a night we spent getting taken in at a Night Club, phew!

Frank Peter, Don and self were walking down 52nd Street – a notorious place for night haunts of all types – best to worst, at about 11.30 p.m., after a show, and decided we would taste a little Night Club life. We walked up and down, and finally decided "Chez Paree" would be the place. No cover charge, no waiting, plenty of dancing, girls, music, bar, tables and Winnie Garrett the "Flaming Red Head". This was the place for us, so in we stepped. Suckers! Given a table right near the stage by a high fellow (Chief thrower out) we watched the show. We discovered in tiny print at the bottom of the Menu, "cover charge 3.50". Well, we were pleased! Deciding not to waste the 3.50. each, I ordered one sandwich, one 7-up, a drink like Soda & Lime, and one Coke. That should cover about 1.00, so it looks as if I loose 2.50, but no! I get the bill. What 5 dollars! This was hard to take – 5 dollars i.e. £2 in cold blood. It's a wonder they do not change the name of the place to the "Den of Thieves". Winnie in her nudity, became unexciting now, as our dignity was hurt and our fighting blood up. We paid our bills and stormed out at about 12.30 a.m. The waiter stormed after us when he discovered he had only 25 cents tip for a 20-dollar bill (should be 10% - 20% of bill).

With that the first and my last experience of Night Clubs, I must now close.

Much love to you all.

BILL.

1633, Elwood,
FLINT 4, MICH.
4/10/52.

Dear Family,

Just dropping in to say hello again. I'm continuing to look forward to your letters. It seems a long time since I last wrote, perhaps it is (I lose track of time over here, as everything is crammed full with something new. New habits, new customs, new scenery, etc.).

The last 10 days have been more of an anti-climax – bored most of the day, with nothing to do at work, and at night I have been writing a report on "Accident Prevention" – how boring! I am lucky, as the other fellows are really hard at it. Up till 1 to 2 o'clock each night, except week-ends, so I've something to look forward to in a fortnight's time.

During the week I sent a package of junk home. Please don't destroy anything, as each thing has some meaning to me, but I wanted to get a lot of the papers out of the way. I hope to send a "Sears & Roebuck" catalogue home, so that you can give me some orders for things (N.B. Send complete size and details for clothing, nylons, etc.). S. & R's. are the largest mail order organisation in the world, and the only decent emporium in Flint. In the package that I sent are tour guides, post cards, etc. of all the places I have visited. Also, a map of Michigan., which you might find handy, and a grand photo of 1952-54 overseas group (take care when opening). One other thing is a complete list of "viewsmaster" needs – ask Andrew which ones he would like, and send over the numbers.

I was hoping by now to have most of my snaps back, but, alas, they haven't arrived, so I'll tell you about them in my next letter. I hope they are better than Don's, as not one of his Ansco films came out. I have spent about £15 in films so far!

Everyone is asking to see a boomerang, so you could send one. Buy a proper one (not ornamental) at a second hand shop, or some place. Also, Koala Bears. How about sending a couple of those stuffed toy ones, or girls purse type, as they would be excellent gifts for friends interested in Australia, e.g., Smith's, Mantner's, etc. Mother, I have written to Mrs. Mantner and told her that her scone recipes are on the way, so I hope this is correct.

My school schedule has been finalised and I am taking:- Electrical Circuits, Industrial Engineering Methods and Processes, Hydraulics of Industrial Equipment, Automotive Body Construction, English Composition, Industrial Accounting, Industrial Development and Industrial Organisation. Quite a handful of subjects. I have placed them in order of importance, the first three are difficult, long and excellent courses, next three useful and interesting, but the last two are typical American "talk" subjects, but we have to do them.

Buick should be quite a place to work – employees vary between 20,000 and 30,000 according to production, which is restricted at the moment to 90 cars per hour. Area of plant is 400 acres and the press shop is over ¼-mile long.

There is a total of 37 miles of conveyor lines in Buick, and about 12 miles of rail track. I have seen all of the plant now. The machinery is unbelievable – special machines for everything. Most major operations, e.g., machinery engine block, are fully automatic. A detailed description I think would bore you. Several defence projects – jets, tanks, motor shells are in hand. Buick are announcing their completely new V-8 engine and body in January next. New machines are pouring into the new motor plant, and production tryout is in progress. I have not received my detailed work-experience schedule yet, but if my suggestions are taken up, it will be good. I'm working with Safety Inspectors – just strolling around the place, looking on this month's assignment.

I've finished writing a letter to Mrs. Hamilton on October 12th. I would spend at least 6 to 7 dollars. Steak, lamb (it's mutton anyway) beef, etc. are most expensive. Fish, chicken, eggs, sandwiches (not like ours) are cheap.

The other day I had fried swordfish and salad (covered with onions, radishes, dressing and garlic, ugh!).

I've just returned from a Chinese restaurant, and had chicken and mushroom chop suey. The chicken must have walked through it on stilts – I didn't see it anyhow. The mushrooms were as big as sixpences, and tasted like toadstools; the rest was a scrawley oniony cabbage mess, interspersed with bamboo shoots (they look like half grown wheat stalks, and tasted worse). I'll stick to Egg Foo Young (egg omelette) from now on.

My usual day means are:- Breakfast, Raisin Bran (Kellogs), two dough nuts and chocolate milk. Lunch:- Peach Pie, Bismark Bun and chocolate milk. Tea:- Macaroni and cheese, French fries (potatoes and chips), fruit cup (salad) and chocolate milk. Cost approx. £1. You can see why I let my hair down and do something unusual, e.g., Chinese food, once or twice a week.

Table manners seem to be non-existent. The louder the noise the more you enjoy your food. Reach. No! Grab anything you want. Generally you take up the fork in the left hand and stab the poor dead piece of animal on your plate; take the knife in the right hand (I do it reversed) and proceed to cut the beast up into eatable sizes (about 2" or 1") drop your knife (anywhere) and transfer your fork to right hand (I leave it in my left), mix up potatoes, vegetables and meat, then proceed to shovel in as much as possible. Chew thoroughly and one of two ways, mouth open or closed (the former is more acceptable). The golden rule:- No less than two glasses of water (iced) are to be drunken at any meal. Well educated college graduates usually drink five to six glasses per meal. Actually this is an excellent idea, and could be well introduced into Australia.

The other day I stopped at a Drug Store for a cup of coffee. I sat down and immediately a glass of water was placed before me. I gave my order, "one cup of coffee with cream", and drank ¾ glass of water, then my coffee, by which time my glass of water was full. On emptying this, I paid 10 cents and went out, my stomach full.

Everything inside is most hygienic and scrupulously clean. Most things you buy, even stamps, are wrapped in germ-proof sealed wrappers. Milk is "de-bugged" three or four times. Yet – on stepping out of a restaurant or just walking along the street, it is customary to spit every 10 yards or so, and not necessarily in the gutter.

Industries delight in building near rivers so that industrial trade wastes can be conveniently disposed, also sewerage of towns – most hygienic!

The temperature for the last week has been about 26°F. Not really cold yet, so others try to tell me. It should be snowing this time next month.

Lots of love to you all,

from BILL.

1633 Elwood,
FLINT 4
MICHIGAN, U.S.A.
12/10/52

Dear Mrs. Hamilton,

Many thanks for your letter, I enjoyed it greatly. I'm pleased about Marg. (growing up, I mean) I knew she would make the grade! Jane seems to have had a grand holiday in W.A. It's great also that you have decided to take the girls to England (I hope you will not be leaving before Oct.1954, i.e. before I return) I am beginning to appreciate how one's outlook and knowledge can be broadened by travelling and meeting other people. Such statements as "you're from Australia, I suppose that is the last country left of the British Empire that are not enemies of America" or "being an Australian, and in America only one month, I can't understand how quickly you have picked up English". One cannot help but ponder about things when stunned by such comments from outwardly sane Americans.

As I have always been an admirer of your kitchen and household gadgets, I thought I would spend the rest of the time on the subject "American gadgets".

Americans are extremely gadget-minded people. The strange thing I have noticed about gadgets over here is that they work. The nearest approach to one not working was in New York, near Central Station. Don Enderby put a nickel in a "personal Wurlitzer" (this is a small speaker situated in front of your counter seat in a Drug Store with several buttons from which anyone of 30 tunes can be selected and played through your little speaker only). It refused to work and we complained. This serious matter was taken before the management, and finally the counter boy solved the problem with three sharp bumps on the seat. It worked, but for recompense for the inconvenience of not playing the first time, the boy let us play a second tune free.

In the American kitchens (I have been in half a dozen or so) you will most likely find an array of white enamel – an electric dishwasher (no good as it is too much trouble to load the dishes in), a clothes washer complete with spin drier, a 9 c.f.t. or larger refrigerator complete with deep freeze, a superb tin opener on the wall (the most used gadget of the American cook) and a gas stove (automatically lit, temperature controlled, and turned off at the set time).

In San Francisco I had a three course chicken roast dinner beautifully prepared before my eyes, in less than ½ hour (from deep freeze, etc.). Everything here can be bought so conveniently prepared. Bread knives or boards are not required, as one buys the bread (rye, caraway seed, which I love, wholemeal, corn or mere white varieties) all cut up (thick, thin or medium) in a sealed cellophane bag. Even stamps can be bought in "germ-proof" scientifically-sealed wrappers. Some things can be carried too far, can't they?

Bottles are never round, they are square with rounded corners. Why? Simple – one can pack a dozen into a freezer with less wasted space – clever, eh!

Bottled milk comes in cartons, but one must decide what flavour – cream, buttermilk, plain, chocolate or strawberry, whatever the decision, one gets "homogenized, pasteurized, vitamin-fortified and scientifically treated milk" according to the label, anyway! I have drank so much chocolate-cream milk that I should be changing colour at any moment. Truly, it tastes wonderful, and no extra cost – a mere 1/ - per ½ pint.

Returning to gadgets. American homes have no mallee root heaps, no hot and cold rooms, no friendly fires, no cleaning of fireplaces – simply air conditioning and heating. One sets the thermostatic clock for 65° in the day, and 70° at night.

Much love,

BILL.

1633, Elwood, FLINT.
13/10/52.

Dear Family,

The pressure is beginning to be put on now. Next week will be really busy when I begin Tech. I have spent this week-end writing part of a report on "Accident Prevention" which has to be handed in on Thursday. Also, I have had to prepare my first speech. I am scheduled to speak on "International Co-operation" with a Dutchman – Ingmar Jankens at a Teachers' Meeting at Flint High School tomorrow night.

Tomorrow is United Nations Day. My sub-topics are Immigration and Atomic Energy. Ingmar's are the Marshal Plan and the Shuman Plan. I'm hoping for the best. It should be a worthwhile experience.

Mother, I don't think I spend all my time in Night Clubs. I have been in one and one only. I'll tell you all about churches here (much different) when I have seen a few more to draw some conclusion.

Next week-end I hope to go to Ann Arbor – University of Michigan, to "Home Coming" (like Graduation, but plus the best football game of the year), and will be staying with an I.V.F'er.

Snow fell yesterday and again today. Quite a thrill. Temperature outside today is 26° Burr! First fall has been 6 weeks early this year – for my benefit, I suppose!

Lots of love,

Bill.

1633, Elwood, FLINT.
22/10/52.

Dear Tim,

I was glad to hear that your operation was a success and hope that you are progressing satisfactorily. Guess you will be laid up again for a little while. Still, you have had plenty of practice at filling in time while in bed this year, haven't you? Like another suggestion of how to fill in time, that is other than listening to test cricket (how are the Aussies going – we are always chipping David Lord and Jackabus Smidt – the two South Africans)? Well, here it is:- Write some big long letters about anything, but try not to repeat what other members of the family have said in their letters (this applies to everyone).

This week I have produced my 50-page co-ordination report on "Accident Prevention". Quite a job, but I've finished it tonight. Feeling a load off my mind, I went down to have a "hot chocolate" with the rest of the boys at the Della (a nearby Coffee Shop). Believe it or not, I was feeling so good that I shun up a light pole (about 30 ft.) for a 2 cent bet!

Tomorrow I am going to be initiated into "Passion Pits", Drive-in-Movies (correct name) with Annabel, so I have borrowed Tony Palmer's '46 "Buick" for the night. (I got my licence last Saturday as a smiling girl approached and asked if she could help me. She did. She arranged to write to the publishers and we got talking she and I. Last Saturday I took her to dinner, then to a show, and afterwards we had coffee and went home. She played me some long playing classical records and we talked about our respective schooling. A most pleasant evening! Flint is not such a bad place after all.

    Love and cheers,

    Bill.

28/10/52.

Dear Family,

I have a spare hour before "supper", i.e. tea, to write to you all again. Today has been a day off for me, so I attempted to do some Christmas shopping. Having wandered around the shops for several hours, I realized that I could buy many things (dollars permitting) which would make your eyes pop out. I'll try to get some stuff away this week by ordinary mail. The declared cost will be about two-thirds of the actual cost. I hope you do not have any trouble with custom duty. Any suggestions for your presents, Mother or Dad? I've fixed the rest, as they're easy. I am sending some books on American home inventions which might give you some ideas for the Mitcham place.

On returning home this afternoon I was caught in a cold snow flurry and froze. With my teeth chattering, I climbed up the stairs, tired. A smile soon spread from ear to ear as I looked through the letters beside the phone (Flint 26749 in any extreme emergencies) and found one from you, Dad, one from Jane, another from Leo, and yet another from Mrs. Hamilton. Having just finished reading all the news, I've decided that it is my turn now.

The "S. & R." catalogue has not been ordered yet, so do not expect that for a while. Glad Tim is getting along so well.

I'm eagerly awaiting tomorrow when I begin lectures and real hard work. The other fellows have become fairly despondent by the pressure of the quantity (not quality) of the work at the Tech. Still, it's good to begin in high spirits.

The position regarding transport is becoming more and more desperate. Brian and Bill Dobell have taken their cars away and we will not see them again until January. Peter Green's "Chevrolet" is not running yet, so we were all (Peter, Don and self) relying on Roy Martin (who is back from Indiana) and his "Buick". However, the side of it was smashed on the way home and at the moment he is outside working on it, poor fellow. No insurance, and no money from either parties.

Enclosed are a couple of colour shots. Please don't let anyone handle them without the covers, as finger prints or sweat will ruin them. I'm seriously considering taking movies instead of stills, as it costs less in the long run. Each exposure now costs me 2/6d. and I can't keep it up. Look at them concave side up towards an opaque light. We flew in directly over the Los Angeles Sewerage Treatment Works and I couldn't resist taking it. (Mr. Hogson might be interested, Dad). The shot alongside it is one of the Sierras near Los Angeles, with a little township nestled in it, which was taken while circling to land. After landing and having unloaded, we walked across the 'drome to the P.A.A. building. As I entered the gate I turned and saw a helicopter landing just beside our plane – hence the shot. After eating, we posted some mail, then walked along the road outside the airways terminal. An impressive line of late model yellow cabs were lined up, so again I weakened. (I would not have taken this snap again, as I've seen enough new American cars to last me the rest of my life – great resemblance, overpowered, chrome-decorated barges!).

The remainder of the photos were taken out of my window of Hotel St. Francis, S.F. I have kept a better shot than either of these two for a colour print, as it has my second prize, so far (if I can afford it sometime, they're 5/-d. each). The square was a magnificent sight.

If you look carefully you can see the Adailai Stevenson procession on the left hand side. Count the number of different makes of cars – 7, 2 T.V. and press trucks, and 3 motor police, sirens, revolvers and all. The cars in the other lane are in the usual traffic jam around the square. From now on, I will send some photos with each letter.

Last week I was a little down in the dumps, due to a feeling of dissatisfaction and "getting nowhere slowly" at work. The main reason for the change was my clearing out of Flint for the weekend. I went to Ann Arbor – the University town. A beautiful place, consisting mainly of one tremendous college campus (University of Michigan buildings and grounds). All American students travel far away from their homes to attend college (University). If they live in California they go to Notre Dame, Ohio. If living in N.Y., then to University of Michigan, or University of Southern California, etc.

Each college has a particular weekend set aside each semester for "home coming" (visiting days) for parents and graduates. This weekend is determined by the football schedule. It's usually held (a) in good weather (b) at the time of the best predicted football game on the list.

I must go to supper now, then over to Annabel's place, as she wants to see the Jubilee Book on Australia. A proper snowstorm raging now I'm still going out in it. One only does such things for the first time, as there's not a soul on the streets.

Having returned from a most enjoyable evening (playing classical records on the radiogram, talking about our different school systems and comparing Australia & America, and preparing an American supper) I'll tell you a little about the snow.

When I went out it was snowing strongly. This snow was the soft flaky and wet variety. Lawns, gardens, trees, cars, etc. everything except the concrete paths (due to the high thermal capacity of cement) was covered with 2" – 3" of fleecy white carpet. In the moonlight every scene looked inspiring. The air was fresh and crisp, and the walk was most exhilarating. Of course, I was well equipped. I've got Bob Holden's snow boots. These are oversize goloshes that fit over the normal shoe, over the ankle and halfway to the knee. The fleecy lined boots that I took with me are excellent as slippers but practically useless in snow, as they absorb water. I had my ski cap folded down over my ears and the beaut. wallaby-skin fur gloves that I bought in Melbourne to keep my hands warm (many people admire these). The "McPherson" cashmere wool brightly colored scarf also goes down well. Actually, I'm most pleased with the selection of clothes that I brought across. Tell Carl that they are not "Bodgy" enough for student wear. Naturally, non-students, i.e. executives, etc. do not dress like us.

Enough of the snow, back to Ann Arbor. I intended hitch-hiking down, but weakened and bought a bus fare in the end. Lucky, I did too, as it was quite cold. In the "Greyhound" bus a little girl of about three years started playing handies. College students (girls) became interested. One of them being attracted to my "cute" accent (I'm quickly getting sick of that line) without hesitation picked the little girl up and dumped her in her own seat and sat down, uninvited, or even persuaded, next to me. Backward, aren't they!!? She tried hard, but I was stubbornly reserved (recovering from shock) for the remaining 40 miles. Poor Barbara will have to invent more catching techniques before she gets her "Mrs." for which every girl here goes to college.

I was met at A.A. bus depot by Mick Coldren (I.V.E. staff worker) and taken to his lodgings, a boarding house hopelessly overcrowded – about 10 students or more on two floors. We watched the T.V. for an hour or so. Eisenhower's Korea speech was interesting but a little optimistic. He will not be able to keep up all his presidential promises any more than Menzies has been able to.

Up early next morning, Mick and I walked through the campus – beautiful buildings everywhere. We saw Engineering, especially the Metallurgical Research Labs. (shown over by Phyll who is Mick's brother) Medicine, Arts, Business Administration, and many other faculties. Mick had to do some dictation so he left me to my own initiative to have a further look around and take some photos. I walked through the University Town (shopping centre) and was attracted to a used car lot. I took to the streets in one of their cars – sight-seeing in luxury. Having had a look around (about 1/2 to ¾ hr. driving) I went back to the lot and told the fellow that I wasn't interested in the "scrap heap" as 2nd and 3rd gears were a little noisy. He wanted 650 dollars for it, and it had done 80,000 miles. Still, it was a great way to have a good look around.

When Mick was through with his correspondence, we walked out to a Fraternity House, or "flash" dental group. Mick used to wash dishes to get free meals there when he was going through college and got to know the cook well. Again, we got a free meal. Ham cooked in ginger ale. Mother it's wonderful.

Guess, I'll tell you the rest in another letter, but briefly the schedule was as follows:- Walked past home-coming exhibits to the football, went to Alumni (Graduate) party on Saturday night – grand time. Sunday – Campus Chapel in morning, dinner at "Old German Inn", Alumni talk in the afternoon, and supper and church at Grace Bible in the evening. Monday morning hitch-hiked back to Flint. Monday afternoon enrolled at Tech. and got books, etc.

Lots of love to you all,

BILL.

1633, Elwood, FLINT.
12/11/52.

Dear Family and Aunt Mollie,

Just to shout hello again before I get some sleep. Thank you Dad, Mother and Tim for your letters. Please thank Mr. Kellett and David Fennell for theirs, and also thank you Aunty Mollie for your cable – it was good of you to remember. Many happy returns for the 16th (I think that is the date, Aunt) I'm sorry I can't directly write letters to everybody that has been so good to me, but next month perhaps.

I had a wonderful (22nd) birthday. For a change I wasn't homesick (it's wearing off quickly how I am too busy to daydream). Your letters gave me a terrific thrill, which was followed up by the beaut. scarf (I wore it on Saturday night) then your cable Aunt, and finally a parcel from the Smith's in Chicago, in fact, everything added up to a most enjoyable day and night. The parcel was a box of scrumptious chocolate revel cookies (biscuits). My, what a memory Mrs. Smith must have to remember the exact day. She sent a thoughtful letter too. The rest of the boys, and myself, enjoyed them very much – only crumbs remain.

The next chapter of my birthday was celebrating at night. The evening nearly began in tragedy. I had borrowed Tony Palmer's "Buick" and was on my way to call for Annabel, and crash! My first automobile smash. I was caught in one of those horrible, but frequent, chain collisions -the last of three cars. Everything happened so quickly – I saw a red light as I was approaching at an intersection at about 40 m.p.h. and when about 200 yds. away the lights turned green and I removed my foot from the accelerator and coasted. The two cars ahead began to take off as I approached them (25 m.p.h.). Then crash! The clown in front stopped dead, changing his mind and trying to do a R.H.T. he collected a "Nash" in his rear end, then I woke up to what was happening, and I nearly pressed the clutch and brake pedals through the floor boards, and with screeching brakes and skidding tyres, I grimly clutched and pulled upon the steering wheel. A direct hit may be avoided if I swing to the gap on the right, between the car and the gutter. Like a desperate friend, I swung the wheels, but in vain, I slid into the R.H. back side of the car. Bang! I had hit him. The sound of crumpling metal did not belong to me, and one rule concerning accidents over here – the car which hits the other vehicle is always at fault – you must be able to stop. These were not very consoling thoughts – however, let's look at the damage.

I had hit a Policeman off-duty (my luck) but he knew the procedure. His R.H. near fender was split and the near bumper twisted underneath it. My, I should say that Tony's front bumper was split, and lay at two awkward angles, one side twisted back and the L. fender badly buckled against the tyre. Mud and pieces of head-light lay all around – small kids gathered round, but no blood – they soon disappeared. The first car that really caused the collision, after momentarily pausing drove on, and we missed his number. With super human strength, I pulled the fender clear of the wheel and examined the suspension. O.K. Got all details them off to Annabel's, 20 minutes late and a little churned up. I rang the police from there and then decided to go out and forget things, so off we went. Uncle Bob's Dinner – I was nearly bilious over the steak and eggs. Saw "Affair in Trinidad" then went on to a Cabaret – home at 3.00 a.m. "All's well that ends well" - this evening certainly did. It was rather awkward telling Tony next morning. An expensive birthday, 40 dollars cold cash (no insurance).

Love,

BILL.

1633, Elwood, FLINT.
16/11/52

Dear Family,

Hiya folks! (That's American for dear family, and appears on most personal letters). I hope you are well Mother and not overworking in your usual manner. That muffler is beginning to be worthwhile now as Indian Summer (late Fall or Autumn) has passed and it is winter.

Dad, I sure enjoy your letters. I rank you second to Tim for interest and presentation. How about telling me more about the Mitcham plans – details I mean. It sounds super from what the others have told me. It will be a credit to you I am certain, when you have finished.

By the way, your books are on the water by now, Helen.

Many thanks for your newsy well-written long letters, Tim. I enjoy them.

Over here it is generally accepted that after three straight dates with a girl you go "steady", then give her your school badge (extra steady, all other hands off) next your graduation ring which ever High School graduate wears (pre-engagement) then the diamond engagement ring, and finally marriage. Quite complicated, isn't it.

How's my little "guy" Andrew? Yes, still working hard at school. Remember me to Miss McDonald when you see her tomorrow, Andrew. The little children, sorry, big little men like you, over here look really cute with their fuzzy ear muffs and quilted lumber jacket on. They have great fun gathering all the leaves that fall in Fall from the many deciduous trees, into a large pile with a hole in the centre. They then play "forts" until daddy comes home from work, when he sets the leaves on fire. These fires smoulder all night until the heavy dews put them out and the smoke hangs hauntingly low in the cold air.

Mrs. Webb had a party for "Authors" tonight and we went down to finish the scraps. There was quite a bit of the 22 lb. turkey left (delicious) and a large slab of cream cake. Also avocado pear salad with garlic bread and wild rice savories. There was hot cider and rum to drink. An enjoyable supper. I'm still very disinterested in bought food – I lose my appetite at the smell of it.

Lots of love,

BILL.

Elwood,
<u>FLINT, U.S.A.</u>
23/11/52.

Dear Family,

It's time to say "hello" again. I am very relieved now, as school period finished yesterday, and I begin at Buick, probably on their 200 H.P. V-8 engine plant, to-morrow.

Tech. was really hectic the last two weeks, piles of assignments and a terrific amount of reading. I've found it hard adapting myself to a different method of learning. For instance, in electrical engineering (by far the hardest subject I have) the lecturer, no, I'll call him a supervisor, comes – says nothing, but simply goes through the assignments (homework) that you have placed on the front table when you enter. He looks over them, doesn't mark them or even tell you the mistakes you have made, but he does mark the roll by them, hence one has to hand every one in. Attendance at lectures is stressed greatly here – 10% off any grade for each lecture missed (it hurts every time I write that word, as these fellows don't know what a real lecture is), also a 500 word essay on the subject matter covered during the lecture (I could write it in one paragraph in most cases). Well, I fail to see why they stress attendance so much, but that's how it is. By the time our assignments are handed back there is about 30 minutes left of the 53 minute period. During this time we just sit, most of the yanks mess about, idle chatter, etc. I strive to catch up on some reading. Now someone usually asks how to do one of the problems that he had trouble with. It is sketchily explained, and either the lecturer or someone picked from the class goes out to the board and works the problem through. This may seem a bit tough, but it's amazing what one can do in such situations. I was scared to death at first, but take it in my stride now, as I realize you do not have to know much to get on top of the normal American students' thinking.

Our training at home is much broader, basic and better. I have found myself thinking from 1st principles, but most of the others get very confused (N.B. don't think they're all mugs). There being only 10 minutes left, assignments are set for the next lecture. In electrical, usually read, to be able to give the lecture, the next two chapters (20-30 pages of solid theory) and 5 to 7 problems. That's travelling, for in four weeks we are one-third through a whole textbook, and I did about 40 problems and wrote up four long lab. reports) N.B. I have four other subjects but thank goodness they're not as bad as this.

Don't get the wrong impression about this self-teaching method of learning. I'm getting to like it, and it is basically around if one really spends time at it (but time is a scarce commodity here). All the Australians have done exceptionally well.

We went to an Episcopal Church the Sunday before last; had to hunt all over the place to find one open (A morning service is usually sufficient here). The four of us went and doubled the congregation, believe it or not. Then halfway through the service the Pastor fainted. I was approached to read the rest of the service, but declined, being unfamiliar with the form (practically identical to, say, St. Margaret's, Woodville). An old gent continued, and we were glad to get home. One never knows what the next new experience is over here.

Well Tony Palmer has arrived with Vic Gosney and we're going to Detroit for the rest of the day.

With love to all,

BILL.

Elwood,
<u>FLINT, U.S.A.</u>
25/11/52.

Dear family,

It's wonderful to sit back and watch others study. Peter, Frank, Don and Roy are all at school while I am working man again. I don't envy them. They will be broke by Christmas, but I'll have two days, perhaps with overtime included, before then.

My works training schedule has worked out well. All my suggestions, except one, have been included – hence, I am well satisfied. The schedule runs something like this:-

Dec., 1952	Metallurgical Department	– Central Lab & Foundry.
Feb. 1953	Metallurgical Department	– Force & Sheet Metal.
April 1953	Tool Manufacturing	– Design & Processing.
June 1953	Engine Plant	– V-8 Assembly and machining.
August 1953	Central Head Office	– Budgetary, Cost Control.
November 1953	Sheet Metal Processing	– Processing.
January 1954	Sheet Metal Standards	– Standards.
March 1954	Sheet Metal	– Plant Eqpt. & Layout.
May 1954	Special Processing assignment	
July 1954	Reserved	
August 1954	HOME SWEET HOME – JUST 87 WEEKS 6 DAYS AND SEVERAL HOURS BEFORE I LEAVE HERE.	

So that is briefly it.

Dad, processing is the U.S. term for "planning and production, designing the tooling, analysing production methods and getting the job into production, etc. and is done by the Master Mechanics' Dept. which is equivalent to our Productions Engineering Dept. Thing are much brighter at work this month. I seem to be accepted into the Metallurgical Dept. and they have taken much trouble to show me some tricks of the trade.

Tomorrow, I start at 7.00 a.m. at the Foundry – next week I'll be with the fellow who hits the cupolas at 6.00 a.m. Brrr! The pleasing feature of this is that I work on until 5.00 p.m. and that gives me several hours overtime. Whacko!

I'll have to finish this tomorrow, as I must go to sleep now to wake up early tomorrow.

Friday, 28th. Sorry I've missed a mail but the last 3 days have been crammed with excitement. I'm enjoying my job immensely – mechanical and chemical testing and analysis of cast irons and steels, Pyrometry and Metallography, and considerable overtime.

Tomorrow I'm working in the morning, actually determining the composition of the melt for the new V-8 engine block. The guys in the Met. Lab. give me a shot at everything, even though I know nil about some phases – still it's an excellent way to learn.

Last Sunday afternoon Tony, Frank, Vic and self went to Detroit to have a look around. It was a good trip, we didn't do anything gay, but simply had a cup of afternoon tea in good old English style, with the couple with whom we board. They are English and have just returned from a trip home. Thence to see the sights – a sprawly and dirty industrial City, but excellent shops in the main central section and large used car lots on every corner – automobiles everywhere. We had a delightful supper at the famous "Brass Rail" in Central Circus, window shopped and then headed for home, coming back with Mick Wylie.

What a treat we will have at Xmas. Turkey and cranberries with pumpkin pie are traditional, and that is exactly what Mrs. Webb so excellently provided. It was the best meal I have had. I was completely satisfied. We had a 25 lb. turkey – it was enormous. Afterwards we had movies – even one on "Advance Australia" which were good. We all got up late had "brunch" and prepared to sit out the football game – Central v Northern Flint High School (traditional like the Intercoll., but much more thrilling). 15,000 sat with us in the snow (it has snowed continuously for two days now and the ground is becoming frozen hard). This is what I wore – 2 pairs of snow boots, 1 set of under-clothes, 1 pair of pyjamas (don't laugh), 1 shirt and sports trousers, 2 heavy pullovers, 1 lumber jacket, 1 sports coat, 1 overcoat, and your muffler, Mum, also my ski cap and large wallaby fur gauntlets. I was one of the few that didn't shiver, but if I had blown my nose it would have fallen off. The novelty of snow and snowball fights has not worn off yet.

Lots of love to all,

BILL.

1633 Elwood,
<u>FLINT.MICH.</u>
10/12/52.

Dear Family,

I'm afraid this will have to be a short letter, as it is fast approaching my bed time (10.00 p.m.). Thank you for all your letters, I, like you, keenly look forward to mail days.

Although still hale and hearty, I'm feeling quite tired, over tired I think, as I'm finding it hard to get to sleep. The last fortnight or so has been really hard work.

Tim, this week's pay cheque will be just over £81 (Australian currency). I'm saving too – to buy a car. The overtime work will help out a lot. I get up at 5.45 a.m., trudge through the snow to a Grill Shop, have breakfast – eggs, ham and coffee, and buy lunch which consists of 2 tins of pineapple juice, 1 pint of chocolate milk, 4 donuts and a piece of cake, a perhaps a peach pie.

I start measuring temperatures at 7.00 a.m.., and at 6.15 p.m. after over 1,100 engine blocks have been cast, I wearily put down my pynometer, wash up and plod home again in the dark. I repeat this 7 days a week. (I haven't seen the sun since "Thanksgiving Day"). My hands, neck and shins are spotted with blisters from molten metal burns (12 on my left hand – I've just counted them). Fortunately, they only hurt when the metal strikes you, and for a few minutes after while the flesh sizzles. What a price to pay for 180 dollars, but this is more than anyone else has earnt here yet so I'm suffering in silence. Don't take it all to heart, Mum, as I'm learning a lot, and hard work is doing me good.

For tea (supper it is called here) I have a hamburger and malted milk – cost 1 dollar (8/- Aust.). Let me explain why this is not exorbitant?? The 'burger has a piece of heated frozen mince meat (we wouldn't give it to dogs at home), 1 slice of cheese, 1 fried egg (Australian special – one never eats eggs with meat here), 2 pieces of lettuce and as much ketchup (tomato sauce) mustard or pickles as you want between 2 halves of a roll. I am a convert to American malteds – Recipe:- 2 shots of flavouring (pineapple for me) 5 to 7 scoops of ice-cream, add a dash of milk, so that the mixer won't stall, then mix until the forth appears at the top of the container, pour into a paper conical shaped glass and suck through straws. Safety precautions – Don't suck too quickly, or in a terrific headache across the eyes forces you to stop. It is essential that in a good "shake" that the straws when inserted will remain in any one position. This is a fact not a fad.

After eating I have ½ hour under the shower, then ½ hour under an ultraviolent lamp of Mrs. Webb's to catch up on my sunlight – beginning to go brown too. Then to bed and attempt to sleep.

I've received the papers that you sent – most interesting reading, please continue to send them.

I've been invited to go to Miami with the Brazilians for Xmas, but as yet I haven't decided whether I will go. I may go to Chicago instead. If the overtime keeps up I will go to Florida, as a warm Xmas is very tempting.

You should receive your presents soon.

                        With lots of love,

                        BILL.

1633 Elwood,
FLINT 4, MICH.
15/12/52.

Dear Family,

Christmas greetings and a Happy New Year to you all! Don't be too disappointed when I tell you that I will not be having a "White Christmas" which is probably what you are telling everybody. The reason is simple. I've seen enough of snow, and am not thrilled with it any longer – dirty, slushy, slippery, sloshy mess, especially in the afternoon when it thaws a little (i.e. when it gets hot enough – I mean over 32°F.) and this is only three or four times a week.

Well, I will be celebrating Christmas Day in Miami with Ron. Bradley (South African) Bob. Black (Belgian) Rene Bernesquet (Frenchman) and 4 Brazilians, and we should make quite an international party. Ron. has bought a '47 "Nash", equipped with wireless, heater and special bed that folds out of the back seat squab trunk so that two can sit in front and two can sleep horizontally while the car is travelling. The car is in excellence shape, and he beat a guy down to 450 dollars – a bargain. The first four of us are going in this, and we reckon on two nights and one day for the 2,000 mile trip. The Brazilians are going in Wal's '50 Buick Special – a beautiful car, but he paid 1,200 dollars for it. They are taking it in easier stages and we are meeting them down there.

We will go down via Dayton to drop Bernie Corbel (French) off, Cincinnati, Knoxville, Jacksonville (stay one day here), then Palm Beach (1 day), Miami (1 day). We won't have time to go right down to Key West, but will cross to the other side of the peninsula, St. Petersburg (1 day) then head back home. The pace will be set by the time left, but we will return a different way, probably along the East Coast. Sounds a good trip for 10 days. It will make an excellent break for me as I know I've been working a little too hard (I've only been out once in three weeks). For instance, to-day we tried out some new Hi-Carbon Coke in the Cupolas, and the boss wanted me in at 2 a.m. to see the changing. I went in early (5.15 a.m.) and I knocked off to-night at 6.15 p.m., only 13 hours hard, dirty work – still the overtime has allowed me to bank several hundred dollars. I intend buying a car, probably at the end of next work month (February). I'm a bit keen on the "Nash", as the bed idea is excellent for trips. Enough of the Sunny South (I hope) but I'm sure looking forward to a swim in the Briny next week.

Don't get the wrong idea from the photos enclosed they were taken in the best Fall (Autumn) week, about three weeks after I arrived in Flint. Trees are all barren and desolate and snow covered now. Magnificent colourings aren't they? Brian and Bill Dobell played golf one Saturday afternoon, and I went too, but wandered off with three cameras, with instructions to get some good autumn tints. That wasn't hard. I had a delightful time – the colourings were breathtaking. I walked through several woods and all about one of the best residential areas of Flint (near the Golf Course), taking shots here, there and everywhere. I used up two films on Bill's camera, and he has thanked me for taking them. They came out even better than mine. Note the two-storied houses which are so popular here – also a small "ranch type", as they call it here means single storied, and is the latest rage if you can afford them (more costly land to build them on, and I think the Architects and Builders pile on the cost just for the uniqueness). One could describe them as a medium priced Australian house, or a good Housing Trust Home. The automobiles in front of the house is a '52 – 4 door "Buick" Roadmaster and a '50 – 2 door Riveria "Buick" convertible.

The two door automobiles are most popular here, and last week I discovered the reason why. Every family has a car, but the kids always open the doors on the four door models, so – shove them in the back where there's no doors that can be opened, but they're most awkward to get in and out of for adults, also they're cheaper to manufacture (two doors less), and the bodies are stronger and more rigid (less openings and more bracings on.

I sent a Montgomery & Ward's Christmas Catalogue off yesterday. Mrs. Dear came to the rescue and gave me hers. I thought for a while I would have to back down from my promise, as Sears wouldn't send me one, and I couldn't get a good one anywhere. I've seen much better than this one, but I think you will be impressed with the variety of goods available in even this one. Montgomery & Ward's are the second largest mail order store – a little higher class than S. & R.'S.

I hope you had as much fun opening the parcels as I had getting them off – had to re-pack the records three times.

Please thank Auntie Glad, Marg. and Joan: Campbell and his wife, Harry and Phyl. Billingham and Dave Pennell for their cheery Xmas Greetings.

I hope you all have a Happy Christmas. Don't eat too much for Xmas Dinner, Andrew.

And if this doesn't reach you in time for Christmas, then – HAPPY NEW YEAR.

LOTS OF LOVE,

from

BILL.

1633, Elwood,
FLINT 4, MICH.
29/12/52.

Dear Family,

Well, after several weeks break it is great to write to you again – and what a story I have to tell.

First, thank you for all your wonderful Christmas letters. I'm sorry I didn't get them before I left for Florida, but what a grand welcome back – 27 letters to read! The mail here, due to Xmas card mania, gets completely over-loaded, and I received your last 3-weeks letters on arrival. Note – this is not the reason you didn't hear from me for so long, I tried hard, but I simply was too tired to write in the limited time available.

I received Xmas cards from South's at S.F., Droogan's in N.Y., Smith's at Chicago (both Gordon's & Bud's families), Kallen's in Georgia (I'll tell you about them later), Gale Harris in Chicago, with an invitation to visit them some time (she's Marg. Hamilton's penfriend); Manter's in N.J., Anabel; Mick Caldron, N.F.; C.E. Wilson, President of G.M; I. Wiles, Gen. Manager of Buick; Bruce Lowe, Training Director of Buick; Harold Dent, Eng. Director of G.M; A.G. Gibbs, Doug, Joyce, and Gundill from G.M.H. Not bad for a beginner!

Enough of cards, as its all very superficial here, but presents have more meaning. Mrs. Webb gave me a lovely tie, and I received your parcel of Koalas (only 15 cents custom examination fee on these) just before I left. These will be very useful as presents for the firm friends (there's many who are only interested in the novelty of being an Australian student) here in U.S.

The tinned meat, etc. was waiting here with the letters. Please don't waste your time or money sending more meat, as Australian tinned meat is no improvement on the frozen meat here.

I hope that my letters have not sounded too much like I'm living on rations – I'm not. I eat well, but have to be careful what I choose that's all. I've only lost 8-lbs. since arriving, and I'm not complaining about that. Please don't think that I don't appreciate your thought in sending it, as I do very much, but I'll be looking forward to Mrs. Warner's cake much more, as cakes are something we just don't buy as such. Thanks, Mum, for all your trouble. Probably the cake is at the P.O. now, as I have another ticket for postage due (only 15 cents custom I expect). I still haven't received my trunk, but it has landed at N.Y. I'll have to track it down somehow.

So sorry I've disappointed everyone by not spending a "White Xmas", but what a time – Miami – Oh, to be there again! Sunshine, sunny sunshine and beautiful beaches. I left tired, overworked and depressed. I've returned healthy, happy and with a much brighter outlook on life – feeling as if I can really hop into another month's serious study.

My, I'm glad I decided to go – a glamorous 4,000, or better, mile trip in 9 days, i.e. 450 miles per day, avge. Amazing, but I don't feel tired. I've deliberately not given you all the details in this letter, as I hope to write fully on this adventure after I've had time to collect my thoughts on it (be prepared to do some duplicating, Dad). To give you a rough idea of the route we took – Michigan, Ohio, Kentucky, Tennessee, North Carolina, Georgia, Florida and returned via Alabama, Tennessee, Kentucky, O.M. – Cities – Dayton, Cincinnati, Knoxville, Jacksonville, St. Augustine, Daytona Beach, Palm Beach, Miami Campus, Tallahassee, Montgomery, Nashville, Louisville, Dayton, Detroit & Flint.

With lots of love and best wishes, Bill.

Elwood,
<u>FLINT. MICH.</u>
1/1/53.

Dear Family,

Well, it's 1953 – my, how time flies – nearly four months since I left you all.

This year has started very well, I saw the New Year in at the Downtown Recreation Club, with most of the other Overseas students who were in Flint to attend the annual event. Before the party I went to the movies, then to a dance at the International Institute with Ron. Bradley (S.A.) Bob Block, Roy Springham and Theo Roland. We slunked away from the Rec. early (about 2.30 a.m.) had some supper, went for a drive, and I turned into bed at 4.45 a.m.; the others staggered in at various times before 6.30 a.m. Tony Palmer and Don Wylie came around early and woke me (at 11.45 a.m.) We make ourselves lunch then I went with Bill Dobell, Don & Pete to Pontiac to visit some of Bill's friends. Enjoyed a pleasant afternoon sitting in front of a glorious pinewood fire. We had fun playing with "Gypsy fire" which makes flames of green, blue, etc (the gum has a sweet smell), talking and looking out of the bay windows at the girls and boys skating on the frozen lake. The Australians all go to the St. Louis' Lakeside Home to swim during the summer. Although the temperature has been below freezing (20°-30°F) for several months now, there is very little snow about, usually there is 2-3 ft. by now, but barely 2" covers the ground. (That's why the flat surface of the many lakes are so excellence to skate on).

Bill, Don, Theo and some others are going north to Grayling (200 miles) or Cadillac, to ski this week-end. I would like to go and try it too, but (a) I have too much study to do (b) I've had an excellent holiday and break (c) I'm saving to buy a desperately needed car (we only have one here at Aust. House now, and the transport position is hopeless).

As the Webb's are away skiing, and we have the run of the house, we decided to have a spread tonight. What a meal – Don and self were the self-appointed cooks (Mum, you wouldn't believe that I do my own washing, ironing, darning and mending, and now cooking – a handy guy). We conveniently worked your tinned meats into the menu which consisted of Soup, Fried Sirloin steak (cost 2.50 dollars for 2 slices) potatoes (boiled) peas, fruit salad and ice-cream, strawberry and vanilla – coffee or tea. We did things properly, and although we received much razzing at first from the others, they looked more than satisfied when they had finished.

I now know that the cheapest way to eat in U.S. is to buy food in bulk at a super market and cook it oneself. Don is toying with the idea of getting an apartment but I'm not a starter, as this place (1633) is like home to me now.

Having made you inquisitive about the Florida trip in my last letter, I'll now describe a little about it to you all. (Don't be perturbed if I wander off on some abstract thoughts or comments every now and again, as I intend to make this my subject for several months. I have made a few notes so I won't forget my impressions, and eventually, you will end up back in Flint – and school, ugh!).

Friday, 19th Dec. I had to talk hard to my boss at work to be let off overtime on this night. Although we weren't leaving until 6.30 p.m. I had to get washed, have supper, pack and buy some odds and ends, films, money from bank, etc.so I left work at 3.30 p.m. and did I have to travel. I ran to the bus, ran all the time between shops. Dad, note the difference in attitude towards overtime here. Men work, and work, and still work if their bosses order them to. The bosses only ask them when there is much to be done, or production is behind schedule. Now, when schedules are out, or a steel strike, or defence contracts or sales dropping, etc., then the men are laid off right and left. A cruel process, as usually they are the same men who, a few months previously, had sweated hard, hours on end, to help management keep production schedules. The insidiousness of this deal becomes apparent when men are laid off in order of seniority (that is the number of years one has worked without absence). This means that a newcome can never get started on his seniority, because he's usually laid off at least once a year unless he happens to be lucky and strike a continuous job first pop. The amazing part to me is that all Americans think their standard of living is so very superior to any other country. My answer: - depends what you judge, the standard of living on. If the basis is manufactured goods, automobiles, washing machines, refrigerators, etc., sure you can "own them" all here (should say have them as the banks usually own them, due to an amazing credit system) but to own your own car, house, and live up to our Australian standard and clothe yourself well, then one has to work overtime, which of course, everyone does. Summing up. Australia has a higher standard for essential things only – by a 40 hour week; but, working a 58 hour week here, which gives no leisure, no time for picnics, races, sports, church, etc. (they get this in concentrated re-played sessions on the T.V. in the few free hours before going to bed, sleeping, getting up and working) then I agree the standard of existence, not living, can be said to be higher here.

To proceed with our trip. I had supper at a Restaurant which consisted of soup, cheeseburger and coffee. A girl waitress was done up a little cheaply, but had made a reasonably good job of herself (a good job if I was in Aust. as girls here, from 12 on, certainly take a pride in their make-up, if nothing else. They're taught it at school.). In conversation with another girl I heard her say that she was too old to get married. When she gave me my bill I asked her how old she was to consider herself above falling for a man with a view to settling down to married life. She replied "Why, I'm nearly 18!" Deep in thought I counted my cash, put it on the counter, looked up and smile. In silence I walked out of the door.

Well, next time, perhaps, we'll begin the trip.

Love,

BILL.

1633 Elwood,
Flint 4, Michigan. U.S.A.
Sun.19th January., 10.00 a.m.

Dear Family and others,

Another short note. I haven't been able to gather enough time together to start my detail Florida trip. Next time perhaps? I got my photos back last week. They're gorgeous – 7 reels of colours, magnificent colour in many shots. As Ron. Bradley and self swapped cameras for most of the trip there are many shots of myself in them. Climbing palms, splitting coconuts in Miami beach and so forth. I'll send some later but I might take some black and white prints off first as the colour prints are good but expensive, 50 c. a throw.

Thank you all (Mum, Dad, etc. Mrs. Warner and Jane) for your Christmas cakes. I received the package with the dried fruit in it just after New Year's Day. My trunk with its "spoil" arrived the same day. Eager eyes watched as I produced the ½ doz. The lucky ones were Mr. Webb, Brian S., Mick, Bill Dobell and the rest was sipped mouthful by mouthful at an Australian House celebration that evening.

Mrs. Warner's cake, the iced one I presume, has received the No.1 applause so far (Yours isn't opened yet Mum). Thank you very much Mrs. Warner. They simply don't make cakes like yours over here.

We broke into Jane's (Mrs. Hamilton's) when we had a break from study at 1.00 a.m. this morning. After such a delightful refreshment we drank some coke and pressed on until 2.30 a.m.

Your presents should be there by now as they were sent a week after Jane's, however, they may have missed a boat and have to wait six weeks for another. Please don't let Andrew ruin his and your records on that heavy gramophone (play them up at Delbridge's school or somewhere). I thought they were good recordings and would be handy when we go to Mitcham. There's a limitless selection of all three speeds here. I'd quite struck on long playing 33 ½ r.p.m., they're good. Hope you like the hose Mum I had to guess your size. Dad, the corn forks are a good idea – you don't have to get buttery fingers now. The Californian Zephyr was where I saw them – most elite. Tim, old chap, nylon to me over here is a disappointment but see what you think of the sox. There's no substitute for wool. I like the hand painted tie – there's many beaut. conservative ones here, in fact, well dressed college people wear a simple plain tie like yours.

Ruth, the necklace I liked, hope you do too. Helen, if you wish, you can give your brooch (scatter pins) to Ruth and have your books or, on the other hand, keep the brooch and consider the books as a birthday present.

Dad, regarding packing, newspapers most acceptable, but put a couple of sheets of old newspaper over outside of them as holes get rubbed into the surface during transport. Packages in general have to be of extra strong ribbed cardboard as they get a terrific pounding. Cakes are best in tins and calico stitched around them. Ask Mrs. Hamilton on this (hers was in perfect condition).

Love to all,

BILL.

1633 Elwood

Flint 4,

<u>MICHIGAN, U.S.A.</u>

Wed., 21st Jan 1953

Dear Family and Others,

At last, I have some spare time and I can give some thought to our Florida trip. I hope you will all come along with me and enjoy the experiences that we will have together.

My, it's late – I dashed from the Grill Shop around to Lambert's Photo Supply. "1/2 doz. Ektachrome 620, please, and remember the 10% discount." "Thank you", and off I half ran, half walked – a little quicker this time as I was 8.50 lighter and time was fast disappearing. 5.30, Rene's picking me up at 6.00 – I haven't even packed yet. Swish! I tore.

I had showered, shaved (on my Super Schick 60 electric razor) and packed when Rene Bernesquet and Bernard Corbel arrived. But I couldn't find my camera – Ahh!, under my bend – the only place I hadn't looked at least three times in the panic. Rene's '39 Olds. appeared in remarkably good shape for such an "old clunker" (a term given to any car whose life exceeds the estimated 7 years). We had to push on steadily to reach Dayton, O., 300 miles away, by 2.00 a.m., where we would meet Ron Bradley and Bob Black. The Olds. was going nicely, a steady 60 m.p.h. The cumulative strain of excessive overtime the steady rocking of the car, and the incessant jabber of French in the front seat. I awoke to the uncomforting sound of a clanging, sputtering engine, and an oil-smoke-filled car, just outside of Toledo. We had come straight down through Ann Arbor, about 100 miles. 200 to go, and either (a) a cracked piston, (b) a broken ring (I'm still sure that's what the trouble was), (c) a big end bearing gone, or even (d) a main crankshaft bearing worn.

We floundered around to various garages – all most pessimistic – our hopes of reaching Florida were rock bottom. I had immediate thoughts of catching a bus to Chicago and spending the time with the Smiths. In desperation, we decided to remove the sparkplug (to relieve compression stress and hence reduce noise) and press on regardless with the five remaining cylinders. We crawled along at 20 m.p.h., then 30, 40, and eventually about 50 miles from Dayton we chuffed past a Nash doing about 30, at the tremendous speed of 55 m.p.h. There was a yell – it was Bradley's Nash, the one in which we were going to travel 4,000 miles in 10 days! Our hopes were dashed to the ground again. He was limping into Dayton too. It was most encouraging when we discovered that he was running in a new engine that he had put in that afternoon. We chuffed on, dropped Berny, who had to work at Frigidaire, Dayton, and met "Brads" at the Biltmore Hotel at 4.30 a.m. We had a clean-up, transferred luggage, parked Rene's "chuffer" and on the way again – to Cincinnati.

"Brads" and myself seemed to take a liking to each other right from the start, so we arranged that we drove together, while the Continentals, Rene and Bob, slept in the back. I forgot to mention that while we had stopped near Toledo, it was snowing. Bitterly cold outside, the heat in the car, of course, was cold and I had to get out and do most of the talking, as my accent was the least noticeable. (I still often get into language difficulties, you probably can't understand this). I've found that it mainly depends on the person to whom I'm speaking, because if they really want to understand you they will, (and first time too).

I nearly froze, I shivered as I tried to sleep cuddled up in my excellent radio and heater, a bed in the back and, best of all, good company, and the nose of the Nash pointed to the Sunny South. We happily drove through, at least a dozen, red stop lights, still going in the early hours of the morn. There was not a sign of life anywhere – and we were anxious to reach Florida.

As we entered Kentucky, the "Blue grass State", I took over and Ron navigated. Williamstown, Corinth, Georgetown, Lexington, Richmond all quickly rolled by. Lexington is the centre of the "Blue grass" country. This bluish coloring was most noticeable in the early morning light. The sun intermittently shone through the heavy, dark clouds. The University of Kentucky is on the banks of the Ohio River, some 300 yards wide, at Lexington. The country, with the well kept stud farms, looks a little like Angaston (minus vineyards, of course). It was most noticeable to see the rail tracks and horse racing influenced again, as I had not seen a race track since I left Australia. California and Kentucky are the only states where racing is a major event. No doubt you have heard of the Kentucky Derby, well that is held at Louisville, the largest city in Kentucky. The capital of Kentucky is Frankfort, on the Kentucky River, and here is Kentucky State College (University) and the grave of the famous Daniel Boone (an early explorer, and, now, a children's legendary adventurer).

Kentucky is the historic crossroads of the nation, lying between the Appalachian's and the Mississippi River, at altitudes varying from 4,000 to 300 ft. The six regions are known as the Bluegrass, the Barrens, the Mountains, the Purchase, the Western Coal Fields, and the Knobs. Mostly very scenic, varying country. Kentucky was the scene of many North v. South battles. The Battle of Perryville in 1862 was one of the bloodiest. The State had divided sentiments as 90,000 enlisted in Union Army (North) and 40,000 joined the Confederates. In 1782 "the last Battle of the Revolution" (when Britain lost control), between a force of Indians and Canadians, and the Kentuckians was fought where now stands Blue Licks Battlefield State Park. Going through this State was an excellent history lesson.

The College at Berea was most impressive – old, and steeped in tradition. The students pay no fees, but earn their way through by working the college dairy, bakery, gift-shop, farm, etc., co-educational, non-secretarian.

We could now notice the difference in the trees – autumn leaves still clung to some. These had fallen months ago in Mich., and only snow clothed the bare branches. We felt we were going south and the seasons were changing with us. This was even more noticeable when returning north (a depressing thought). I didn't think I would ever be in London, but we drove right through this little town. I took a photo of a sign post for record purposes – "In the heart of London".

After Corbin, a railroad junction for the coal mines nearby, we decided to detour and see the Cumberland Falls. The weather was misty and overcast, but the few extra miles were well worth while. The Cumberland Falls, State Park, is heavily wooded, with mostly pines. The views would have been marvellous had the weather been clear – but this was not the right time of the year. The Falls themselves were the best I have seen. Similar to a small Niagara, 65' high and 125' wide. At night, it is said, that a moonbow can be seen in the mist below the falls. We had a good clamber around the rocks and visited a delightful Cabin-Hotel. Brads of course, was full of his great Victoria Falls.

I also missed the scampering rabbits on the road. We saw more dead dogs (10) than squashed rabbits (1). Coal shale outcrops were often seen in cuttings as we neared the Tennessee border, the land getting a little dryer, the sun a little warmer.

The car had developed a bumping on the L.H.S. which we all agreed was the shock absorber – we thought many nasty things about it. The engine was purring along nicely and we increased speed to 50 m.p.h.

As we crossed the border into "Tenn-err-see" and then stopped at a dirty, destituted dump called Jellico, we knew we had left the beautiful Bluegrass country in Kentucky.

I have lots to tell you about Tenn. next time.

Much love to all,

Bill.

1633 Elwood,
Flint 4,
Michigan, U.S.A.
Sat., Feb. 1st, 1953

Dear Family and others,

Hello, once again. I suppose you have all returned from your holidays very fit and well rested. I hope you are in good writing form as I've missed your letters lately. (I've been guilty too.) I'm still enjoying it here but have been a little miserable the middle of the last month. I can tell you now as I am well out of the doldrums. It's bitterly cold out, temp. dropped to 3°F. the other day, but the average 24 hour temp. is up (I find myself saying "up" now) around 25°F. One has to be extremely careful about what one eats (plenty of fruit juice) and when one showers (never before going outdoors) as disregard of these factors have drastic effects. I have been caught out – never again. This caused me to miss all final months exams and I'm afraid negative grades will result – I can't worry about it but I'll try and work harder next month, last in the semester (term), to make up (virus throat and influenza laid me low).

It's good to be at work again, although I've had to take it easy as I still cough and splutter a little. The Metallurgical Dept. – Sheet Metal Press Shop 2 weeks and then in the Forge Press Shop for the remaining 2 weeks. I'm learning a terrific amount. My job at the moment is Assistant to the Assistant Factory Metallurgist – a good deal.

Just before I fell sick, Sunday 3 weeks ago, Brads and I went and spoke at a Friends of the Baptist Church Meeting at Flushing, a small town 20 miles from Flint. The talks went very well and we were presented with tastefully chosen ties wrapped up most daintily with fancy pink ribbon. (Americans are ribbon mad, they tie everything up with it.) In the late afternoon we drove on to Detroit as Ron had to speak again at the Redford Presbyterian Church "African Missionary Meeting". A crowd of 400 were present – a very alive, friendly, Christian Church. We attended Fireside, a group of young people, 20-25, and played many enjoyable games afterwards. Churches don't have evening services here.

Tomorrow morning I'm driving with Roy Springham down to Redford to go to the 11.00 service. We hope to get an invitation to a home to dinner and then tour Detroit tin the afternoon, attending the Fireside Meeting before returning to dull old Flint at night.

This afternoon I'm going down with Frank Pound, Peters, Theo. Roland, N.Z., to see Greenfield Village at Dearborn (Ford's) and the Ford Museum of Industry where there is a special Sports Car Show. We then go on to an ice hockey match (Professionals) before going home.

Next weekend many of the Overseas fellows (with self) are going up to Grayling (10° below) to ski. This should be fun.

The following week end I'm spending writing another wretched report.

Leaving the week-end before returning my 3rd months' school to take Brian back to Cleveland and see the city sights there.

Much love to all,

Bill.

1633 Elwood,

Flint 4,
<u>MICHIGAN, U.S.A.</u>
Monday, February 2nd, 1953

Dear Family and Others,

I hope you all found something of interest in our journey through Kentucky. We will continue doing a steady 60 m.p.h. through the "Land of the Hillbillies" – Tennessee, finally stopping for an adventurous night at Gatlinburg with "The Lone Ranger", then across the "Great Smokies".

Crossing the hilly border one immediately notices the desolation of the hard, flood years of the 30's. The country is poor, much red clay with dark, dirty-black, coal-shale outcrops appearing intermittently. This was a long way from "The State in which anything will grow" that we had heard about. Everything looked a ruin – houses built cockeyed with weathered palings, abandoned machinery in the barren, undulating dry hills. We were in the headwaters of the famous Tennessee Valley Authority (T.V.A.) which supplied a desperate need in the depression years – work, and hence money.

Each year the farmers were able to plant their meagre crops in the valley and hillsides, watch them come up, toiling day and night or an existence, then – swish down came the floods from the surrounding hills sweeping everything in front of them.

These destructive elements were tamed by a series of dams, locks, etc. throughout eastern and central Tennessee. Prosperity came to the central and western part of Tennessee and on our return journey north, we see the mighty worth of this immense scheme (T.V.A. cost approx. Equivalent to our Snowy River Project).

As we drive on south with the sun in our eyes, already the land gradually improves from destitute Jellico, and La Follette, Clinton to marble-faced Knoxville, spread eagled in valleys on hills. Knoxville had grown tremendously in the last 10 years being the home for the staff workers in the adjacent Oak Ridge Atomic Energy Plant – an immense, concrete powerful-looking block building. Temporary homes for workers everywhere. We missed the Norris Dam as we missed the turn-off. This is where some of the hydro-electric power is generated.

The sun set prematurely, as we drove into the shadow of the high, distant Great Smoky Mountains – smoky because, like the N.S.W. Blue Mountains, a dense blue haze always envelopes the high peaks.

The "Smokies", as they are nicknamed, are in a large National Park, some 60 miles long, and 20 miles wide. The Tennessee-North Carolina border bisects the beautiful park longitudinally, and the Blue Ridge Highway follows a similar path. I'll leave the color print to do the describing. This crossing was adventurous as slippery ice covered much of the road.

Then we descended into the Cherokee Red Indian Reservation, - a glorious place – but no Indians in head-dresses, etc., Andrew. Again I leave the photo to describe the bear incident. I didn't run with a "bear" behind, but I nearly lost my "knee action".

Gatlinburg, at the foot of the mountains, is a delightful little place with amazing tourist capacity, 5,000 beds available, yet it didn't appear any bigger than, say, Mount Compass. Motels, Touratels, Hotels, Apartments, Cabins, all snuggled into small nooks and crannies. Many cabins, were built overhanging the babbling brook that wound through the Settlement. And so I fell into bed thoroughly tired, but wonderfully contended – shared it with a Frenchman.

Before retiring we walked along the clean, winding, main, and only, street to find a place to satisfy our empty bellies. We were enjoying our fried chicken at the back of a restaurant and in walks three gentlemen. Bob Block, who is always very abrupt, looks up. One of the bunch began to take offence, Bob and Rene simply continued eating, while Brads and I were almost hysterical. We couldn't stop. The big boy gets up, hops across to our table, and with his hands on his six shooter and displaying his sheriff's badge, threatens innocent Bob (except for his one utterance) "If you have something to say then say it! But don't just sit there and pull silly faces." We stopped laughing – you could have heard a pin drop, all eyes and sympathy of other locals on us. We fortunately said nothing. How, I don't know. He cooled off, then stormed out, mounting his thoroughbred (a 1952 Ford Sedan) and drove off. All of us, waitresses and customers, laughed ourselves silly. He was the newly appointed deputy sheriff – hated by all – he had made himself foolish. That may have easily been "goodbye", but I'm glad I can still say it now.

Love,

Bill.

1633 Elwood, Flint 4, Michigan, U.S.A.
Sun. 8th Feb. 1953

Andrew, I hope you like the stamps.

Dear Mother, Dad, Helen, Ruth, Tim & Andrew,

Letters seem to be flowing again now – thank you. A few comments before continuing our trip to reach Florida tonight.

I've turned Presbyterian it would seem, as last Sunday I spent an enjoyable day at the Redford Church in Detroit. I spoke at a Young People's Fireside Meeting, and tonight I'm going to a young adults' group at the First Pres. Church in Flint. I'm feeling dangerously fit now as my throat has completely cleared up. All's right with the world. The last fortnight I've been "Assistant Assistant Metallurgist for Sheet Metal", a most interesting job. The press shops are huge – 380 large presses in one over ¼ mile long, and over 500 in the small press shop about 300 yards long. They stamp 1000 (short) tons of coil steel each day, 2 shifts, 16 hrs. At Woodville we stamped about 100 tons/8 hr. The new '53 Buick models production has risen to 2400 per day, 8 hrs. Amazing isn't it. Tomorrow I'm going into the Forge Shop to see the 2000 ton drop & steam presses in action. – I will be studying the metallurgy of forgings and forging dies.

During the last two weeks I've made several more friends. Howard Bowman & I worked together most of the time on sheet metal scrap problems. He is a graduate of the University of Arizona & invited me to his home for dinner last Wednesday, together with Phil Palmer, a graduate from Uni. of Mich., both are Metallurgists. Howard's wife, Ida, and baby daughter, Cheryl, are most charming. They've just bought a beaut 21" T.V. set and we had fun watching it. If you pick your programmes, you can see and listen to ballet, opera, vaudeville and other excellent live artist shows. Last night I was there again, and saw the famous "Jimmy Glennan Show", the most extravagant and classy program on TV. Due to the 25 million audience it draws, the advertising nights cost 700.00 per hour, and it runs for 1 ½ hours.

Returning to our trip South, we still have many miles to travel and many exciting episodes to encounter. We are at Cherokee Indian Reservation standing in front of an Indian hut. A black bear skin is nailed to the neatly chopped log cabin wall. A wrought iron cooking pot hangs on a tripod over the remains of a fire. An eerie-looking horse skull also adorns the cabin wall. Each side of me stands a Continental student. Bob Block from Belgium in his usual carefree stance, and Rene Bernesquet, a Frenchman (2nd year student, Dad) with his determined facial expression and camera. "Brads" took the shot (he is 1st yr. Dad, but he and Jackabus Schmidt, the other S. African, arrived in N.Y. late, and missed the party photo taken in Detroit.) ("Pete" is Peter Green, 1st yr., married from Melb., "Don" or "Moose", as we've nicknamed him, is Don Enderbery, 1st yr. from Sydney; Frank or "Fearless Fagin" is 1st yr. from Melb. These were my travelling companions and we're all like brothers now. No four guys could have more different personalities. I won't comment further now, as I'm like you – rearing to get to Miami. Tony Palmer is 2nd yr. from England; David Lord (a super guy) 2nd yr. from S. Africa; Bill Dobell is 2nd yr. from Melb., as is Roy Martin. One is continually in the company of these fellows, and apt to forget you have no idea who The Good Lord, etc., is.)

I would have loved to have heard "Unto These Hills", an excellence Indian play – presented by a cast of 1800 Indians in an outdoor hillside auditorium at charming Cherokee – however tourist season was over, and the show had packed up for the winter. Approx. 8,000 Cherokee's live on the reservation. We drive on along the twisting hills across the toe of North Carolina, we stop for a snap of a Moccasin Bend in the Fontana.

The mountains changed to hills, the hills changed to rolling undulating open country. Deep red soil and the fields covered with dried cotton, corn or tobacco stalks wherever one looks. Corn cobs were stored in stacks with a pole stuck in the centre and looked like yellow beach tents standing in fields.

Being Sunday morning and still in the land of the hillbillies every station had hillbilly church services (organ, banjos, guitars, yodellings – the complete treatment). The hand-clapping drawly spiritual at the moment is called "I'm heading for higher ground, up closer to the Lord". We pressed on regardless – Clayton – Cornella – Athens, saw Uni. of Georgia here – Maddison, Eatonton, the birthplace of Joel Chandler Harris, the creator of Uncle Remus (Andrew, you ask Tim to tell you about Brer Rabbit & Brer Fox and the tar baby) on to our next stop to Milledgeville, the State capital from 1807 until 1867, but today Georgia Military College occupies the Old State House. We looked for Montgomery Street and had no trouble finding it. As we drove along this street we noticed many fine old homes with porches and majestic colonial-type columns supporting the front eaves. In the dusk one house was a particularly good example of Georgian architecture & Rene jokingly said "I think we stop at this mansion". I drove on, but had to turn about as I had passed the number. By strange coincidence we did go into the "mansion" and Mrs. Frank Kaler, Rev. Brian McDonald's sister Mollie, was thrilled to see me. Frank is an English master at the College, and the children, Susan & Chris., were most intrigued by the nationalities and different accents. Mollie was eager to hear about Brian. She looked a little tired as she had a nasty gum boil, but was otherwise well. Brads & I helped Susan cut the Christmas tree to a suitable size and hauled it inside. We had an enjoyable supper and talk, but had to bid fond farewells after 2 ½ hours, as our aim was to reach Jacksonville before morning. Mollie & Frank had spent some time in South Africa, so found much to talk about with Ron. Both of them & family would very much like to come to Aust. To visit Brian and enquired about air fares, etc. But I think it would be a little too costly at the moment. Perhaps, when the children are away at College, they may visit you Brian.

Along the Uncle Remus Highway again, driving in turns, all night at 60-70 m.p.h., on through Dublin (we certainly travelled the globe on this trip – London, Athens, Melbourne, Sydney, Hollywood and now Dublin). McRae, all I remember here was taking the wrong turning & going back, then Alma and Waycross, where I awoke. From Waycross to Folkaton we slowed down as dense fog covered the road. We were travelling both alongside and through the large 600 sq. mile famous Chefenokee Swamp – waste land used as a wildlife sanctuary and through which the immortal Swannee River wanders. I was all eyes as we crossed St. Mary's River and read the large neon sign "Welcome to Florida". – The fog immediately disappeared, super highways appeared and we tore on – racing empty fruit trucks along the straight highway to Callahan and then Jacksonville (3 a.m.). Jacksonville was disappointing – very dirty in the colored section and commercialized in other parts.

Brads & I were driving and feeling fine so we decided to head for St. Augustine and here the real sightseeing of the trip began. We hadn't seen the Atlantic Ocean yet, so we decided to sleep, looking across the still silent ocean, on the beach at St. Augustine. Bob disappeared – he had taken us literally and took his sleeping bag and slept on the sands. Ron, Rene & I slept in the car & Ron & I awoke at 6.30 to find Bob missing. We went looking for him and took our cameras as a beautiful, tropical sunrise was probable. It was refreshing walking along the fresh, untrodden sands, not a soul to be seen and a "cool-warm" tropical breeze made it a joy to be alive. Then a magnificent sunrise – our first in Florida – to welcome us. We watched the continuously changing orange, red and yellow hues, entranced by God's presence rising slowly over the still sea.

Much love to all,

Bill.

Elwood
<u>FLINT, MICH., U.S.A. 28/2/53.</u>

Dear Mother and Family,

Mother, I hope you had the happiest of days on the 2nd. So sorry I missed the celebrations.

Tonight, Pete, Brads. & Roy Springham (English) and I went to the movies, and saw "Full House" with an excellent set of short stories – most enjoyable, and presented just like Somerset Maughan's "Trio" or "Quartet". I had never seen such heavy snowfall; in fact, it was a blizzard. I could hardly see to drive, the windscreen wipers going flat out, my nose close to the window, and the heater full on, we crawled along the ice-snow-covered roads at less than 10 m.ph.. Cars were sliding and skidding in all directions. It's an uncanny insecure feeling driving on ice. You have to try to walk or drive on it to realise just how slippery ice can get. It's impossible to steer, accelerate or stop anywhere near normally, as the car is likely to go frontwards, backwards or either sideways careering all over the road.

After parking in a Lot. 200 yards from the Theatre, we dashed through the 16°F. blizzard in a crazy-crooked path to the foyer. Here, we brushed the loose snow-frosting off our overcoats. Snow is an experience I wish you all could enjoy with me. It's amazing stuff.

Due to my catching up on missing tests, etc., I've been kept more than fully occupied during the last week and will be this week too.

I've been most anxious to go skiing one week-end and see if I can break my leg as some people do (not seriously). Perhaps next work month, I've no time now. I was tempted this week-end, as the Webb's invited Roy Martin and myself to go with them, but I guess there will be other times next year.

Last week-end Peter and I drove Brian back to Cleveland. We had a marvellous time. The car went well (600 miles in two days). We left Flint at 2.00 p.m. on Saturday, and arrived back at 11.p.m. on Sunday.

The country was prettier in Ohio than around Flint. In Cleveland we couldn't make out what made everything so attractive, and then Brian realised what it was, and said "look fellows! Green grass!", and so there was – on the brown withered lawns, gardens, side-ways, etc., a greenish tinge could be detected – new sprouts of green. Spring must be close now – in Ohio, anyway.

Much love to you all, <u>BILL.</u>

Elwood,
FLINT. MICH. U.S.A.
4/3/53.

Hi Folks,

The prints are beauts, aren't they?. I've just returned from the Camera Shop with them and I am beaming with smiles. Descriptions are on the back.

School work is descending on me in ever increasing quantities, but I'm going to clear out to go North near Grayling to Waters (Snow Village) with Peter Green, Roy Martin (both Aust.) Rene Bernesquet and Berne Corbel (both French) to try another new experience – skiing. It should be fun. I hope I don't get sunburnt (from reflected infra-red off-snow surface), as did Roy last week. "Brads" may be taking a load up in his car too. My car is going well now. I've had a new pinion bearing put in the differential, the wheel bearings tightened and aligned, gear linkage replaced, brake and clutch adjusted, and the engine tuned – cost only 35 dollars – a little different to Australia isn't it, Tim? I've got a reasonably good car now, although I've lost some money on it for yearly depreciation already. This is inevitable. Dad – thank you for sending the dollars. I'll be going along to see a film next week in the Flint Adventure Series, entitled "The Land Down Under". If it's as good as the previous ones – "Wild Game in the Rockies", "Switzerland", "Mediterranean Shores" and "Polynesian Playgrounds", it will be well worth seeing. I bought a season ticket (3.50 dollars) but certainly have not regretted spending the time or money. Professional cameramen-speakers put on a full length film, very similar to Fitzpatrick's Travel Talks, but much better as a (more intimate) live commentary.

Let's wake up with a stiff back from lying on the front seat of the "Nash", which is parked on the foreshore of St. Augustine, Florida, and rise with the magnificent sunrise to have breakfast and a wash in a small restaurant, then off to see the sights of famous St. Augustine.

To get an idea of the City, we drove up and down the streets. St. Augustine is the oldest place in U.S.A., because it was a well-established Spanish settlement when the Pilgrim Fathers landed in the "Mayflower". It was discovered by a Spaniard, Ponce de Leon in 1513, and founded by another, named Menedez, during 1565. Sir Francis Drake plundered and burnt the colony in 1586. The city was also razed to the ground by other privateers and in 1756 Costillo de San Marcas, an impregnable fortress, was built. Today, this powerful ancient fort is a National Monument, and provides many tourists (like us) with much enjoyment, instead of the protection afforded to Matanzas Bay against foreign intruders, for which this fort was famous. This castle stands today, the oldest masonry in America, seeming proud of her unconquered record. The powder magazine, the dungeon, the chapel, and the centre quadrangle with its derelict windlass well were sights worth pondering at for hours – but we must move on.

The city still retains much of its Spanish architecture – immense, magnificent Hotel Ponce de Leon, like five Teachers' Colleges (Adelaide) combined, with a centre courtyard into which we peeped inquisitively and watched workmen lay beautiful turquoise tiles on the walls of the new outdoor hotel swimming pool (50 yds. x 20 yds.) A little way behind the pool was a group of grass tennis courts – the first I had noticed in the States (no wonder we win the Davis Cup – nobody plays that stupid game here, that is in the North) California and Florida are the only States where it is anything like a major sport.

We didn't drive down Treasury Street, as we couldn't. It is only 6'1 wide, but Brads. did try some that were 10 ft.

A Presbyterian Church (Spanish style again) we went into was rather eery greyish-white cold looking marble throughout, except for dark, solidly built mahogany pews. A guide showed us around but I was glad to get out into the lovely sunshine again.

Two cabbies were waiting outside for other tourists. What a sight! Old moth-eaten horses all dressed up flowers, pulling 4-wheeled old fashioned black cabs and beside them were the drivers. Darkies in tails, top hat, pink waist coats and red bow ties, and a great big smile, full of white teeth, were waiting beside their cabs for the party. I ran out of film, hence missed a good shot.

We move on along U.S.I. over the Spanish-type-causeway-arch-bridge, and I was surprised to find we were soon on the open road. Somehow, I had imagined all the Eastern Coast of Florida to be one glorious surfing beach with houses along the foreshore. I did not see this, but I wasn't disappointed.

First there was a mangrove-looking growth, with an intermittent Alligator Farm or Seminole Indian Trading Post pushed into a clearing. This became denser and more "jungley" looking, and Jungle Gardens, Parrot, Monkey or Snake Farms were there to catch the tourist "suckers". Everything is the "biggest in the world".

Then came land similar to the tidal swamps behind Grange, in fact, it was similar to driving along Military Road. This used to be infested with 'gators – it still looked a little treacherous. Soon civilization began to appear and we were at Marineland. Again, prices jacked up for the tourists benefit, and we grudgingly paid 2.50 dollars to enter (remember Florida is the wealthy man's playground over here).

I had seen Sydney Aquarium, but this was an Oceanarium – in fact the only one in the world (this time I might have been told the truth). I had often seen it in the movies before – you know – feeding the dolphins – sorry porpoises – under water, and also by making them leap out of the water. I've got a shot in colour taken at 1/500 sec. with the whole animal out of the water, and the water splashes just hanging in the air – it's a glorious shot.

Listen again next week for more exciting adventures in another episode of "Murrell in Florida".

Tons of love,

BILL

16TH April, 1953.

Dear Family,

I hope you are all well. I'm fine, although the weather certainly is not. It snowed today quite heavily but it has all melted again now. I can appreciate the meaning of the words to the song "April Showers" now. Each day for the last fortnight we have had some rain.

As there has been rain and also enough heat (40°) to melt the ice on the winter frozen Great Lakes, much water is now flowing over Niagara and tomorrow I'm off to see this great sight.

Today I got my final grades for my first semester, and I'm quite pleased. (Also, my grades for the work I had to catch up, ugh!)

Electrical Circuits	82%	Industrial Engineering	85%
English	88%	Industrial Organisation	87%
Hydraulics	87%	Industrial Development	78%
Automotive Body Construction	93%	Manufacturing Accounting	87%

These grades are well above the usual American student. It's practically an established tradition that the Overseas students fight it out for the first decile (top ten in school) especially the Australians, Germans and Englishmen.

I don't know whether this will bore you, but the following are the subjects I'll be taking for my second semester: -

E.N.31   Standards of Plant & Equipment Engineering.
E.N.33   Economics of Tools and Equipment.
E.N.49   Materials Handling and Storage.
E.N.31   English – Report Writing.
E.N.30   Industrial Economics.
E.M.31   Job analysis and Wage systems.

These subjects should prove even more interesting than last semester's, but there is still plenty of work. However, I don't intend to get sick this time (I'm feeling most fit, and am enjoying food at last), on the other hand it will be summer, and there's more things to do, such as swimming, etc. Enough of Tech – let's head back to Florida.

(a)   "It's night, and as we drive over the causeway into Miami (downtown) across the water our eyes are attracted to the multitude of flashing neon signs. "Pepsi-Cola" is "Coke's" big opposition – slightly more fizzy, but more in a larger bottle for the same price – it's selling point.

(b)   We drive downtown where the shops are filled with many suggested Xmas gift items fit for all purses. Between two main stores, straddling a very busy street stands a gigantic colossus – Santa Clause, as he is always called here. "Santa" stands some 2-3 stories high, and is a masterpiece of illumination engineering. Actually, he waves his arms to you, but I caught this on a time exposure just right. I'm most pleased with Ektachrome, as this was outdoor film obviously used as night.

    2.   (a) We rise early next morning and drive around the palatial homes on the off-shore side of Miami Beach overlooking the fashionable Canal (Man-made lake). It is as pretty as it looks – most of the homes feature the Spanish architecture – stately and serene looking, yet still maintaining an air of old times gallantry in the buildings.

    3.   (a) The "A.A.A." (Aye, Aye, Aye – as one America repeated after me when I said it), anyway you've guessed right, it's the American Automobile Assoc. of which I'm a member (by the way I never abbreviate it now as I've learnt my lesson) and who advised us to go way across Miami suburbs to see Florida's finest Racecourse. I'm glad we went for two reasons (1) I could compare the tracks with those in Aust., and (2) we had to pass through some of the less luxurious suburbs of Miami, which forcibly showed me that they had a poor section – a "nigger" coloured (as people politely say) section, and the simple mediocre section in this most luxurious place (from the surface). Well here it is. We drive up a magnificent palm lined entrance – it was breathtaking, then we go up in the grandstand and view the track. If I hadn't known I was on a race track I would have guessed the sight to be a huge botanical gardens.

In the pond in the centre of the course is the largest bevy of Flamingo (except natural breeding grounds in Arica, etc).

I wished I had a telephoto lense to catch these picturesque pink birds at a closer range."

Well 'bye for now, With lots of love,

BILL.

BUICK, U.S.A.
4/6/53

Dear Family,

This morning I woke and all was dark, lightning and thunder resounded through the charged air. It sure is a strange summer here. Looking outside now (12.30pm) the sun is shining brilliantly on the trees causing the many shades of green to be easily distinguished. I squint as I look down on the car park, and become dazzled by the reflected light from the windshields.

This car park is a good example of union and management friction in American industry. It is one of the best pieces of chaos I've seen. Cars are parked skew-whiff all over – no organisation. Last Friday I had a R.H. door stoved in by someone in a hurry. About 900 cars are crammed into this mess each shift. Management at Buick realised the situation and drew layouts up so they could pave the lot, and organised the parking for 1,000 cars, but they insisted that 20 spaces be reserved for office personnel coming in late at 8.00 a.m. instead of 6.30 a.m.

The union said "No", it is for employees, and here is to be no favouritism. So, Buick straightened their backs and replied "O.K." the parking lot stays as it is and we will not spend one more penny on it – hence the disorganisation has progressively increased.

I travel to and from work with the supervisor of Standards of the Sheet Metal Plant in a 1953 Buick Riviera Hardtop – a good deal. The day before yesterday he invited me to watch the Coronation on his T.V. and to bring the rest of the Australians across with me (he lives in Elwood, too).

The films were rushed to U.S. in Canberra Jets, being processed on the way over. We saw the full length show on the T.V., although we didn't get to bed until about 2.00 a.m. G.M. put it on as one of their key programmes.

Sir Ralph Richardson commented on the proceedings along with famous American commentators.

The whole background of the story of the traditional pageantry was well explained and many points of interest that a person watching the actual scene would not note as significant were pointed out by the commentators. The views inside the Abbey were better than if you had had one of the best pews, this was due to the myriad of cameras and various special lenses used.

The T.V. lacks only one thing – colour. Even this has been achieved, but only in experiment so far.

The weekend up in Charleroix was fun, although we didn't actually sail. The weather was bad. The boat was in the water, but much work had still to be done on it and we helped all we could.

June 7th – I'm sunburnt on the face and arms after 5 hours of golf today. The Webb's have moved and I hope our new landlords are as good. Peter Green's wife and young daughter Heather arrived on Friday.

All the best,

Lots of love,

(Sgd.) BILL.

<u>FLINT, U.S.A.</u>
10/6/53.

Dear Family,

If the news of the Flint tornado reached the South Australian papers, I hope this letter (on the first outside mail since the disaster) will put your minds somewhat at rest, because I'm quite O.K., as I was not touched.

In case the news didn't reach you, which I hope it didn't, as I know you would worry unduly Mother, I'll try to tell you about this twister. Michigan rarely has tornadoes, but they are common in the lower mid-western states at this time of the year. They are even more uncommon in Flint, as never before has anyone been killed. Today 127 are dead and many others (about 700) are hospitalized.

The three small whirly-whirlies, as you would call them, joined high in the sky near the northern outskirts of Flint at 8.30 p.m. on Monday. I noticed the thunder, lightning and the gradual darkening, but I continued writing a "thank you" letter to the Harris'. I then jumped in my car and went downtown to post the letter and also bought two sports shirts. The shops were closing, due to a severe storm warning at 9 p.m., instead of 9.30 p.m. or 10.00 p.m. (late closing on Monday, Wednesday & Saturday nights – a good idea for workers).

The damage was done by then, as the huge twister – the biggest in Michigan history and the largest since the war in U.S.A., lowered and hit Northern Flint at 8.37 p.m. It swept all in its path in a strip some 300 yds. wide and 8 miles long. Hundreds were homeless, many killed instantly (about 90), and many others are still in hospitals all around. Martial law has been declared and thousands of G.I.'s (Police) and demolition squads have come into Flint. The area devastated is only 2½ miles from 1633 Elwood.

I went through the area on my way to Bay City (for Buick) on Tuesday. Cars hurled 400 ft. and practically turned inside out, and debris lies everywhere. As much concentrated destruction as if an elongated A-bomb had exploded. But I repeat, I'm unscathed, as are the rest of the Australians.

Lots of love,

(Sgd.) BILL.

www.ingramcontent.com/pod-product-compliance
Lightning Source LLC
Chambersburg PA
CBHW042355280426
43661CB00095B/1113